It's a Jungle Up There

1. Western Samoa
2. Biosphere 2
3. Cameroon, Africa
4. French Guiana
5. Florida

Bird's-eye view of our canopy research sites (illustration by Barbara Harrison)

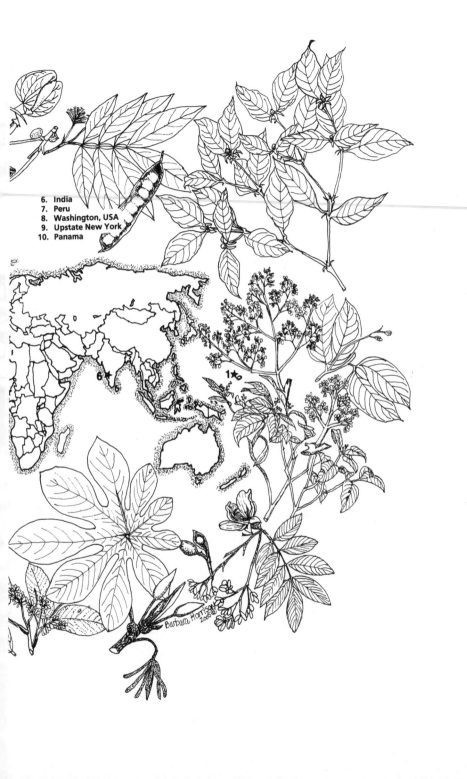

6. India
7. Peru
8. Washington, USA
9. Upstate New York
10. Panama

Barbara Harrison©
2005

It's a Jungle Up There

It's a jungle up there (illustration by Barbara Harrison)

It's a Jungle Up There

More Tales from the

Treetops

MARGARET D. LOWMAN

EDWARD BURGESS & JAMES BURGESS

Foreword by Sir Ghillean T. Prance

YALE UNIVERSITY PRESS / NEW HAVEN & LONDON

Epigraph to Introduction from *The Lorax* by Dr. Seuss, copyright ®
and copyright © by Dr. Seuss Enterprises, L. P. 1971, renewed 1999.
Used by permission of Random House Children's Books, a division
of Random House, Inc.

Epigraph to Chapter 9 is from *The Faithful Gardener: A Wise Tale
About That Which Can Never Die* by Clarissa Pinkola Estés.
Copyright © Clarissa Pinkola Estés, Ph.D. Reprinted by
permission of HarperCollins Publishers.

Set in Galliard type by The Composing Room of Michigan, Inc.
Printed in the United States of America by R. R. Donnelley,
Harrisonburg, Virginia.

Library of Congress Cataloging-in-Publication Data

Lowman, Margaret.
  It's a jungle up there : more tales from the treetops / Margaret
  D. Lowman, Edward Burgess, and James Burgess.
    p. cm.
  ISBN-13: 978-0-300-10863-7 (alk. paper)
  ISBN-10: 0-300-10863-X (alk. paper)
    1. Lowman, Margaret.   2. Ecologists—Australia—Biography.
  3. Women ecologists—Australia—Biography.   4. Rain forest
  ecology.   5. Forest canopy ecology.   I. Burgess, Edward, 1985–
  II. Burgess, James, 1987–   III. Title.

QH31.L79A3 2006
577.34′092—dc22
[B]

                                              2005054133

A catalogue record for this book is available from the British Library.

The paper in this book meets the guidelines for permanence and
durability of the Committee on Production Guidelines for Book
Longevity of the Council on Library Resources.

10 9 8 7 6 5 4 3 2 1

We dedicate this book to parents who struggle to balance career and family and still seek connections to nature for their children, and to young people who search out nature in their daily lives.

And to Michael Brown, a master at juggling career and fatherhood.

Contents

Foreword

Meg Lowman, a pioneer of rainforest canopy research, here brings us more of her adventures in the treetops. She is a renowned scientist who can interpret her findings to a wider audience than just scientific colleagues. This is also the main goal of the Eden Project in Cornwall, England, where I work. Eden, with its five-acre rain forest, is another indoor canopy where we plan to build a walkway. The purpose of Eden is to interpret the importance of plants to people and to promote their sustainable use. I am therefore delighted to introduce this book, whose mission too is to increase public understanding of the science that is carried out in forest canopies. Several chapters describe the author's efforts to promote sustainable use of plants, such as propagating orchids in Cameroon or building a canopy walkway in Samoa to promote ecotourism to conserve the forest there.

Forest canopies harbor about 40 percent of all biological species, so their study is vital. Since her first book, *Life in the Treetops,* canopy research has made great progress through the work of dedicated scientists such as Meg who are afraid neither of climbing to the tops of trees nor of the deprivations of field-work in remote places. This sort of work is bound to lead to adventures that are worth telling, and here we have a wonderful mix of adventure and good science. Here is a university professor who is equally at home lecturing or writing for schoolchildren and the lay public, as can be seen in the chapter on the Jason Expedition. She has obviously also been remarkably successful in educating her own children. How exciting that her two sons contribute their comments to each chapter!

Professor Sir Ghillean T. Prance, FRS, VMH
The Eden Project
Bodelva, Cornwall, United Kingdom
(Former director of Kew Gardens, London)

Preface

My story of science and family began long ago and far away, early in my career when I became a new mother in the outback of Australia. In a country hospital of twenty-three beds, Eddie was the product of thirty-six hours of labor without drugs or injections. When the delivery table broke some twenty-eight hours into the process, my sheep-farming husband cleverly fetched the tool kit from his truck and repaired its broken leg. James, thankfully, emerged into the world after only ten hours of labor some twenty months later. In that rural environment, sending a wife to the hospital was not much different from sending a pregnant cow to the cattle yards. It was simply a biological event, and I respected that.

As a farmer's wife, I was the major child-minder while the men worked long hours with the livestock. It was an unarguable separation of duties. In the boys' infancy, they often went to the woods accompanying their mother, who lived by Thoreauvian tendencies. As a threesome, we had our share of adventures while exploring the treetops, as well as episodes of relative tedium counting and measuring myriad leaves and insects. In the process, mother and sons bonded not just with nature but also with one another. We shared special abilities: how to walk quietly in the woods, where to find a tarantula, how to stalk a lyrebird, how to avoid brown snakes, how to create a hypothesis in science, and how to rig a rope on a tree using a slingshot.

Although for the most part we have selectively fond memories of that time, we also recall occasional mishaps. For example, Eddie got his ears nipped by parrots during a research trip into the Queensland rain forests, and James endured sheep blowfly maggots hatching in the woolen fabric of his crib blanket. We drank our share of water laced with slime molds and dead sheep carcasses. We inevitably consumed hundreds of flies on meat pies; and we all gave several pints of blood to the leeches that lay in wait on the rain-forest floor.

During my children's early years, after I became a single parent, writing was my constant companion. I wrote scientific papers by day as part of my career, and became preoccupied with journaling as a nocturnal hobby. On Friday and Saturday nights, when my young boys went to bed early after a big day of play, play, play, I escaped to my grammatically correct adult world of complete sentences and nondangling participles.

Using diaries kept throughout a lifetime, I wrote about my rainforest treetop adventures, a laptop my constant companion. The manuscript was both solace and therapy. I struck up a relationship with Yale University Press that enabled me to turn my experiences into a book contract. My mission was to write about field biology for the public. My editor hoped to encourage young women in science via my adventures in the treetops. Since young boys play hard and need lots of sleep, I actually found time between batches of chocolate chip cookies and statistical analyses of field data to complete that first draft by 1996.

Entitled *Life in the Treetops,* the book was intended to inspire a few young women or educate a small portion of the public about the importance of rain-forest conservation. But through some miracle of the canopy gods that I will never quite fathom, a journalist in New York City read my small volume. Her review, featured on the cover of the Sunday *New York Times Book Review* on August 8, 1999, spotlighted *Life in the Treetops* and gave it a broader readership than I would have thought possible for a scientific publication.

It was a eureka moment for me. I learned firsthand that communication about science is almost as important as the science itself. All the experiments in the world may not save a rain forest as effectively as a clear message to the public. Some reviewer I never met had advanced the cause of rain-forest conservation, perhaps more than my twenty-five years of technical work. Her article caused me to reassess my priorities and seek to communicate science more effectively to the public.

I postponed writing a second book to focus on parenting instead. It was difficult to make this family-oriented choice, especially when a fairly lucrative book contract was offered by a big publisher. But my boys were becoming teenagers, at a time of life when they needed me more than as infants. Despite the mythology, I enjoyed this critical age in their lives, focusing my nonworking hours on them instead of on book chapters, and savoring their adventures instead of reminiscing about mine. Four years later, in 2000, as I gasped for breath while my teens galloped at a pace that left me slightly ragged, I contemplated another book with a theme more relevant to my children's young adult lives. I wanted to depict not just my own perceptions of juggling science and family, but also those of my sons.

The return to writing was joyful and provided another shared experience for our family. I had become the director of the Marie Selby Botanical Gardens, which involved more time sitting in a padded chair than climbing a tree. Leaving the treetops was a difficult career choice, but the leadership platform allowed me to focus on another lifelong goal: making "plant conservation" a household phrase. As the new director, I was charged by the board of trustees with prioritizing public, rather than technical, communication of science. In effect, I took a sabbatical from field research and tackled the mission of bringing plants and people together. It was a pleasure to pursue this new assignment, and to seek effective ways to educate the Gardens' visitors about botanical conservation. I have thick files of letters from adults and children who were exposed to the importance of plants during my tenure as director. One, from 7-year-old Bryn Morgan in Cleveland, reads: "It's fun to have a scientist friend. Meg makes me feel happy and excited about being a scientist when I grow up. I love the rain forest and my favorite part is the canopy because I love climbing trees." Letters like this made my new position particularly rewarding. (I look forward to visiting Bryn in her laboratory someday in my dotage when she is a famous scientist.)

My writing time was limited, however, because administrative duties dominated all waking hours. In 2002 the Gardens' vision for achieving plant conservation and education became mired in board politics and ego wars. I had become a national spokesperson for plants, ecosystems, and science education; but the new board of trustees preferred a narrower focus prioritizing bromeliad and orchid displays. Reluctantly, I left the padded chair and moved to an intellectual community at New College of Florida that shared my sense of environmental ethics. Back in the educator's role, today I have the responsibility of training environmental stewards of the future; as a professor of biology and environmental studies, I was even encouraged to complete this book.

My first book embraced stewardship through two pathways: research in tropical rain forests (career goal); and parenting (family priority). Of necessity, such juggling prompted me to seek creative ways of balancing the boys' needs with my unconventional career. Now in this sequel, my saga of exploration and research in forests of the world continues. The chapters address new canopy research questions in Western Samoa, French Guiana, Peru, Puerto Rico, Panama (again), Cameroon (again), and my own backyard of Florida. Using different forest types, I explore new methods of canopy access to answer those questions. This time I have shifted my priorities from pure scientific research to conservation and education outreach. On each expedition, an education or hands-on conservation program became part of the scientific process encapsulated in my account. Also new in this second book, my sons (now 20 and 18) wrote narratives to complement my chapters. Their thoughts on science, on boyhood, and on local as well as global issues provide a refreshing perspective when compared to that of their mother, who has weathered more pitfalls in her journeys. What a privilege to share this authorship with my children—no longer boys but young men with strong messages to convey via their own written words.

As parents in this uncertain world, we seek to endow our children with skills to navigate "the jungle out there." Balancing children and career remains a significant theme for most adults, regardless of career choice. For those of us who are baby boomers, caring for our aging parents has become a second phase of "parenting." I hope that my adventures as both a parent and a scientist will help those of all ages, as they learn from my mistakes as well as my discoveries. And I hope that our family adventures in "the jungle *up* there" will bring out the Tarzan or Jane in our readers, young and old, inspiring curiosity for the natural world and encouraging them to promote conservation of their natural heritage.

Acknowledgments

One of the blessings of turning fifty years old is sharing an evening with old friends and musing over our life-long journeys. Suddenly, the chaos and uncertainty pale. We marvel at what we have done, the road we have traveled, how we have survived, and best of all how we have done better together than apart. Teamwork is critical to both career and family. I used to tell my staff at every monthly meeting that there were only three requirements for success at their jobs: "1. Work as a team. 2. Seek excellence. 3. Have fun!" That prescription holds true for almost all elements of life. It is comforting to share memories with close friends after fifty years of survival. Collectively, our success stories in different vocations derive mainly from trust and teamwork.

I am led to believe that my next fifty years may be more about memories than about action, as the biological limitations of aging overtake my enthusiasm for adventure. But I look forward to seeing how it all unfolds. For now, I have been blessed to travel through life with many exceptional friends and family, especially two wonderful children, Eddie and James. Our family unit, joined in 1997 by a stepfather, Michael, has been nothing short of inspirational. We are grateful to our extended family, who tolerated our blowgun collection in the living room and other idiosyncrasies. John and Alice Lowman have been instrumental in allowing their daughter and grandchildren to pursue science and in encouraging all of us to dream bigger than most children from small rural hometowns. Our brothers, cousins, uncles, and aunts all tolerated collections of natural tidbits throughout our respective childhoods. Our teachers were inspirational in their shared gifts: John and Lee Trott, who were natural history mentors first to Meg and then to Eddie and James; Eloise Malinsky, who taught Eddie and James that chemistry is the building block of all life; Linda Janoff, who gave the boys their strong foundation in writing; Bijli Myers, who made mathematics for both boys one of the most elegant scientific languages on the planet; and other teachers at Pine View School in Osprey, Florida. The professors at Princeton University continue to strengthen Eddie's and James's love for science, while their mom and stepdad vicariously enjoy a second college career via the boys' enthusiasm.

Other close friends have served as mentors and friends to us: Gerri Aaron, Deane and Rex Allyn, Paula Benshoff, Stephen and Elizabeth Booth, Barthold Bouricius, Charlene Callahan, Patricia Caswell, John Cranor, the Reverend Susan deWyngaert, Kristina Ernest, Nathan Erwin, Joel Fedder, Robin Foster, Francis Gatz, Sandra Gilchrist, Mark Hunter, Robert Johnson, Michael Kaspari, Robert Kluttz, John Kress, James and Tamara Ley, Saul Lowitt, Dulce Martinez, Elzie McCord, Michael Michalson, William (Randy) Miller, Mark Moffett, Randy Morgan, Nalini Nadkarni, Bernard Nkongmeneck, Michael Pender, DC Randle, Robert Richardson, Bruce Rinker, Stephen and Rosalba Schimmel, Lavinia Schoene, Timothy Schowalter, Michelle Schweber, Timothy Scoones, David Shaw, David Sicree, Donald Weber, and Philip Wittman.

We are grateful to the families Arbucci, Buszin, Caswell, Ferguson, Folit-Weinberg, Heymann, Lamensdorf, Miller-Morris, Peters, Roth, Sateesh, Schaub, and Schur, and to the Amazon travelers who accompanied Meg on her ecotravel adventures; to Robert Ballard, Donald Carr, Joseph Connell, Paul Cox, Francis Hallé, Harold Heatwole, Thomas Lovejoy, and Peter Raven, who were our international conservation mentors; and to supporters of research expeditions over the years, which include Jason Foundation for Education, National Geographic Society, National Science Foundation, New College of Florida, Sarasota County, Marie Selby Botanical Gardens, TREE Foundation, and Triad Foundation. The Hermitage (an artists' retreat operated by Sarasota County Arts Council) kindly hosted me to finish and edit this book.

Beryl Black, Susan Fernandez, and Jane Minshall kindly read and edited sections of the book, as did the eleven outstanding students in my New College tutorial, The Role of Women in Natural History. Vivian Wheeler crafted some of our awkward sentences into presentable prose; we were fortunate to be the beneficiaries of her professional editing of this sequel after she had polished *Life in the Treetops* so beautifully. Barbara Harrison masterfully illustrated many chapters with her endearing pen-and-ink drawings. Last but not least, the staff at Yale University Press, in particular our editor Jean Thomson Black, contributed untold hours of dedicated perseverance. As neophytes in the world of writers, we are forever grateful for Jean's professionalism, humor, friendship, and patience as we followed a less conventional lifestyle that led us to write as a family about science, and to write as scientists about family.

James' Timeline— Growing

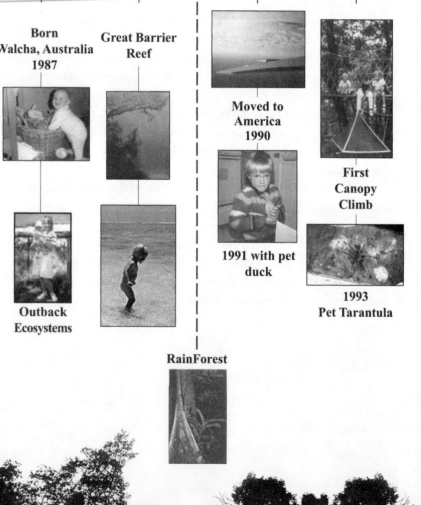

Early Education
Toddler in Australia

1980's

Childhood in
America

1990's

**Born
Walcha, Australia
1987**

**Great Barrier
Reef**

**Moved to
America
1990**

**First
Canopy
Climb**

**1991 with pet
duck**

**Outback
Ecosystems**

**1993
Pet Tarantula**

RainForest

James's chronology of his youth as he and Eddie juggle family

up with a Scientist Mom

Research as a Youth

Late 1990's to 2005

Jason V Belize 1994

First Science Project

Biosphere 2

Peru 1998

Panama Canal 2001

Entomophagy* at Explorers Club 2003

Antarctica 2004

*eating insects

and their mother's career in field biology (photographs by author)

Introduction

I am the Lorax. I speak for the trees.
I speak for the trees, for the trees have no tongues . . .
—Dr. Seuss, *The Lorax*

When asked about their mother's occupation, my sons usually reply, "Well, she climbs trees for a living." My two boys were raised single-handedly for many years by a mother who is passionate about science and conservation. As a rain-forest biologist, I have been on many expeditions to remote jungles, and my sons have often accompanied me. We have shared adventures in the Amazon, dangling from trees together, walking on canopy bridges, learning medicinal plants from a shaman, eating insects, spotting scarlet macaws, and just getting muddy. In the course of my scientific exploration, the boys have sampled mud on four continents—not an intentional goal of our research but a sideline that they absolutely relished. Both have an insatiable curiosity about the natural world, probably as a result of growing up in a household with a mom-scientist. My children have an extraordinary tolerance for biology at the dinner table that ranges from discussions of insect poop and how to measure it, to Latin names of beetles that are bandied about like sports teams. Family debates may focus on how to rig new gadgets for sampling in the treetops; or we may spend entire days in a forest searching for one specific leaf (the proverbial needle in a haystack).

But we have also had conventional family activities such as cooking, sports, reading, visiting Grandma, getting muddy (again!), or discussing book reports. Whether it was the thrill of discovering a previously unknown species or of buying new shoes, our family life expanded my view of the world far beyond my career perspective. As a single parent, I usually had no choice but to have my children accompany me as "field assistants." They taught me to think beyond the relatively narrow perspective of analytical science. Experiencing the world through three pairs of eyes has enriched my life far beyond relying on my view alone.

In my first academic job interview after Eddie and James were of school age, I was asked by the search committee members to explain what unique qualifications prepared me for a leadership role at their institution. The committee had copies of my résumé and knew of my multiple publications and grants, so I decided to give an answer that was not part of the written record. I replied, "Raising two boys single-handedly while juggling a successful field research program." This particular hiring committee, all white males who were older than I, obviously did not see any connection between their question and my statement. I did not get the job.

Having since risen through various levels of leadership in my career, I have bent over backward to promote a child-friendly work environment where family values are compatible with career. This advocacy has not been easy, particularly in remote regions such as the Australian outback or the interior of India, where notions of gender equality are often regarded with suspicion. Even in recent years I worked for a board whose chairman criticized prioritizing a family-friendly workplace and protested the hiring of women. But I have stuck to the belief that intertwining family with career can create a positive and productive work ethic, for both women and men.

Much has been written about the struggle to achieve a high-powered career, and perhaps an equal amount about the pitfalls of parenthood. Books on these two subjects usually prioritize one over the other, frequently treating them as two disparate agendas. Few rejoice over the combination of parenthood and career or advocate their compatibility. I believe that juggling the two activities enriches our everyday life with some sense of balance. Balance — what balance? I am the first to admit that my ability to keep work and family in perspective is far from perfect, and that my family has been very patient with me. There have been times when I was determined to complete a manuscript on a Sunday night when the Simpsons premiered on television. At other times, during their final exam week, I have cajoled the boys to wake in the middle of the night to view asteroid showers. From my children, however, I have learned more about balancing life, values, and career than from any self-help book or professional development course. I hope that I never cease to learn from them, and that they feel reciprocity in this mutual learning process along their path toward adulthood.

Unlike most of my friends, I pursue a career that has become a political hotbed. I am a forest ecologist specializing in tropical treetops and their biodiversity. The issues of species diversity, ownership of plant genetic materials, the fate of our forests, and sustainability of tropical ecosystems spawn great scientific and political debates. The acceleration of deforestation during my children's short lifetime, and throughout my career of twenty-five years, has caused me to rethink my priorities and goals as a scientist. If I continue doggedly to identify and study the ecology of a few new species, publish in obscure scientific journals, and slowly climb the traditional scientific career ladder as defined to me in graduate school, my rain-forest research sites will be cleared long before I am retired, and most of the organisms I study will have become extinct (some already are). But if field biologists were to seek conservation applications for our research projects and allocate some of our time to educating the public about science, perhaps we could avert impending disasters such as global climate change, destruction of rain forests, loss of fisheries, and episodes of coral bleaching.

Likewise, parents must do their part as stewards of the planet. Our children are not well educated about how our planet works or aware of how to become conservation-minded consumers. They need nature in their daily lives. Science literacy will be our downfall if we do not tackle this important challenge. As conveyed in my earlier book, *Life in the Treetops,* I am not content to contemplate these crucial issues after I retire. That will be too late. Our children's best inheritance is not stocks or automobiles; it is fresh water and healthy forests. Aldo Leopold summarized this philosophy so well almost sixty years ago: "Our bigger-and-better society is now like a hypochondriac, so obsessed with its own economic health as to have lost the capacity to remain healthy. The whole world is so greedy for more bathtubs that it has lost the stability necessary to build them, or even to turn off the tap. Nothing could be more salutary at this stage than a little healthy contempt for a plethora of material blessings. Perhaps such a shift of values can be achieved by reappraising things unnatural, tame, and confined in terms of things natural, wild, and free" (*A Sand County Almanac*).

If I were to specify to my children the single attribute that has best served me throughout my life, it would be passion. Passion for nature led me to a career in science. Passion for exploration led me to canopy research. Passion for people led me to advocate teamwork. Passion for conservation led me to use canopy walkways for ecotourism and education. Passion for children led me to participate in science education programs. Passion for a global vision enabled me to endure personal setbacks such as mishaps with orchids and egos. And passion for both my career and my family inspired me to seek ways to balance the two.

This book is aimed at a broad public audience: youth who express curiosity about a career in science, citizens who care about the environment, women who juggle the challenges of the career track and the biological clock, students learning about science or cultures, men and women who balance parenting and careers, scientists who use technology to develop new research, field biologists who work in remote areas. This book is also written for curious readers who simply wish to visit the rain forest in their armchairs or to experience family life through the eyes of a biologist. My primary goal is to encourage people to make science a larger part of their day-to-day framework for decision-making. My second goal is to illustrate that science as a career integrates well with families if one is creative and thinks outside the box. Third, I hope to educate readers about the importance of forest ecosystems and their conservation.

All of the chapters in this book reflect my enthusiasm — my passion — for scientific exploration and family life. The two are intricately intertwined. I could not begin to separate research projects from family vacations. Nor could I consider sole authorship of this book, since my children were such an integral part of my research. In each chapter I write about the science, the question asked, the canopy access method developed to answer that particular question, and the conservation or outreach elements of each expedition. My children write how they felt or what they dreamed on our journeys together, either using their diaries from early expeditions or writing more recent essays on how their mom's work affected their lives. For example, how did they feel when their mother wanted them to join her in katydid-hunting in the middle of the night in the Amazon? Did they dare admit to their friends that our dinnertable conversation sometimes focused on how to find beetles on giant stinging trees?

After having guided my sons through the pitfalls of their childhood, I do not want to disappoint them in their adulthood. As a parent and a scientist, my gift to them is the incentive to provide sound science for resource management that will conserve the ecosystems on which we all depend. I believe it is our children's most important inheritance.

OUR FAMILY TREE, BUGS AND ALL

By Eddie and James Burgess, aged 18 and 16

Like most families, ours has had its share of adventure. But while many children's adventures revolve around the chaotic life of the urban jungle with its city blocks and shopping malls, our adventures took place in a real jungle with towering trees and tribal villages. Dinnertable reflections commonly recall fishing for piranhas or encountering an anaconda. And we all have had a good laugh about the day in the canopy of Blue Creek, Belize, when we got drenched by eleven consecutive thunderstorms. We've never been to the state of Texas, but we have been to the Amazon village of San Antonio, Peru.

Not only did jungle adventures become a staple of our family folklore, but elements of these journeys invaded our everyday life. A tarantula always seemed like a more suitable pet than a dog or a cat. Crickets served as a tasty hors d'oeuvre were a fine source of protein. Our backyard contained no ordinary set of swings, but rather a full-fledged canopy walkway. And our playroom included a microscope, always with a fresh vial of army ants to investigate.

Our rain forest exploits constitute the most exciting chapters in our lives to date. When we share our jungle adventures with new people, they always say "Wow! It must be so great to have traveled to all those cool places!" And though we try to maintain some level of modesty, the honest answer is "Yes, it has been awesome!" The rain forest is truly one of the most awe-inspiring places on this Earth. The sheer abundance of life there is enough to make us dizzy. We have sensed the importance of this ecosystem, not only in terms of the cultures that live there (and those that don't) but also on a more spiritual level that can only be perceived through personal experience.

Here is our story, intermixed with our mother's version so that readers can gain both perspectives. In the process of sharing our mom's career, we learned a lot about creating solutions to problems, about teamwork, about asking questions and formulating experiments to answer them, and about other points of view. We also learned to love Oreo cookies (even when melted or squished), to munch on insects when offered, to check often for leeches, to drink lots of water even when we weren't thirsty, to walk in darkness, and to be flexible. It is our sincere hope that everyone has an opportunity to experience these jungles before it is too late. It may be wishful thinking, but perhaps with a little extra effort our generation may someday share the wonders of tropical rain forests with our own children.

1 Why Canopies Are Exciting

*I*ndeed over all the glory there will be a canopy. It will serve as a pavilion, a shade by day from the heat, and a refuge and a shelter from the storm and rain.
— Isaiah 4:5–6

When my children were toddlers, we passed many hours on our sheep and cattle ranch in rural Australia watching the livestock seek shade. They squeezed together under the few remaining gum trees in the midst of our sun-baked, wind-swept paddocks. If you were a dingo searching for dinner, it would be easy to head for one of the few shade-giving trees under which stood a smorgasbord of lamb chops and steaks. The canopy was not only important to animals that benefited from its shade, but also critical as a home to the many other organisms that made up the forest ecosystem. We would catch Christmas beetles, count caterpillars, track down goannas (Australian lizards), observe koalas, and monitor magpie nests.

In the past decade, tree canopies have attracted intense attention in urban centers, not just in forests. Like livestock in the outback, humans have discovered that shade enhances the quality of life. Shade provides recreation: we read, garden, picnic, swim, party, dine, and seek romance in shady places. Shade enhances our economy: we save money on air-conditioning, building maintenance, paint, cars, and even heating by creating canopy cover in our neighborhoods. In our typical headlong impatience to sanitize and modernize our cities, we tend to cut down trees without understanding their importance. In Florida, where development is epidemic, builders often clear all trees, including mature, hard-to-replace live oaks, before building homes. Then the new owners struggle for many years to restore a shady canopy around their house. Despite our increased knowledge of the benefits of tree canopies, we still follow this shortsighted, "cut-it-down" attitude toward our forests. Why are tree canopies so underappreciated and understudied, yet so essential to life?

Almost thirty-five years ago, when I was in tenth grade, the first Earth Day was celebrated. Almost thirty years ago, when I was in college focusing on environmental studies, I clapped with joy when the Endangered Species Act was legislated. Yet since then, an estimated 800 million or more acres of tropical rain forest have disappeared. Other ecosystems too are disappearing — the Florida coastline, North American old-growth forests, wetlands, and coral reefs.

I cared passionately about this vanishing natural world, enough to pursue it as a vocation. In 1978, while a graduate student living in Australia, I started climbing rain-forest trees because I was curious about what lived at the top. I asked questions: How long did evergreen tropical leaves live? Why didn't insects eat up all that green, which they obviously found so delicious? How did that green material manage to fuel all the food chains on earth? How did foliage defend itself from predators, since plants cannot run away from their enemies? This was my world.

Almost every child climbs trees, and I had figured out how to continue this wonderful pursuit as an adult. I frolicked in the forest and became an expert on forest canopies. I never envisioned, however, that my world of the treetops would become critical to the future health of our planet. But one of my colleagues turned the world of canopy biology upside down.

Quite by chance, Terry Erwin of the Smithsonian Institution discovered such abundance of life in the treetops that forest canopies became a hot spot, or epicenter, of field research. Terry sprayed several canopies in the tropics with a mild insecticide (a procedure known as fogging), and all of the arthropods fell to the ground in a heap. He could then count and catalogue the insect residents of an entire tree. From that initial harvest of insects in Panamanian rain-forest trees, he calculated that there might be 30 million species on our planet, not 3–5 million as previously estimated. As one of a handful of scientists studying the treetops in the early 1980s, I suddenly found myself in the spotlight, along with Erwin and several other canopy biologists.

Why was Terry's discovery so astounding? As field biologists who focus on species diversity, we seek to catalog, identify, and understand the role of all creatures. It is not simply a naming game; the ultimate purpose is to understand the structure and function of an ecosystem, even as we seek to know how the components of a car engine operate to create an efficient machine.

Our challenge of discovering and identifying the organisms on the planet is not easy. Finding a new orchid in the treetops is 90 percent perspiration and 10 percent luck. All of these organisms — orchids, beetles, birds, vines — are part of what we call biodiversity, otherwise known as the variety of species on Earth. Over the past two decades, the term "biodiversity" has become politically and scientifically important, as human activities have accelerated ecosystem degradation and subsequent loss of species throughout the world. Our new awareness of the complexity of ecosystems suggests that disruption of their function will be extremely difficult, perhaps impossible, to repair.

In the 1800s, at the dawn of modern biodiversity, Charles Darwin estimated that approximately eight hundred thousand species inhabited the Earth. (I can only imagine that the Queen of England was most impressed by his scientific prowess in calculating this apparently enormous number.) Nearly one hundred years later, however, Terry Erwin's collections from canopy fogging raised Darwin's tally more than fortyfold. Similar data sets all over the world, including those of Nigel Stork in Malaysia, Yves Basset in New Guinea, Joachim Adis in Brazil, and my own work with Roger Kitching in Australia, have confirmed Terry's initial figures. We now believe that the treetops are home to perhaps the greatest biodiversity on the planet. (Only the soil ecosystem may exceed canopy biodiversity, but we have not yet learned how to make an accurate count of the microorganisms underfoot.) E. O. Wilson, an eminent biologist at Harvard University, has raised Terry's original estimates. By including the canopy, soil, and oceans in his extrapolations, Wilson speculates that as many as 100 million species may inhabit our Earth.

Forest canopies are merely one example of a region on earth that was out of reach to scientists until as recently as twenty-five years ago. When I and other scientists first used slingshots to propel our ropes into the treetops, we did not yet fathom that this green leafy "machine" was a critical component of global health. Now forest canopy scientists, along with reef ecologists, ice physicists, soil biologists, water chemists, and many others, have become the physicians of the planet. We work against a near-impossible timetable in hopes of unraveling the critical mysteries of how our planetary home functions.

With access into forest canopies, our knowledge of biodiversity and the creatures constituting the machinery of forest ecosystems has burgeoned. Accordingly, the role of canopy biologists has changed. No longer can we dangle leisurely from the trees and simply contemplate the beauty of orchids and poison dart frogs; instead, we are caught up in a battle against time to provide answers before the chainsaws dominate. In short, we cannot afford to sleep! To date, biologists have catalogued only 1.5 million species of the alleged 30 million, or perhaps 100 million, species. The pace is slow: taxonomists calculate that we are classifying only the inordinately small number of 7,000 new species per year. Our work is cut out for us. The notion of sorting, counting, and naming 100 million species is daunting. The ecological task of determining which species are critical to essential processes such as photosynthesis, nutrient cycling, and decomposition is even more challenging. Stewart Udall, former U.S. Secretary of the Interior, once said, "Over the long haul of life on this planet, it is the ecologists, and not the bookkeepers of business, who are the ultimate accountants."

Exactly how many is 100 million species? Is there a way to make that enormous number meaningful to those of us who are not mathematicians? We can say that if two hundred scientists discovered and identified one new species every day for the rest of their lives, they would need almost fifteen hundred years (including weekends and holidays) to complete the task of identifying the estimated biodiversity on Earth. Even more urgent than names alone, we need to determine benchmarks for forest canopy health. How many trees and which species are crucial to maintain the global machinery that we call a forest?

Is biodiversity important? Can ecosystems function and remain healthy with fewer species? Unfortunately, no one has the answers to these vital questions. We have not studied our forests long enough to understand the biological processes that are critical to their health. To return to the wisdom of the *Sand County Almanac,* Aldo Leopold said in 1949, "To save every cog and wheel is the first precaution of intelligent tinkering." This statement, made almost sixty years ago, holds true today. We must preserve all the pieces of ecosystems until we know which are essential to their operation. Forests, after all, are efficient machines that produce energy, medicines, materials, fibers, and foods — and they carry out ecological processes. Their well-being invariably affects human health. Forests may well survive the extinction of some species, but which of these losses exceed the critical thresholds beyond which forests can no longer produce oxygen, cycle nutrients, decompose leaf litter, and carry out all the other services essential to our life on Earth?

These are major issues for our children and their children, as they grow up to become the next stewards of our planet. I hope that we can provide them with an education in science that will equip them to seek solutions. But we scientists need to do more than practice sound science: our research needs to be accompanied by public education and applied conservation, to foster a new environmental stewardship. Forests doubtless house uncharted discoveries for young explorers — new medicines from tropical canopies, exotic fragrances, unique seasonal patterns, unknown creatures buried in the soil. Exciting as the possibilities are, people are not likely to save something they do not understand. Despite the flurry of ecological research over the past twenty years, the Earth has lost an estimated 21 percent of forest habitats. Somehow, scientists have not communicated effectively to the public to ensure stewardship of what they study. Sustainability of our forests is best achieved through education and conservation.

In accordance with this philosophy, I have focused on understanding the energy transfer from leaves to the creatures that consume them (called herbivores), and explaining the importance of this process to the public. Herbivory, the process of foliage consumption, is my scientific specialty. I could thus be described as a professional leaf detective. The major herbivores are insects (such as beetles, caterpillars, walking sticks, true bugs) and mammals (koalas, sloths, and other vegetarians).

The topic of herbivory is complex. Why do insects prefer some leaves to others? Do they like to feed at different heights in the canopy, or on leaves of a certain age? Do they eat by day or by night? In my opportunistic world of canopy research, I sample many leaves, branches, seasons, years, trees, and forests, in order to address the question of how herbivory varies over space and time. I have measured nearly 250,000 leaves in my quest to understand defoliation in forests. My colleagues have jokingly appointed me honorary president of the Leaf Lovers Club.

Measuring leaves is often tedious, even downright boring, work. My database for each leaf includes length, width, area, age, toughness, and types of herbivore damage. Occasionally it also incorporates chemical analysis. Not having access to adequate electrical supplies or a digital computer in the wilds of Cameroon or other remote forests, I have frequently relied on graph paper, tracing leaf samples and counting squares during my nonclimbing hours. To persuade colleagues to count graph-paper squares for me, I have been known to bribe them with Oreo cookies — my staple for survival in the jungle.

Back home, I delight in the speed and accuracy of a digitized leaf-area meter hooked up to a computer. My results have documented leaf life span and mortality, the latter frequently caused by herbivores (also referred to as insect pests).

Why is herbivory so important? First, the process whereby insects consume leaves and in turn transfer this energy to the forest floor via their bodies and their frass (droppings) is critical to effective nutrient cycling among the various layers of the forest. Herbivory also creates a catalyst for the production of plant chemicals that defend foliage from animals that would otherwise eat it. Complex relationships have sometimes developed between specific herbivores and their ability to digest the chemicals in a certain type of foliage. This chicken-and-egg scenario is never resolved. Leaves evolve toxins that deter foliage feeders, and herbivores evolve ways to digest those toxins.

The interactions surrounding herbivory are constantly changing, but the end result is a plethora of chemical compounds (many of which have exciting medicinal properties). As ecologists, we become detectives seeking clues to who eats what, what camouflages whom, whose tissue is defended against whom, and which different plant or animal defenses are triggered by chemical or physical traits.

I accidentally stumbled on this ecological battleground. When first undertaking my studies of leaves, I never intended to study insects. I only wanted to find out about leaf growth and turnover of photosynthetic material within the canopy. But the fact that creatures kept nibbling on the marked leaves piqued my curiosity. I began looking at the herbivores in tandem with the leaves and became intrigued by their complex interactions. I also found out that measuring leaves in forest canopies is no simple task. What appeared to be a matter of merely picking ten leaves and measuring their defoliation became a complex chronology of birth, growth, survival, struggle, and death in the treetops. Most insects eat young leaves, but a few also eat older

The infant Eddie carried by his mom as she surveys eucalypt canopies in the outback of Australia (self-photograph by author)

tissue; some insects feed on lower canopies and others on the uppermost foliage; some herbivores take big bites and others simply suck juices.

In no time I had amassed a data set of over a hundred thousand leaves. Even in my initial canopy research in Australia, some leaves lived nineteen years, extending beyond the duration of my anticipated fieldwork. I faithfully checked all marked leaves throughout their lifetimes each and every month, including times when I was pregnant, had toddlers, or juggled my housewifely duties as the wife of a sheep farmer. Some tree species had leaves that lived only six months; those longevity surveys were completed rapidly. I became fascinated by the dynamics of leaf populations in the treetops, and devoted my time to trying to understand the lifestyle of this highly productive component of our planet.

This long span of data collection showed me that, when measured accurately, leaf-area losses in forest canopies approach 15–25 percent per year, a fairly high turnover of green material falling from the treetops via insect digestion and becoming part of the soil below. Scientists measure these processes of energy transfer to understand what keeps forests healthy, just as a doctor measures our blood pressure, heart rate, and other indicators of human health.

My herbivory measurements in Australian dry forests were perhaps the biggest anomaly of my research career. In *Life in the Treetops* I chronicled how eucalypts, with their resilience to fires, insect outbreaks, and droughts, suffered as much as 300 percent leaf-area losses per year. How can trees endure that high level of attack? In this case, beetles defoliated some trees three different times within one year, resulting in an enormous percentage of annual defoliation (table 1). Such high levels of herbivory cannot be sustained and led to what was termed "eucalypt dieback," which killed millions of Australian trees. Defoliation by insects is both good and bad: it creates a direct transfer of energy from the treetops to the forest floor, stimulating growth and forest health when moderate amounts are eaten; but it can also result in tree mortality if outbreaks or severe defoliation occur. In my job as an ecologist, or leaf detective, I seek to understand this balance and predict changes in forest health with changes in insect numbers (also called "pest pressure"). With the onset of global climate change, or with excessive logging, the proportions of insects may increase, causing widespread canopy defoliation or even death of entire forests.

My efforts to integrate research on herbivory in forest canopies with conservation and public education are highlighted in my field

Table 1. HERBIVORY IN FOREST CANOPIES OF THE WORLD
(percentage of leaf area lost per year)

Forest type	Foliage eaten annually (%)
Temperate deciduous	15
Australian eucalypts (or dry sclerophyll)	15–300
Cloud forest	26
Subtropical	16
Warm temperate	21
Tropical	12–30
Temperate coniferous	1–2

expeditions to remote regions including Africa, French Guiana, Peru, and Panama. For example, hot-air balloon surveys in Africa and French Guiana documented canopy biodiversity of lowland tropical rain forests on two continents. With but little extra effort, I created materials suitable for public education through documentary films. Francis Hallé, mastermind behind the hot-air balloon canopy access method, starred in an IMAX film. Likewise, I shared my research on plant-insect interactions in French Guiana with young people in a National Geographic film called *Heroes of the High Frontier*. Later I partnered with local botanists in Africa, training Pygmy villagers to identify their orchids and supporting orchid farming as a sustainable economic initiative for conservation.

In Samoa, our Canopy Construction Associates walkway team designed a treetop walk for ecotourism, not just for scientific research. The revenue from the walkway created a sustainable economy without logging the village's forest. The notion of using canopy walkways for both research and conservation has become a model for other regions. In Peru and in Panama, millions of students joined me in

Eddie (*left*) and James (*right*) in the rain-forest village of Blue Creek, southern Belize (photograph by author)

canopy research via a distance-learning project called the Jason Expedition (formerly the Jason Project). With the help of a film crew, we may have inspired a cadre of canopy scientists to follow in the next generation!

Throughout my career, my own children have participated in most of my field expeditions, by necessity but also by choice. They counted leaves, patiently watched herbivores feeding on foliage, lived in remote huts, brushed their teeth without running water, ate mystery stews over campfires, addressed their own hypotheses, and generated their own data sets. This sharing gave rise to the coauthorship of scientific papers as well as this book.

The prioritization of science education for young people has never been more important than it is today. Science literacy will provide the environmental solutions for the future. The treetops also represent an arena for exploration and discovery. Canopy research is a catalyst to

James (*left*) and Eddie (*right*) brushing teeth without running water in a hut in the jungle of Belize (photograph by author)

recruit young people as future scientists, and to encourage scientists to become stakeholders in conservation. Scientific data and technical publications are necessary, but they are assuredly not enough.

TALES OF ROSELLAS

By Eddie, as happened in 1986

One of my earliest memories of the natural world is my experience with the crimson rosellas at O'Reilly's Guesthouse in Queensland, Australia. About 3 years old at the time, I was accompanying my mother on one of her research excursions into the rain forests of Lamington National Park, near the guest house. At this tender age, I fancied myself an ornithologist and took it upon myself to memorize the calls of every Australian bird in the field guide. Mom claims that even her ornithologist colleagues were impressed with my accuracy in identifying avian fauna.

Considering my fascination with our feathered friends, you can imagine how delighted I was to discover that O'Reilly's was home to a host of Australia's most magnificent birds — including the notable crimson rosella. These brilliant red-and-blue birds were often so tame that they would eat seed right out of your hand. (As it turns out, feeding wildlife is not an ecologically sound practice, but at the time this was not widely known.) Unfortunately, the food I offered did not satiate one particularly voracious rosella's appetite and he decided to make my fingertip the second course. In case there is any doubt, let me assure you that rosellas are not exactly known for hav-

Eddie surrounded by crimson rosellas in the Australian rain forest (illustration by Barbara Harrison)

ing soft beaks. The wound the rosella inflicted bled for what seemed like hours. Needless to say, I was not too happy. How could such a charming creature have betrayed me?

You might think that this traumatic experience would deter me from further ornithological pursuits. On the contrary, I went on to become a bird-watching instructor at a summer camp and have kept a life-list to track my bird sightings over the years.

I believe I learned a valuable lesson that day back at O'Reilly's: I could survive nature. Too often today I find that our society is afraid to experience nature. People think that all the pesky critters of field and forest are out to get them, and the discomfort they may suffer will outweigh the satisfaction. In my experience, though, none of these discomforts are insurmountable. When I look back on my time with the rosellas, what I remember most vividly is their brilliant plumage, not their sharp beaks. It is my hope that children today will not become too sheltered from the "dangers" of the natural world. The risk of getting a little muddy or a little bitten is well worth the reward of curiosity and appreciation for the natural world.

2 Canopies for Conservation: Climbing in Samoa

How wonderful are islands! Islands in space, like this one I have come to, ringed about by miles of water . . . Islands in time . . . The past and the future are cut off; only the present remains. Existence in the present gives island living an extreme vividness and purity. One lives like a child or a saint in the immediacy of here and now.
—Anne Morrow Lindbergh, *Gift from the Sea*

Samoan proverbs:
Ua afu le laufale.
The floor mats are sweating. [Visitors are overstaying their welcome.]
La lafoia i le fogavaʻa tele.
Cast it on the big deck. [Have patience and forgive those who trespass against you.]

Ingredients for adventure:
A tropical island
An endangered rain forest
An indigenous village with a tribal council devoted to conservation
A funky old bus
A few canopy scientists

The scenario:

The government wants the tribe to pay for a new school.

Logging their rain forests will pay for the construction.

The question:

In terms of conservation, is there a better way of paying the debt?

FEBRUARY 12, 1994. SCENE I. We arrived in Western Samoa at dusk. The airport was situated along a beautiful blue sea, with coconut palms just behind the single runway. We passed through Samoan customs in a crowded, humid hallway typical of most tropical airports. On this trip, Eddie and James stayed home with their grandparents, and I traveled with several colleagues. Our bags arrived — oh joy! We piled into a dilapidated taxi to travel for an hour into Apia, the capital city. Our drive gave us some evening glimpses of Samoan life. Children were walking down the roadside, coming home from school. Men sat cross-legged in their prayer huts, taking part in traditional evensong sessions commonplace in each small village. Many homes were open-pole construction, so we observed dinner preparation or, in many cases, family prayer sessions.

The colors and scents of Samoa were vivid: gnarled cinnamon-colored breadfruit (*Artocarpus altilis,* family Moraceae) voluptuously bursting from its green canopy; velvety-textured red lanterns of hibiscus (*Hibiscus rosa-sinensis,* family Malvaceae); brilliant yellow bananas (*Musa* sp., family Musaceae); pungent frangipani (*Plumeria rubra,* family Apocynaceae); and tall green sentinels of the ti plant (*Cordyline fruticosa,* family Palmae), whose foliage cured fever, headaches, eye ailments, and inflammation. Plants were not the only colorful portion of the landscape. Homes were painted light blue, bright yellow, pink, or other bright colors; even the lava rocks lining garden paths were decorated with red, blue, or aqua, as if to compete with the bright colors of the bungalows and landscape. Samoan cottages, called fales, featured practical tin roofs that captured fresh water and channeled it into a cistern for drinking and cooking. It was obvious that the Samoans lived with utmost respect for their unique island ecosystems.

Robert MacArthur and Edward O. Wilson pioneered the concept of island biogeography, through their renowned research on the numbers of species that settle into a finite space. Three underlying principles prevail:

1. The number of species and the species composition of an island are dynamic and constantly changing.
2. The number of species and the species composition are determined by an equilibrium between the immigration of new species and the extinction of those already present.
3. The rates of immigration and extinction depend on the size of the island and its distance from the mainland (which they call the *species reservoir*).

More recently, human activities have disrupted the natural process on the islands and introduced exotic (i.e., non-native) species. These alien species often become pests. For example, the cane toad (*Bufo marina,* family Bufonidae) was introduced into Australia from Hawaii ostensibly to kill the sugarcane grubs. This toad not only failed to eat the grubs, but it has decimated native wildlife and spread at an alarming rate throughout the continent. In North America, the house sparrow and the grackle are now unwelcome residents brought in by unsuspecting colonial settlers. Both have significantly displaced native bird populations and caused expensive damage for farmers and city dwellers alike. Even more threatening are the gypsy moths, released by accident in Boston after being transported from Europe in the mid-nineteenth century. Since then, they have caused billions of dollars' worth of tree death and defoliation throughout eastern North America during outbreak years.

Islands are especially vulnerable to exotic species, because the chances of an alien species displacing a native population are high. At last census, Hawaii listed over 350 threatened species, most of them the result of the pressures of human activities. The likelihood that an island ecosystem, once disrupted, can regain equilibrium is remote. Although the challenges for the conservation of islands are enormous, solutions can be achieved by creative thinking.

Island rain forests are some of the most threatened habitats in the entire tropics; once they are deforested, no seed sources exist to facilitate their regeneration. The composition of an island rain forest is a unique product of chance and climate, with no two islands exactly alike. Most have become vegetated over thousands and even millions of years. The odds of a seed landing on a remote island shore are slim. It takes chance events such as catastrophic cyclones, passage through a bird's stomach, physical attachment to (and subsequent detachment from) a swimming or flying animal, or airborne travel. These one-in-a-million incidents lead to the unpredictable dispersal of plants to other islands. Thus, South Pacific islands have varying compositions of vegetation. Although it is possible to assess ecosystem succession by the complexity of vegetation, it is not possible to predict which plants will establish themselves on an island, because so much of their dispersal depends on chance.

Harold (Hal) Heatwole (an extraordinary ecologist who is an expert on sea snakes, tardigrades, ants, and other zoological creatures) and I conducted many surveys of the vegetation on Australia's Great Barrier Reef Islands when I was his postdoctoral student in the early 1980s. We found young islands with zero to five plant species established, and older islands with fifteen to thirty species established. The latter formed a more complex ecosystem that in turn provided a means for settlement of insects, followed by reptiles, amphibians, birds, and finally mammals. On Heron Island, perhaps the most widely studied island of the Great Barrier Reef, we recorded approximately thirty-six native species of plants (plus thirty exotics, species that were not native but introduced by human actions). In contrast, a two-year-old island of only 15 feet in diameter, Howard's Patch, had no plants at all on its small, newly emerged surface. We first discovered, named, and stepped (actually frolicked) on Howard's Patch in 1984, and in subsequent years mapped its gradual expansion. Perhaps the birth of an island is as closely akin to parental joy as island biogeographers ever feel about their subjects.

Paul Cox, internationally recognized ethnobotanist, has been working for many decades on the islands in Western Samoa. Paul's second home outside the United States is the village of Falealupo on the island of Savai'i. The island healer, a wise woman named Pele, taught him over many years how the Samoans use plants as an apothecary. Paul's research on South Pacific islands and his stories about healing have brought many different plants to the attention of pharmaceutical companies and ultimately to the world of medicine. On this trip, he and I partnered in developing an ecotourism project that now serves as a model for the application of canopy research to conservation.

Normally, the self-sufficient island of Savai'i did not need the outside support of an ecotourism industry. However, in the early 1990s a cyclone demolished many thatched schools and other government buildings throughout Western Samoa. As a consequence, the Samoan government mandated that all villages must build storm-proof cinderblock schools for their children at a cost of approximately $65,000 per school.

The village of Falealupo on the island of Savai'i had no cash economy to cover this cost. Its yearly per capita income was equivalent to less than US $100. The people fished for food and used plants from their preciously guarded rain forest for medicines, clothing, and homes. The forest was not only a treasure trove of economic plants and their derivatives, but also a breeding ground for endangered flying foxes (*Pteropus samoensis,* family Megachiroptera). The villagers, believing that flying foxes harbored the spirits of their ancestors, considered them sacred animals. Spiritually, economically, and biologically, the forest provided all the needs of the village and had done so for generations.

Since the villagers had never participated in the economics of the outside world, they did not know how to finance their school. Loggers offered to buy the villagers' rain-forest timber on contract, thereby providing cash income to pay the debt. However, loss of the forest would virtually ensure extinction of the village. Without food, shelter, fabrics, medicines, and security for the spirits of the ancestors, the lives and heritage of the villagers would be destroyed.

Paul Cox had a novel solution: why not build a canopy walkway, whereby tourists would pay to enjoy a walk through the treetops and money would be raised to pay the debt? When the Seacology Foundation in America offered to provide a bridge loan plus seed funds to initiate the ecotourism project, the plan seemed a real possibility. Paul came to visit me in Florida to talk over his plan. If we combined our skills in ethnobotany and canopy research, perhaps we could make a positive difference in island rain-forest conservation. It was a wonderful idea and a new conservation partnership.

With Paul and two builders from Canopy Construction Associates (CCA), Phil Wittman and Bart Bouricius, I traveled to Samoa in February 1994 to discuss with the village chiefs the concept of a canopy walkway in Falealupo. Accompanying our expedition were an executive from Neuskin Corporation (a cosmetic company that had helped fund Paul's ethnobotanical research), a reporter from *Vogue* magazine in New York, and a staffer from the Seacology Foundation. I subjected my body to the barrage of injections required for that remote region of the planet. Laden with gifts for our hosts, film, ropes and climbing gear, water and snacks, we flew to our rendezvous point in Western Samoa. We met at the Aggie Gray Hotel, formerly a getaway for Ernest Hemingway and today a tropical paradise for those who find their way to this beautiful, off-the-beaten-track British outpost.

FEBRUARY 13, 1994. SCENE 2. In the hotel we awoke to the sounds of heavy rain, a typical tropical shower during this season of monsoons (called cyclones in the South Pacific). Our final destination was Savai'i, about 25 miles from the mainland of Western Samoa. We saw the rough seas and felt grateful that Paul had booked us on Samoan Air, the tiny airline that serviced the island as a more rapid alternative to boat transport.

After we were weighed in (some of Bart's heavy climbing gear was set aside for a later flight), a torrential downpour blackened the skies and we felt less comfortable about our choice. The little propeller plane took off despite the challenging conditions of rain, wind, and weight. I imagine that our Western prayers were not nearly as effective as some of the Samoan chants. Miraculously, we survived the stomach-lurching flight and landed at Savai'i's tiny airport. A minivan was waiting for us — old and patched together, but quite adequate for travel on the island's narrow road that saw almost no other vehicular traffic. In the late morning, we approached the village of Falealupo, passing small family-operated roadside stands selling soda pop (mostly Coke), crackers, and candy bars, obvious social gathering spots for the youth on a hot day.

In Falealupo, the entire village had congregated in the meeting-house. As if by magic, they seemed to know exactly when we would arrive, without the assistance of clocks, telephones, or electricity. Evidently our visit was a significant event, and the village had prepared an enormous feast. Paul had briefed us by explaining that nothing occurred in the village without the unanimous approval of all fifteen chiefs and that the walkway represented a relatively radical idea for this small village. Not only was the school debt large and unprecedented, but encouraging tourists to come to the region was a novel and perhaps frightening notion.

We disembarked from the van, wearing our newly purchased lava lavas. These were traditional, colorful, cloth wraparound skirts, worn instead of pants. The twist-and-tie mode of securing the cloth around one's waist required much practice! Bart, with his 230-pound frame, looked almost like a clown in his colorful lava lava and in construction boots that threatened to trip him with his every step. Without a moment to use the toilet (in whatever form it existed) or freshen up, we were led into the center of the meetinghouse amidst great cheering and fanfare. Everyone shook hands around the circle and said "Talofa lava" [greetings]. The feast had begun!

It was quite a trick to sit cross-legged on straw mats covering a cement floor, with tightly binding lava lavas, and at the same time deal with sore ankles that were not used to mashing against the hard floor for five hours. Chiefs in training and young women served course after course of food, creating a busy and colorful scene in the meeting hut. We sat, spellbound, as the chiefs orated in Samoan about their origins, their ancestors, their culture, and their precious rain forest. Small and light, I was able to sit with ease like a Samoan. Unfortunately for Bart and Phil, the only polite mode of sitting was cross-legged — no legs outstretched. Pointing one's toes at anyone was an insult. (Midway through the ceremony, poor Bart stretched his legs and courteously hid his pointing toes by pulling the mat on top of his feet. He simply could not endure another minute of crossed legs, which left his ankles black and blue and his back sore for days.)

In the center of our circle was a large wooden bowl with a muddy liquid. This ceremonial drink, kava, was made by fermenting saliva with the roots of a tropical shrub (*Piper methysticum,* family Piperaceae), an important medicinal plant in the South Pacific. I called it the consensus plant, because after drinking several cups the entire group of chiefs voted "yes" to an issue. This mildly intoxicating plant numbed our tongues, and eventually our brains, in a pleasant and gentle fashion.

Kava was the main ceremonial drink in Fiji, Samoa, and most of the islands throughout the Pacific. To drink in traditional style, I imitated what the chiefs did: slapped the right knee, accepted the kava cup, poured several drops on the floor, drank a sip and said "manuia," which meant "good fortune." The chief presented each of us with a kava stick, a very special gift that meant we were highly respected by the leaders of the village. To me, it was like receiving an Oscar. My kava stick continues to be one of my most valuable worldly possessions. I have carted it all over the world, and I share its power with friends who are sick and/or in need of spiritual guidance.

The chiefs themselves were unique in mannerism and dress. All had full body tattoos, which signified that they were good husbands. Samoans believed that the pain of tattooing was equivalent to childbirth, so a man who had been tattooed was considered a better husband because he would be more appreciative of his wife. Young men who chose to undergo the tattoo process stood in the ocean every night because the cool salt water soothed the agony inflicted by the tattoo process. In Samoa, a full body tattoo extended from the neck down to the knees.

During the welcome ceremony, each chief spoke at length in Samoan about the village debt, the school, and the proposed canopy walkway. At one point, it was obvious that they were talking about me: one chief pointed and uttered the words "monkey woman" in English in the midst of his Samoan dialogue. Everyone laughed. We were

A Samoan chief is about to present Meg with a sacred kava stick during
a ceremony in the village of Falealupo (illustration by Barbara Harrison)

also issued Samoan names during the ceremony. I was christened
"Mati," meaning fig. What a wonderful tree with which to be associated! Was it just chance that, for most of my professional career, fig
trees have been my inspiration?

We ate fare new to my imagination during the course of the day.
The feast, served in gourds and coconuts set on the floor, lasted for
hours, and we were graciously served first. The custom was that no
one would eat until the guests had consumed their fill. This meant that
everyone else watched hungrily as we all had to eat huge quantities of
mysterious foods: chicken stew, taro, coconut, breadfruit, and yam
were somewhat recognizable. But I will never forget the strange pud-
ding-like substance served on a banana leaf — what was it?

Coconut milk made a tasty thirst-quenching drink, and its large seeds served as a wonderful cup once cracked open. We Americans were honored with a drinking straw in our coconuts and a crooked spoon that came with the custard, touches of Western culture that they had procured on our behalf. No one else had these unique commodities for dining. Where did they find straws on this remote island, I wondered? Women fanned our plates to fend off flies. A banana leaf for a plate and a coconut husk for a glass served as clever, recyclable products. What an honor to participate in the feast of a lifetime (at least of my lifetime)! And after much kava, we had even more cause to celebrate because the tribe unanimously approved the canopy walkway project.

Following the feast we stayed with the village healer, Pele, in her falé (hut) and were privileged to observe her fascinating techniques of medical practice. Well over 80 years old according to Paul, she was a walking encyclopedia of knowledge about plants and their medicinal properties. Bart, who suffered from chronic athlete's foot, was given a poultice of leaves, and his affliction soon disappeared despite many years of unsuccessful treatments in the United States. The reporter from *Vogue* had a queasy stomach. She reclined on a mat while Pele gently waved ti leaves over her body as a diagnostic effort. Suddenly, the healer jerked back and communicated to Paul Cox that the woman had some foreign body in her uterus. Incredibly, she had an IUD. Pele had diagnosed this from noninvasive techniques passed down over many generations.

A few of the medicinal plants about which Pele instructed us included:

Zingiber zerumbet (family Zingiberaceae), shampoo ginger — for washing hair

Ficus obliqua (family Moraceae), fig — sap used to kill parasites in stomach; also for inflammation

A Samoan healer holding the shampoo ginger, whose fruits are squeezed to produce a soapy substance. Other medicinal plants described in text are depicted (illustration by Barbara Harrison)

Artocarpus altilis (family Moraceae), breadfruit — antiviral and anti-
fungal qualities
Piper methysticum (family Piperaceae), kava — for internal distress as
well as for ceremonial activities
Rhapidophora graeffei (family Araceae) — for inflammation
Cananga odorata (family Annonaceae) — for asthma

Later on, I was fortunate to spend a day hiking with another healer
(called shaman in South America, but healer in the South Pacific), and
I learned even more about Samoan uses of plants. As we traipsed
around the interior of the island, he indicated that virtually every plant
had a practical application. A significant find on the island was *Homa-
lanthus nutans* (family Euphorbiaceae), a common roadside tree that
colonized cleared areas (also found throughout Australia). It is used
in Samoa to treat yellow fever. Because of this antiviral property, Paul
arranged for the National Institutes of Health to test this plant for
AIDS research. Even the enormous fig (or banyan) trees, the designated site of the canopy walkway, has an important medicinal role. Fig
leaves create a poultice for inflammation, and a mere teaspoonful of
their milky latex kills stomach parasites in children. One of my fa-
vorites was the ordinary ginger plant; its exudates, when squeezed
from its bulbous fruits, serve as shampoo. After using it, I had very
clean hair despite the plethora of tiny insects that came along with the
plant juices. Perhaps I went home with some new biodiversity on my
scalp!

The shower experience was memorable. In the center of the village
was a single spigot attached by a long pipe to fresh, cold water. Everyone showered at this site, with no shower curtain or private shed constructed around it. To complicate matters further, Samoans showered
modestly without removing their lava lavas. They soaped up as far as
possible and soaped down as far as possible, and then "they showered

the possible" (as my childhood summer camp counselor used to say when referring to the male anatomy — the notion of a boy washing his possible reduced us teenaged girl campers to giggles). The Samoan shower was anxiety-ridden for us Westerners. I wondered if I could really get clean. Would my lava lava fall down? Would anyone be watching when I soaped my possible? What critters lived in the water supply, and was I ingesting them? Or were they ingesting me?

Even more challenging was the double lava lava shower. If truly filthy, a showeree would take off the dirty lava lava and replace it with a clean one, still under the shower, tying one over the other and then dropping down the dirty one. I was happy to wear my dirty lava lava rather than struggle to exchange it for a clean one and risk exposing my possible.

In spite of our difficulties with the logistics of living in the village, we spent all our waking hours talking, measuring, and thinking about the canopy walkway. Many were the hours we debated with villagers over the potential walkway site. The chiefs wanted the bridge to start at the school roof, as a symbol of connection between the school-children and the forest. But no one could artistically create any aesthetic or economic design to cross the 75-foot field between the school and the forest, other than to build a bridge on telephone poles. Although the wooden pole structure would make a wonderful board-walk that was structurally pleasing in this beautiful remote island situation, it was an expensive proposition.

The villagers also wanted the walkway to span a cleared area planted with bananas and eventually embrace an enormous emergent fig that was well within the forest interior. After the storm that had flattened the old school, the fig was severely damaged but now was regenerating. Its stature was notable in comparison to the other trees in the forest, most of which had been even more severely pruned or toppled.

The fig had multiple stems and lots of branches for epiphytes, and could easily support a platform for viewing the rain forest. We clambered around in the fig canopy for an entire morning, sketching and measuring different branches and assessing their strength. It would have been simpler to design a short walkway within the forest and around the emergent fig, without any link to the school or construction over the banana fields. But we were inspired by the enthusiasm of the chiefs, who wanted the structure to remind their children that education was tied directly to their forest heritage.

Our last day on Savai'i was spent at the most senior chief's house — the nicest accommodation and the principal home in the village. It was an open-air wooden cottage, with four rooms including kitchen area, living room, and two bedrooms. An old mattress, probably the only one on the entire island, was offered to me for sleeping. Villagers traditionally slept on rattan mats on the floor or in hammocks. Probably the mats or hammocks were cooler and healthier than an old, damp mattress, but it was extremely generous of them to offer me one of the creature comforts of Western society as a gesture of hospitality.

It was also evident that the chief's daughters were "off limits" for flirtation, and the family kept a watchful eye on our group of American men. While we were in residence, a Peace Corps volunteer who was helping to build water supplies throughout the island came to visit. During his short stay, he was scolded by the chief for flirting with his daughters. (Small world that it is, I caught up with this man many years later in Sarasota, Florida, where he had returned to live with his Samoan wife, the chief's daughter!)

The chief and his family were excited to see photographs of my children. They felt sorry for me. It was inconceivable to them that a mother would leave her children for ten days. Their priority was family; to them, quality of life translated into living with one's family in one place. In contrast, our westernized lifestyle has reinforced the concept that success is measured by acquisition of material goods, even at the cost of employment that requires extensive time away from family. The culture of Savai'i assessed well-being by the presence of family, not by material possessions. To the villagers, ten days without their children was probably a greater hardship than an entire lifetime without shoes or television. Their sentiments made me lonelier than ever for Eddie and James. My only consolation was to collect photographs and stories to share with them upon my return.

To show their appreciation for our visit, the village invited us to witness a tattoo ceremony. Paul wanted to record some of their ceremonial songs to preserve this cultural tradition. We went to the tattoo hut, our demeanor hushed and respectful, since we were the first outsiders allowed to witness this important coming-of-age ceremony. It was drizzling. It was also Valentine's Day (although there was no romance in this painful process). We were given permission to use cameras and tape recorders, but not to talk.

A young man, perhaps 18 years old, was lying on the floor surrounded by the tattoo artist and four other young men with partially completed tattoos. Samoan teenagers underwent the tattoo process together, taking turns each day until all had completed the process. It took about a week to receive a full body tattoo. Each design was different, and obviously the tattoo artist was highly respected throughout the village. Tattoos were expensive and cost up to a year's wages, usually paid in pigs and crops. An additional fee of five fine mats (that collectively took one year to weave, we were told) often completed the transaction.

Tattoos originated in Samoa, where they are made with the juice of the candlenut tree (*Aleurites moluccana,* family Euphorbiaceae). They have since spread to other cultures, but different materials are used.

In Samoa the fruits of the candlenut trees are burned and their soot scraped from the fire pit to mix into a purple liquid. A small hammer made from turtle shell and animal teeth pounds the juice into the human skin. This application is obviously painful, and the group sang louder as the victim moaned in agony. The songs were meant to comfort him, and everyone switched places throughout the day.

After a momentary feeling of nausea, I became fascinated by the use of plants and natural materials in the tattooing process. Thinking of these Samoan men experiencing extreme pain as a symbol of their loyalty to their wives and out of respect for childbirth, I was awestruck. It was reassuring to know that the young men of the village were not *required* to have tattoos, and many went without. Perhaps new ways of testing a husband's loyalty will be forthcoming in younger generations, but a strong sense of tradition existed throughout this village. The only way to lose face as a young man, we were told, was to begin the tattoo process and then drop out with an unfinished tattoo. The entire family was outcast for this behavior. It was all or nothing in the tattoo business on Savai'i.

In addition to sharing the tattoo process, we were privileged to visit the school and meet the principal and teachers, highly regarded citizens in the village since they had the all-important task of teaching the children. We brought gifts for the school and were invited to present them in the classrooms. Eddie's elementary school back in Florida had collected school supplies (notebooks, markers, pencils, staplers, and other goodies), which we had shipped in boxes along with our luggage. The new school was quite simple in its construction — a cement block structure with a line of classrooms connected by a sheltered walkway for rainy days. There were windows but no screens, and one simple toilet block. I visited a fourth-grade class. The students were shy but polite, all wearing blue-and-white uniforms. They loved the

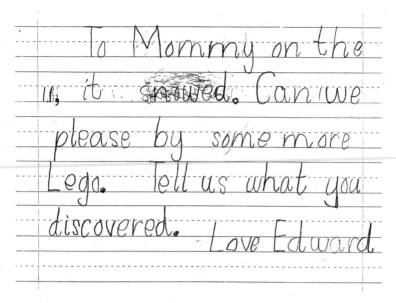

To Mommy on the 11, it snowed. Can we please by some more Lego. Tell us what you discovered. Love Edward

Eddie's note to his mother while she was in the remote regions of Western Samoa

toys: a Frisbee (their first), a troll doll, and a matchbox car were vastly different from their conventional repertoire of playthings. It was fun to watch the children amusing themselves with their familiar soccer balls and generally cavorting on the open field outside their school — no shoes, no hats, no cell phones, and no backpacks to lug homework.

We spent the last rainy evening prior to our departure making a few more measurements of the school and surrounding vegetation. Bart was satisfied that he had enough information from which to create a design and order supplies from halfway around the world, a challenge in that we could not even phone the village to get additional information. The chief was pleased with our "dignity and grace" and claimed that "we acted like chiefs." The village waved good-bye, and we hopped into the old, run-down minibus that was packed to the hilt with our belongings. Humidity and sweat had undoubtedly expanded the dimensions of all our clothing, and we had to be careful stowing our kava sticks. We went home facing many logistical challenges, but with strong enthusiasm to complete the detailed drawings and estimates for this project.

On the way back to the airport, Paul took us to view the flying foxes. Another village was hoping to create a preserve for these sacred animals, which they called *pe'a vao*. Many rain-forest trees were dependent on flying foxes for pollination, including species of plant families such as myrtle (Myrtaceae), bignonia or trumpet vine (Bignoniaceae), silk floss (Bombacaceae), and pea (Leguminosae). Flying foxes, by eating fleshy fruits, dispersed seeds and contributed to forest diversity and regeneration throughout the Pacific. Thus, they merited conservation for their ecological role as well as their spiritual importance throughout Samoa.

Reflecting on the spirituality of the Samoans, I felt enriched by their culture. I now had a special Samoan name, an intimate knowledge of their lives, and my very own kava stick blessed by the chief. I clutched that lifelong treasure all the way home.

We arrived at Western Samoa's international airport some ten hours early. Paul went in another direction, and the three of us from Canopy Construction Associates faced the prospect of a long day. To my surprise, a robust and important-looking gentleman cornered me in the airport lobby, demanding to know who I was. He immediately mistook me for royalty because I was carrying a kava stick. When I explained what we were doing, he was even more delighted. Mr. Afioga Polataivao Fosi (also known as the Brown Hawk because he was former professional heavyweight champion of Western Samoa) was Minister of both the Environment and Women (two portfolios amusingly lumped together). He insisted that fate had decreed that he would be our guide for the entire day, while we awaited our flight back to Hawaii.

Sniffing an opportunity for even more adventure, we hopped into his Mitsubishi Pajero (with driver) for a tour of his achievements on the island. Very few cars were on the road, and certainly none as nice as the minister's vehicle. We went to his office, where he told the secretaries that he was out for the day. Next we went to his house, where he picked up a lavish picnic for our outing. Then he took us up into the hills to view the hydroelectric project he had created: power for the entire island from a single dam. The landscape appeared natural and wild, but was in fact a newly created lake resulting from the dam.

We went to his favorite beach for a picnic. The minister's royal picnic table awaited us, although others appeared to have permanent tables there as well. We enjoyed a wonderful meal, with fresh fruits and fish and soda pops, returning to the airport at sunset to catch our flight. I felt as if we had made a friend for life, and the minister promised to assist us in the challenges ahead. (Importing strange items such as telephone poles and reels of stainless steel cable for the canopy walkway project would undoubtedly require a minister's support.)

The uneventful flight home bore the sad emptiness of leaving behind new friends, especially people who loved their forests so much. The mother in me, however, had mixed emotions; I was anxious to see my children and share this experience with them through pictures and stories. They would have grown and changed even in the ten days I was away, and there would need to be a great deal of catching up. I regretted that they could not always accompany me on these adventures involving new cultures and people; however, the chief was adamant that I must bring my family when I returned to build the canopy walkway — a notion that brought great joy as I daydreamed throughout the long flight home!

THOUGHTS ON LEADERSHIP: SAMOAN CHIEFS
AS A GLOBAL EXAMPLE

*Recollected by Eddie and James, Aged 9 and 7 at the Time
of Their Mother's Visit to Samoa*

The day my mom brought back her kava stick from Samoa was a memorable one. Although we have not yet had the chance to visit this tropical island nation, our mom's stories of her adventures there enriched our views of the world beyond Sarasota, Florida. The story that sticks in our minds is her meeting with the tribal leaders. We remember listening in awe as she explained how the chiefs sat cross-legged for an entire day to learn from my mom and her colleagues about the walkway and about ecotourism. She told us how the members of her team were welcomed like royalty and invited to join a celebration feast. The tribal chiefs' process of learning from the experts, openly expressing personal concerns, and then celebrating together struck us for its openness, honesty, and hospitality. These elements are lacking in our own government. In today's global politics, too much time is spent sidestepping the real issues. If more of our leaders could simply level with the matters at hand like the Samoans and treat each other with humility and kindness, we think our Western world could do greater things. The West prides itself on its advanced level of civilization with its endless supply of creature comforts, yet the civility of the Samoan's decision-making process makes us wonder which culture is more civilized in a deeper sense.

MARCH–DECEMBER 1994. SCENE 3. Although our daily lives back in Sarasota eventually settled down, the project in Western Samoa had not receded into the Florida sunset. On the contrary, Bart and I spent hundreds of volunteer hours (during off-work time) tracking down suppliers of telephone poles in Australia, locating ships that would carry them, engaging appropriate professionals to join our team, and measuring and calculating timber and hardware. My phone bill at home reached an all-time high. None of us was willing to give up on this conservation project. Bart and I exchanged many conference calls and finally arrived at a budget, but not without glitches. For example, the Australian shipping company would not guarantee that the telephone poles would arrive intact; they felt the requested poles were too long to guarantee safe transport. This left us with a dilemma: Should we order extra poles, but at great cost? Figure out an alternative? Buy shorter poles and disappoint the chiefs? Or simply pray they arrived intact? Ship them from the States at an absolutely astronomical cost? Meanwhile, Paul Cox anxiously urged us to lower the budget for all aspects of the project, since it was a conservation mission based on charitable contributions.

Finally, the budget was firm. It was higher than anyone had anticipated, but the final structure was within the specifications of the village chiefs. Our struggles, however, were not yet over. The next roadblock was our team of builders, who worked by the American conventions of contracts, insurance, and liability coverage. "What?" they exclaimed, "Go to Samoa and build something without specific maintenance contracts? Without guarantees of the deliveries of equipment? Without a definite timetable? With significant cyclonic rains? To work for half price because it's a conservation mission?"

The logistics with the builders became more difficult than the supply orders. Bart and I became frustrated, and finally at the final hour, when we needed to confirm air bookings and begin inoculations for the team, we had to admit that the project was at risk. We simply could not guarantee delivery of the goods within budget or assure the crew that their contracts were watertight.

With a very heavy heart, I called Paul. He was not surprised, but he was disappointed. It was a sad day for conservation, for the villagers and for those of us who had invested our hearts and souls in the project. I lay awake many long hours trying to find a creative solution but could think of nothing. It was the first time I had admitted defeat in my passion to promote conservation. We were beaten by the challenges of getting equipment to a remote site, and by the American fear of liability. Drat and double drat.

Our only consolation was that we now had some workable designs to build canopy walkways for ecotourism, to provide a sustainable income from forests without logging. And the children of Pine View School in Sarasota, Florida, had sent several more boxfuls of toys and school supplies to Samoa, strengthening the international ties of friendship.

POSTSCRIPT, 1995

Paul Cox was not to be defeated. Through our canopy network, he located a young couple from Maine with construction skills who were willing to go to Samoa, to build a canopy structure for the village without insurance or assurance. Stephanie Hughes and Kevin Jordan simplified the original design so that it required less hardware. The chiefs also compromised and agreed to a revised design.

From our measurements, photos, and diagrams, a beautiful platform was built around the emergent fig tree, omitting the bridge from the school to the forest. (That had required the expensive and questionable telephone poles, as well as a shipload of timber.) The structure generated funds for the village without logging the forest. The simplicity of design also ensured ease of maintenance, so less liability was associated with its construction. And one year after their visit to Samoa Stephanie and Kevin had a baby girl whom they named Falealupo, in honor of the village. Despite our failures, both an ecotourism project and a potential canopy biologist were born from our efforts in Western Samoa.

ETHNOBOTANY IN FOREST CANOPIES: A CAREER ASPIRATION?

By Eddie, Written in 2002 at Age 17, Inspired by Paul Cox's Work in Samoa

For almost one hundred fifty years, scientists have recognized the importance of the knowledge of local people living in the tropics, and their sustainable use of plants for medicines and other important everyday applications. Professor and Mrs. Louis Agassiz said in 1868: "A large number of the trees forming these forests are still unknown to science, and yet Indians, these practical botanists and zoologists, are well acquainted, not only with their external appearance, but also with their various properties. It would greatly contribute to the progress of science if a systematic record were made of all information thus scattered throughout the land: an encyclopedia of the woods, as it were, taken down from the tribes which inhabit them" (Richard Schultes and Robert F. Raffauf, *The Healing Forest*).

Over a century later, botanists have not undertaken such a comprehensive survey. Worse, many valuable medicinal plants are being lost as tropical regions are cleared, burned, and logged. The promising field of ethnobotany deals with the study of people's interaction with plants in their environment, especially the use of plants for medicinal purposes. Rather than direct scientific experimentation, ethnobotanists attempt to gain knowledge of forest plants through the indigenous peoples of the area. This approach often yields excellent results, because many indigenous tribes have lived in forested regions for thousands of years and have an immense knowledge of their local plants and uses.

Although humans interact with plants more commonly on the forest floor, the numerous plants in the forest canopy cannot be overlooked. Accompanying my mom on many canopy research expeditions, I have observed and appreciated some of these plants and their uses in tropical villages where we have been privileged guests.

Lianas, epiphytes, and many other host-dependent plants found in the canopy serve important functions for humans. Fibers, foods, medicines, fuel sources, aesthetics, and special ceremonial functions are some of the most important uses of plants from the treetops. Pioneering surveys by scientists such as Bradley Bennett, Paul Cox, Richard Schultes, and Mark Plotkin have provided me with wonderful reading about tropical ethnobotany.

It seems surprising that only a small handful of pharmaceutical companies have played a role in the conservation of tropical forests as potential apothecaries of the future. However, I have read that large multinational companies prefer artificial manipulation of chemicals in the laboratory. I hope to contribute someday to our knowledge of medicinal plants, and in the process to assist with a global vision of sound forest conservation ethics.

3 Indoor Canopies: From Baseball to Biosphere 2

The scientist. He will spend thirty years in building up a mountain range of facts with the intent to prove a certain theory; then he is so happy in his achievement that as a rule he overlooks the main chief fact of all — that his accumulation proves an entirely different thing.

— Mark Twain, *"The Bee"*

As both boys learned to read and write, they became wonderful field assistants.
They traveled easily, their lithe and spindly bodies adept at curling into pretzels
in the small spaces of prop planes or rickety trucks on dirt tracks. Exuding that
wide-eyed wonder that children naturally share with all those around them, they
were an inspiration to their scientist mom. Best of all, they were curious and
loved to count insects, find leaves, or discover new things. We entered into a new
phase, changing from mother as child-minder and gatekeeper to mother as ex-
pedition leader, with all three of us constituting a team.

1994. This was a year full to the brim with science and family activities, and Eddie and James shared this bounty. Two visits to Biosphere
2 were barely sandwiched in among many other long-term research
projects. In addition, the boys' perceptions were changing daily as
their horizons expanded through school and other adventures. Eddie, aged 9, started a special health class in gym, in which he learned
various facts of life to supplement his knowledge. I ordered a book
entitled *What Is Happening to My Body: For Boys* that immediately circulated to all his friends. In no time it was chocolate smudged and tattered around the edges. The boys sequestered themselves behind
locked doors to study the pictures, memorize the text, and giggle.

This course on manhood coincided with tryouts for Little League,
another American rite of passage — especially in Florida, where baseball can be played year-round. Eddie's first baseball game created family chaos, ranging from losing him in the large baseball complex, lock-
ing my keys in the car with the motor running, and other crises
conveniently lost in the recesses of my brain.

Little League did not integrate easily into our lifestyle. It seemed
that whenever I had weekend work at the Gardens, I was also called
to man the hot dog stand at the stadium. The practices were long, hot,
and dusty. And the games seemed to attract parents who loved to
shout aggressively from the stands, as if more decibels would trans-

form their kids into instant sports stars. Perhaps sensitive to their mom's frustration, the two boys ended their baseball careers early and moved on to other sports. (We also tried soccer for a season; but after several encounters with fire ants both sons turned to tennis and eventually to rowing, where they enjoyed long and dedicated high school careers.)

After Eddie's retirement from baseball, we had more flexibility to travel for science as a family. In early March of 1994 we escaped to Cape Canaveral on the east coast of Florida, where a colleague had invited me to lecture at the National Aeronautics and Space Agency during the week of *Endeavor*'s space launch. NASA booked us at the Holiday Inn, with direct views of the launch pad; in anticipation of this historical event, my dad joined us. We went to bed early, setting our alarm for 1:00 A.M., just before liftoff was scheduled. The evening was rainy and cloudy so we were not optimistic. Miracle of miracles, it had cleared when we arose in the dark and went out on our balcony. An indescribable sight: the entire sky blazed with a great white light, and a delayed roar suddenly drowned out all sounds around us. Three generations watched in awe.

We were fortunate to have a family pet that did not preclude frequent travel. Harriet, our tarantula, ate one cricket every few weeks. The neighborhood kids watched her cage like a TV screen when the boys placed the sacrificial cricket inside for dinner. Although she never barked, she was a relatively effective watchdog. Spiders, at less than a dollar a month, are not expensive to feed. The boys developed quite a fondness for Harriet. At one point early in his writing career, James even dedicated his class valentine to Harriet. I was not jealous, because I got a Valentine's breakfast in bed, with eggs, bacon, and fresh raspberries, while Harriet received only her single cricket! Harriet was initially named Harry, but then she grew enormous. (Male spiders grow less than half the size of their partners.) The other advantage of

+10

Dear Harriet,
You are my *lovely Valentine*.   I *adore* your
ribbon-like spinnerets. I am *devoted* to your
hairy legs. You defy all *tradition*. I have great
fondness for you.   You have lots of *kindness*. You
pounce as fast as a *Cupid's arrow* and *cherish*
your crickets. The *lace* you make is beautiful.

your *beloved*,
James

James's ode to Harriet, our pet tarantula

her being Harriet and not Harry was longevity: females live up to
fifteen years, whereas males live only about four years.

Our next scientific sojourn that year was to attend a National Science Foundation workshop at Evergreen State College near Seattle.
The initial plan was for Grandma to come and baby-sit, but she developed bronchitis and had to cancel at the last minute. The conference organizers kindly offered to fly the boys out and to provide childcare.

Laden with the requisite books and toys, our flight to Seattle was
smooth. We took a shuttle to Olympia and unpacked at the Ramada
Inn where the conference was to be held. Eddie, now a budding
young scientist, dutifully brought four apples in paper bags as part of
an experiment due in school on his return. He was testing the effects
of dirt on apple-rotting (examining ways to speed up decomposition), a process that required daily observations. We housed the apples in a drawer with a "Do Not Disturb" sign on it and hoped for the

best. Miraculously, the hotel staff left the drawer alone, despite its odor. We then carted the apples, still in their ragged paper bags, to three different hotels so that Eddie could continue his observations over the week. Oh, the challenges of keeping up with science homework, even in elementary school!

The conference was very tiring for me, juggling intellectual ideas during the day then sharing my bed with a wriggly 6-year-old at night, not to mention all the jumping on the bed in his dirty, wet clothes. I could never understand why young boys simply have to jump on beds. Each morning, the baby-sitter rescued me from my child-minding duties so that I could focus on canopy science. One day she took the boys up Mount Rainier. Perhaps it is just as well that I did not know the details of jumping into snowdrifts without warm clothes, and of frozen hands and feet. Another day, the conference group stayed at an old country hotel with a spa. Each of us was given a coupon to enjoy a hot bath, so I naively sent the boys off into the men's baths, only to have them reappear seconds later, giggling uncontrollably. The older men inside were stark naked in deep hot tubs — definitely not a child-friendly sight.

On the last day, the boys brought their books and sat all day in an office while we scientists conducted a wrap-up workshop in an adjacent conference room at the field station for the Wind River canopy crane. By the end of the day, the boys had met and talked with most of the scientists during breaks. They were ready to go home. Poor Eddie managed to complete five pages of math homework on the return flight, only to leave his notebook on the plane. Aside from this minor catastrophe, we were happy to have shared yet another science adventure. Several weeks later, I got a letter from a Russian scientist named Boris, saying "Your children are treasures. The world is in good hands." His letter became a special keepsake, eulogizing this particular trip in our family memory.

My next "expedition" in September was an international workshop in Arizona. Biosphere 2 was a first-ever attempt to create and maintain ecosystems under relatively controlled conditions. Could valid experimental science be conducted on artificial ecosystems under the confines of a glass dome? When Darwin sailed on the *Beagle*, he had no scientific hypothesis to test, and no museum awaiting a quantitative collection amassed in scientific fashion. Instead, he was a "thinker-observer . . . on a long, eventful voyage." So stated Roy Walford, the "inside" physician for the Biosphere 2 crew who lived under glass for two years. Walford saw the first phase of Biosphere 2 as another serendipitous scientific adventure similar to the voyage of the *Beagle*, whereby the eight "crew members" made many discoveries but entered their glass world without strict scientific notions of what was to be discovered.

Biosphere 2 was an enormous glass structure built to artificially recreate conditions for life, perhaps on another planet. In this case, the planet was under a dome of glass in the Arizona desert. The question was, could human beings in a closed environment produce food, oxygen, and all the essentials for life as we know it? Biosphere One is our natural Earth, which has created the perfect conditions for human life over many millions of years. This process of replicating it in the Biosphere 2 experiment proved expensive: keeping eight human beings alive under glass for two years cost approximately $200 million. It was a simple matter of multiplication to extrapolate to the 6.5 billion people on the entire planet. Based on the budget of Biosphere 2, it would cost close to 8.125×10^{16} (approximately \$81,250,000,000,000,000, or 81 quadrillion, 250 trillion) to artificially support all the people on Earth for just one year — obviously a preposterous idea. The artificial scenario of Biosphere 2 provided a renewed appreciation for the ecosystem services that our Earth provides naturally and without cost, to sustain life on our planet.

As human activities continue to degrade natural systems, we may need to pay enormous sums to repair the ecological services that are essential to life on Earth. In fact, we already pay for some ecosystem services that used to be free. As a child, I never dreamed that someday I would buy a bottle of water in an airport or purchase water coolers for both workplace and household use. Americans pay billions of dollars annually for pure water, something that we used to take for granted. What is next — air for sale?

The amazing benefit of ecosystem services is that they function while we sleep; even more incredible is the fact that ecosystems will continue to provide our planet with these services if we only leave them alone to function naturally. Economists and biologists working together estimate the value of services provided by global ecosystems at a staggering $36 trillion per year. In other words, if we had to artificially create services currently produced by natural ecosystems, the price each year would be almost as great as the gross world product, estimated at $39 trillion. Obviously, this cost cannot easily be borne by the next generation, so the best solution is to set aside adequate expanses of ecosystems and allow them to continue their services that keep the planet healthy. Consider the water supply of New York City: construction of filtration plants would have cost an estimated $8 billion, but $1.5 billion sufficed when forests in the Catskills were successfully purchased outright to serve as natural watersheds. Similarly, the tropical rain forests provide essential stability for the global climate, as well as carbon storage and high levels of productivity that benefit the entire planet. Scientists recognize the importance of conserving vast areas of tropical rain forests, but are challenged to decide who should pay for these areas. It is an unfair economic hardship to burden the tropical countries alone, when the rain forests actually benefit temperate countries as well. The question is not only who should pay, but how much? And could such a program be enforced?

Eight crew members lived off the ecosystem services of Biosphere 2 for two adventurous years, during which many measurements including the costs of survival were quantified. The inhabitants struggled, because the complexity of replicating planet Earth had been vastly oversimplified; they simply could not produce enough of the essentials to survive. After the eight Biosphereans emerged, a second chapter for the enormous glass structure began.

Biosphere 2 was turned over to Columbia University as a rigorous experimental chamber to test scientific hypotheses. The structure itself occupied 3.15 acres (just over 1.4 hectares), and was termed a glass-enclosed mesocosm. It contained different ecosystems (biomes) including desert, rain forest, savanna, thornscrub, mangrove marsh, coral reef, ocean, and agricultural plots. Plants, animals, and soils were imported, and sun remained one of the few locally natural attributes (although it was reduced by half because of the glass). Air was circulated with blowers, pumps, and two enormous adjacent "lungs" (approximately 165,000 cubic yards in airspace) that expanded and contracted to relieve the pressure of the air throughout the day and night.

These biomes served as the ultimate artificial chambers for conducting controlled ecosystem experiments on biogeochemical cycles. No one entered or exited without careful monitoring. Strict scientific codes were followed, and various hypotheses were tested in different biospheres. Studies of biological and chemical processes were conducted essentially to mimic the entire Earth, using these small microcosms of measurable space. Such research is classic ecological experimentation, in the sense that scientists subsample entire populations, in the hope of answering big questions. Careful experimentation can yield answers without measuring an entire population. It was hoped that Biosphere 2 could provide an accurate subsample of our planet in order to manipulate different environmental factors and observe the impacts.

Biosphere 2 provided vivid insights into the value of ecosystem services. Our Earth has evolved over billions of years to function as a well-oiled, complex machine. It provides natural services such as air-conditioning via wind currents, energy production via plant photosynthesis, and water purification via stream flow, to name just a few. The goal of our international conference at Biosphere 2 was to determine if this unique artificial set of ecosystems could be utilized to resolve major scientific questions. Approximately thirty scientists attended from all over the world, each to apply his or her relevant expertise to research within the biomes. To me it was old home week, for several of my Australian and European colleagues were part of the contingent. I was honored to participate in this "think tank" aimed at restructuring Biosphere 2 from an adventurous science experiment to a rigorous indoor hypothesis-testing environment. My parents willingly flew down from upstate New York to serve as surrogate parents for their grandchildren. (In actual fact, I should probably have co-authored many publications with my mom and dad as essential "collaborators" throughout my scientific career.)

My role at the workshop was to evaluate the rain-forest ecosystem, and specifically to discuss ideas with the directors about the possibility of constructing a canopy access system there. This rain-forest biome had been established under glass in 1991 to simulate a rain forest in the New World tropics. Ghillean Prance (at that time director of Kew Gardens in London) was consulted to create a plant list, and his efforts culminated in the planting of some 282 species within this relatively small plot of 17,000 square feet. Approximately 61 percent of the plants survived, leaving 172 species in a tiny tract of under half an acre (0.19 hectare), less than a fifth of Biosphere 2's domed interior.

The rain forest had five purposes in Biosphere 2:

1. Create a sustainable ecosystem to stabilize atmospheric cycles in the domes, and to study biogeochemical cycles;
2. Contribute to the diversity of the landscape by housing more species than the other biomes;
3. Produce food and other materials (medicine, cacao, etc.);
4. Provide aesthetics for the Biosphere 2 inhabitants.
5. Serve as a model for restoration ecology

Amazonian plants, as well as Puerto Rican species, predominated in the rain-forest biome and were planted in eight subhabitats: lowland rain forest, ginger belt, varzea, cloud bowl, surface aquatic systems, bamboo belt, mountain terraces, and cliff face. After having been transplanted from their countries of origin, many of the trees fell down. Analyses showed that in the absence of stress from natural winds, trees do not produce adequate root systems or "stress wood" to stabilize their structures. An important lesson was learned for growing a rain forest under artificial conditions.

My mission to serve as an ambassador for canopy research was successful. Several weeks after my return from the workshop, the director of research at Biosphere 2, Bruno Marino, invited our team of walkway builders, Canopy Construction Associates, to design a canopy access system for the rain-forest biome. *Indoor canopies* — a new challenge for our team, who had been so accustomed to working in remote jungle settings with their physical rigors of weather, tall trees, multilayered tree heights, and sometimes rotten branches.

I recognized that I had well and truly worn out my baby-sitting credit with my parents, as well as our collective bank account for airfares. How could I manage to accept this exciting scientific opportunity in Biosphere 2? I was honest with Bruno and explained my dilemma. He quickly replied that the boys could come along to the site and he would arrange for childcare during my consulting hours. Having children in tow was an extra responsibility, I lamented, but the notion of sharing the Biosphere 2 project with my sons was an exciting family opportunity. In our household, *exciting scientific opportunities* frequently turned into *exciting family opportunities.* Over many years, the extra planning and logistics undertaken by the team leader (aka Mom) created lasting family bonds from experiences shared. It was rare that the boys did not wish to participate. James reminded me that once, as a teenager, he was desperate to stay home from Peru for a birthday party, a fact that he immediately forgot once we arrived in the steamy jungle of the Amazon and he learned how to use a blowgun.

Off we went to Biosphere 2 — once again with science homework, library books, electronic games, climbing apparatus, measuring equipment, camera gear, and extra snacks for those moments when children get hungry after hours. A driver awaited us at the Tucson airport, and we sped off almost as if on a magic carpet ride. The desert was spellbinding and a new ecosystem for our family. In fascination, we watched tumbleweeds vault across the highway, spotted saguaro cactus looking like sentinels in the sand, and exclaimed over houses with backyards like sandy moonscapes. What a different world from the East Coast suburbs! Our favorite souvenir from the whole trip was a small, shriveled tumbleweed that the driver allowed the boys to chase along the roadside; it served for many months as a stick-sculpture centerpiece adorning our dining room table.

The entrance to the Biosphere 2 domes reminded me of seeing the City of Oz across the poppy field. From far away, the vaulted glass structures appeared like a mirage in an otherwise hot and desolate landscape. We were deposited at the Biosphere Hotel, our home for the next four days. After dinner and a full night's sleep, we walked to the research offices the next morning, ready for work. Bart Bouricius,

Eddie and James outside the entrance to Biosphere 2 near Oracle, Arizona (photograph by author)

my partner in walkway construction, was also on-site for the consulting job. Having been unable to locate any childcare within twenty-five miles, Bruno seemed delighted to bring the boys on our tour. We had specific instructions not to leave anything inside the domes, so we heeded the call of nature before entering through the submarine-like, sealed doorways. We brought only cameras and notebooks. Eddie had been charged by his teacher with conducting a science experiment within Biosphere 2 in exchange for missing school, so we all cast about for ideas. Conducting science experiments in remote locations was becoming a family obsession, for mom and kids alike.

We toured the human habitation region of the sealed dome, viewing bunkrooms, kitchen area, library, and general lounge space where the infamous team of eight had spent many months monitoring their existence inside Biosphere 2. We heard tales of chocolate bars and beer smuggled behind the sealed doors. Both boys were wide-eyed imagining life inside this stationary ship.

As we walked, Bruno asked James to carry a rope into the next biome. Dutifully he picked up the coil, only to have hundreds of cockroaches dart out and jump quickly into his clothes. The result was a fairly upsetting, albeit harmless, tingling sensation. Instantly, an idea for Eddie's required science project came to mind. Two insect outbreaks dominated the biodiversity of Biosphere 2: cockroaches in the human living area, and sugar ants throughout the terrestrial ecosystems. It was not surprising that in an artificially maintained environment one or two insects would become pests. The small sugar ants, almost innocuous to humans, were so abundant that they ran in the hundreds across our feet and up our legs. Fortunately they did not sting but were obviously distracting as they tickled the hairs on our legs and elsewhere. Perhaps the ants' bird and lizard predators had become extinct over time in the dome; or the ants may have been mistakenly transported inside by humans, like exotic species that travel to a new continent in the real world. We did not hear the true history of the ants' introduction, and perhaps no one knew with certainty. Calculation of their population densities, however, created a fine science project for elementary school.

Eddie and James set up their survey sites, including their own shoes, to count the abundance of ants in different biomes. They stayed busy all day, while Bart and I measured the rain forest and discussed materials for the canopy access system. At the end of the day, we exited from this legendary world that had been the isolated home of eight people for almost two years. We could not help marveling at how claustrophobic the inhabitants must have felt within those glass domes, with the added challenge of growing their own food. Their

Robinson Crusoe–like existence was the subject of many animated dinnertable conversations over the next few days.

At the end of our second day (fortunately after the boys had completed their ant surveys), a loud and irritated voice came over a loudspeaker at the command center, "What are those children doing in the biome?" We might have been hearing the Wizard of Oz himself. Bruno, our host, sheepishly replied, "They are accompanying our consultants who are constructing the canopy access system." The agitated reply came: "Well, this was not approved and furthermore no children have ever officially been permitted inside the Biosphere." Too late, the boys were definitely inside, behaving themselves rather well, I thought to myself, and now it turned out to be against regulations. Promising not to return, they were allowed to complete their day inside. To allegedly be the first official children working in Biosphere 2 was an unexpected "honor" for Eddie and James. Not surprisingly, they reacted with disappointment to their eviction. In later years, Eddie commented wisely that such adult restrictions may serve to deter children from pursuing science.

Bart and I returned the third day, leaving the boys within the confines of our hotel room. Armed with Nintendo, movies, and other addictive toys, they were cajoled to safeguard each other's welfare, and a few staff members offered to check in on them. It may have been for the best, since James had suffered food poisoning from our dinner at the hotel and was not fit to spend a day inside the biome. I suffered from the same malady, but had no choice other than to return inside the glass dome and complete our tasks. My stomach growled ominously as we traipsed back inside.

Biosphere 2 posed a unique challenge in terms of building an access system that would serve ecological research and also exceed the high levels of safety required. It was our first assignment that required utilizing OSHA (Occupational Safety and Health Administration) standards; the remote tropical locations where we usually construct walkways do not even know about the existence of such standards. The canopy access that we designed for Biosphere 2 was a model system for situations that demanded the highest safety standards to access the treetops. Not surprisingly, it was much more expensive than any other system we had developed.

The rain-forest biome where the canopy access system was to be installed had been planted initially with fast colonizers and secondary forest species, none of which had common English names (including *Clitoria racemosa,* family Leguminosae; *Carica* sp., family Caricaceae; *Leucaena* sp., family Leguminosae; and *Cecropia schreberiana,* family Cecropiaceae). In this artificial setting, however, succession favored only four species of trees that had managed to reach the upper canopy: bombax, or *Ceiba pentandra,* family Bombacaceae; *Hura crepitans,* family Euphorbiaceae; cecropia; *Arenga pinnata,* family Palmae; and clitoria. I was overjoyed to see some of these "old friends" from earlier fieldwork. Perhaps unexpected events such as the death of several pollinators may have altered the natural progression under the glass dome.

Bart and I attached ourselves to the space frame with metal clips and harnesses, and scampered through the treetops with greatest of ease as compared to a natural jungle situation. In almost no time, we had the four species of canopy trees mapped and a simple design to present to the Biosphere 2 staff. Along the way, I must confess to one of my most embarrassing research incidents: I threw up behind a bombax tree in the rain-forest biome. Having wondered for many years about the impact of my addition of nutrients to that small space, I am happy to learn that no catastrophic growth anomalies were observed as a result of my metabolic "contribution."

Our final design allowed access along two axes in the canopy via a double cable system. The system facilitated both horizontal and vertical access to the major canopy species, and the double cables provided safety measures that far surpassed any system we had installed in nature. The cables (Permacable™) were attached to the space frame and allowed a load of up to 5,000 pounds for any fall, as required by OSHA fall protection standards. Fortunately, a fall from the rainforest canopy of Biosphere 2 would at most result in a tiny bump, compared to falling from the monolithic trees of the Amazon jungles.

All individuals who used this indoor system were required to complete a comprehensive training program on the hazards of canopy work. Bart and I were amused. Compared to the danger of crossing the street in New York City, I far preferred the risk of climbing trees! The Biosphere 2 staff went on to conduct intensive research on physiological processes in the canopy of their artificial rain forest and published important findings on photosynthesis rates between canopy and understory foliage in their struggling artificial rain forest. In addition, our system allowed their research staff to address questions about the interactions between the atmosphere and plant respiration.

Biosphere 2 also taught important lessons for the design of experiments to test ecological hypotheses. The Biosphere domes attempted to house entire ecosystems under glass. The concept of miniecosystems had the advantage of complete control over all incoming and outgoing elements. It also provided exact data on species, population dynamics, and experimental manipulations. In addition, Biosphere 2 illustrated some of the constraints of experimental design. How do we know if an artificially created ecosystem is an exact replica of the natural system? And can we accurately control all the myriad variables between plants and atmosphere, even in a small space?

This challenge was greater than had been anticipated. The rain forest in Biosphere 2 lost many of its trees because no natural winds encouraged the normal compensatory growth of root systems. An exotic ant entered the system and became epidemic. Birds did not survive because the forest plot was too small. The cement base of the structure absorbed critical amounts of oxygen over time, creating unexpected skews in the atmospheric gases. Biosphere 2 provided experimental chambers to test some hypotheses with great accuracy, but failed to answer other questions owing to the constraints of the size and the relatively short life span of the system. Biosphere 2 was in essence a large-scale test tube. I hope it will remain a living laboratory in which future students can explore and learn. (Note: As this book goes to press, Biosphere 2 is for sale.)

With our tumbleweed carefully packed as carry-on luggage, the boys and I flew home from our adventures at Biosphere 2, wiser with our newfound knowledge about designing experiments in artificial conditions. We were full of appreciation for our natural Earth and all the ecosystem services that it provides free, especially when compared to the expense required to maintain living systems under glass in the Biosphere 2 project. To paraphrase Mark Twain, scientific research — although it aims to answer questions — often proves that we still know next to nothing about the world in which we live.

1994 — DIARY OF MY RESEARCH IN THE BIOSPHERE

By James, Aged 8

Day 1. Today was our first day in Biosphere 2. It was awesome! The biosphere was a huge place full of plants and animals, separated from the outside world by glass domes. Scientists used it as a lab to study ecosystems. Five ecosystems were growing inside, including a rain forest and a desert. My brother did a project on ants in Biosphere 2. He wants to be a scientist when he grows up, and even wrote it in his "goals assignment" back at school.

Day 2. My mom always said, "Science is everywhere." Whenever we had free time, she would design a little experiment for us to conduct. But my brother designed this one all by himself, and I think he did a good job. He counted the numbers of ants in each ecosystem. I helped him count them and ended up having ants crawl all over my legs! They didn't bite, but they tickled! We stood three times for one minute in each habitat and counted the number of ants that crawled on us. The most ants lived somewhere between the rain forest and the coastal ecosystem.

Day 3. (Forgot to write)

Day 4. Flew home. We got good results except for one problem: my brother lost his notebook on the plane going home. Now my mother says, "Science is everywhere. But don't ever forget to mail home an extra copy of your data!"

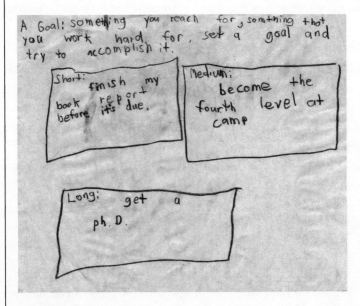

Eddie's goals at age 9

After our family trip to the Biosphere, it did not seem as if the year 1994 could get any better; but it did. In the fall, both boys entered the same school, a milestone for any parent who also occupies the roles of chauffeur and breadwinner. The bus ride was a great lesson in social interactions, and through the years we lost shoes (allegedly thrown out the windows by girls), missed the bus on occasion, and encountered bullies of all shapes and sizes. Sometimes the boys arrived home before I did, although, like most working moms, I tried to minimize that occurrence.

Even in our urban setting, the boys managed to find unusual situations where their knowledge of field biology came in handy. For example, on Halloween night I came home exhausted from a particularly long day at work and got ready to take the boys trick-or-treating. Stopping in front of the mailbox, I found a hand-written note in James's nearly illegible script. It read "Caution — black widow inside." Chuckling at this Halloween prank, I reached in and grabbed the mail. Inside the house, James was excited about his discovery. He absolutely insisted that the mailbox contained not only a black widow, but also her egg case. Still smiling, I walked out with him to shatter his myth. Peering into the dark back wall of the mailbox, I could barely discern a small black silhouette. Squinting really hard and using a flashlight, I was flabbergasted. The characteristic tiny red hourglass of this deadly spider shone in the flashlight beam, and adjacent to her black body was a tawny egg sack. Indeed, James's powers of observation would have impressed even the most experienced arachnologist. In large-scale surgical precision, we used a broom and a jar to carefully transplant the spider and egg sac to a more benign location in our back woods, much to the gratitude of the postman who left a thank-you note the next day. No one had informed me that black widows habitually seek out mailboxes in Florida. Evidently the size and relative sanctuary of the dark box offers a perfect habitat. It seems a little species identification knowledge can be a lifesaving skill.

We completed our rounds of trick-or-treating, having the tale of a real black widow to liven up this ghoulish holiday. After stopping at all the neighbors' homes, gloating over their sugary booty, and putting away the requisite goblin costumes, the boys collapsed into bed.

As a single mom, I rarely had time to myself, each day transiting quickly between work and home. Those rare moments when I actually breathed alone in a room were sacred. Looking ahead on the calendar, I knew that I literally would be without rest for the next two months. The pressure of the upcoming First International Canopy Conference was looming. Sometimes I wondered how I got myself so involved. Our botanical garden, or more accurately I as the director of research and conservation, was hosting the gala canopy event of the decade. As chair of this first conference, I had carefully planned my Biosphere trips around the conference schedule. Preconference months required an extraordinary amount of attention to detail and preparation — late-night phone calls to scientists in India and Australia, block bookings at local hotels, contracts with caterers, rental of appropriate audiovisual equipment, to cite but a few of the logistics. I kept a log of the crazy moments, of which only some examples are appropriate for printing. They included:

1. One month after the hotel reservation deadline, we learned that approximately 75 (of the 175) speakers had "forgotten" to book their rooms. Our staff scrambled to make telephone calls and secure enough reservations.

2. One epiphyte ecologist from Oberlin College absentmindedly forgot to book his room, he anxiously confessed, only to find out later that he had actually booked two rooms, proving himself doubly absentminded.

3. One keynote speaker was "lost" on the Gobi Desert — no one could locate him until several days before his scheduled talk.

4. One Sri Lankan scientist requested that his ticket be delivered via International Express Mail, and he paid a surcharge for camel delivery to his rural field location.

5. My administrative assistant was evicted by her landlord in the midst of the conference planning and had to take several personal days away from work to move.

6. A large contingent of Pacific Northwest scientists was planning to bring tree hammocks to hang in our public gardens, ostensibly to save money on lodging. Knowing that our visitors (and especially my board of trustees) would not appreciate that sight, I was able to convince them at the last minute to share motel rooms instead.

7. My dishwasher (at home) broke down, one day after the warranty expired.

8. A colleague from Cameroon sent a fax of his flight details that came through as a squiggle of black lines. I framed and hung it, as testimony to the immense struggle to communicate with our delegates from thirty-five countries.

Despite the mishaps, the First International Canopy Conference was a great success. A glutton for punishment, I also chaired the second conference in 1998, just four years later. In the second round, I felt more confident in our organization and also funded more scientists from additional countries. Not only was my knowledge of conference logistics expanding, but our international community of canopy biologists was also growing.

Scientists attend meetings as speakers or registrants more frequently than they chair them. On average most scientists attend one, occasionally two, annual meetings per year, to interact with colleagues and share new findings. As a scientist at a small institution, I found it particularly important to attend international conferences to learn about new discoveries firsthand. It was a professional obligation both to my workplace and to my field of research to stay up-to-date. As one's stature increased in a given profession, it was typical that conference attendance was paid by outside grants or societies, not by one's home institution.

Because conferences were an integral rite of passage into the scientific profession, I kept journal entries for each one. Ironically, the adventures coming and going from meetings sometimes seemed as insightful as research forays into the jungle. For example, a conference in India provided insights not just about the profession of tropical biology, but also about how some 2 billion people lived and shared limited resources in a crowded country. Another conference in Panama had a cast of such eminent speakers that I took Eddie and James so that they could hear some of the world's best ecologists debate their latest theories. Although scientific conferences tend to prioritize "conversation instead of conservation," these get-togethers offer important opportunities to formulate future action plans for conservation as well as research.

DINNERTIME DISCUSSIONS: MY BEST TEXTBOOKS

By Eddie, Aged 16

"We are developing a new rapid herbivory mapping technique to better assess canopy ecology," my mother explains between mouthfuls. "Fascinating! With more ecological data we can further analyze nutrient cycles between flora and fauna," a student replies. I glance up from my ravioli to relish the moment. Here I am, dining with my family and the usual mix of scientists, professors, and graduate students, taking part in a conversation that to me seems normal, yet would probably baffle many of my peers whose table conversations normally relate to last night's episode of *American Idol.* While the rest of the world worries about the status of the stock market, I listen to a technical discussion about the status of our ecosystems.

Our family dinnertable conversations are by no means conventional, yet they are nonetheless important. I am thankful for all the information I have gleaned from scientists and scholars during conversations such as this. Over the years, my brother and I have hosted many houseguests and attended a multitude of conferences with my mom. At the dinnertable with my family, I have gained more insight into the inner workings of scientific discovery and the natural world than any textbook could hope to provide.

Our conversation continues through dessert. I wonder if anyone else has ever eaten crème brûlée while talking about the mating habits of a garden spider? A professor rattles off some more scientific names. His eyes burn bright with passion and excitement as he joyfully regales us with his latest fieldwork faux pas. Field biology has that effect on people. I have seen many scientists become animated over subjects as simple as insect excrement (called frass by bug experts). No other professionals I have encountered can claim such enthusiasm for their discipline.

4 Orchid Farming in Africa: Creating Sustainable Canopies

*E*ach town should have . . . a primitive forest, of five hundred or a thousand acres, where a stick should never be cut for fuel, a common possession forever, for instruction and recreation.

— Henry David Thoreau, *The Journal of Henry David Thoreau*

A hot-air ballooning research expedition in Cameroon, Africa, was one of the highlights of my career and my lifetime. Still, one of the dilemmas of such research in tropical countries is what I call the one-way street of scientific results. Frequently, biologists return to their homelands, then analyze and publish their results in a technical journal read predominantly by colleagues from developed countries. The outcomes never have any positive impact on conservation in the country where the research took place. I feel an imperative to undertake research that promotes conservation as one measure of success. Such initiatives will undoubtedly save habitat, first and foremost. Naming species or understanding ecological processes may take a secondary role to the urgent issue of simply finding economic ways to conserve habitat. If we do not conserve rain forests, all of our data will reference extinct organisms or sites that used to be.

1993–1996. On our successful treetop exploration via hot-air balloon in Cameroon, I had calculated herbivory for many African rainforest canopy trees. We recorded leaf miners in the cardboard tree (*Pycnanthus angolensis,* family Myristicaceae), caterpillars on the umbrella tree (*Musanga cecropioides,* family Cecropiaeae), ants in the cola bush (*Cola marsupium,* family Sterculiaceae), and also spent the night in an emergent tree censusing the abundance of arthropods. Rain poured down during that dark endeavor; nonetheless, lifelong memories of the sights and sounds of the African jungle were created.

That expedition team consisted of forty-nine male comrades and me, a fairly dismal ratio in this day and age when women in science are theoretically on the upswing. But this ratio foreshadowed the 2005 controversy in science departments as prestigious as those of Harvard University, where the proportion of women in leadership positions is relatively small. As with most expeditions, I went home from this one determined to work even harder to encourage young women students as well as colleagues to pursue tropical biology.

Back in America, almost three thousand miles from the Pygmy villages of Cameroon, it was satisfying to provide more information about the ecological processes in African rain forests, and I published some technical papers to that end. Such information can be useful in forest management worldwide, as we learn the intricacies of the complex operation of tropical forests. But I wondered how my newfound data on canopy ecology and herbivory of the African rain-forest trees, vines, and epiphytes could be better utilized. Was there any measurable positive impact on the Pygmy villagers near our hot-air balloon site? And what was the fate of the lowland tropical rain forests in western Cameroon that were threatened by the pressures of logging, literally as we sat at home analyzing the data collected in these beautiful tall trees?

One of our host scientists for the expedition, Bernard Nkongmeneck, was a botanist at the University of Yaounde in Cameroon. An assistant professor, Bernard was earning the equivalent of US $800 per year after expenses. His family of five struggled to obtain eyeglasses, medicine for his wife's heart condition, even shoes to fit his growing children.

With our combined expertise on forest canopies, Bernard and I decided to team up after the balloon expedition to design a conservation project for the forests in Cameroon. Corresponding for almost two years, we continually exchanged ideas. In 1994 I obtained a grant that paid his fare to attend the First International Canopy Conference, held at Selby Gardens in Sarasota, Florida. Bernard was grateful to have this opportunity in America to network with other scientists, shop for his family, and develop professional collaboration. During his visit, he and I coauthored a grant application to National Geographic's research foundation. A project that would funnel funds into Cameroon would be like winning the lottery for Bernard, since botany did not merit major financial support within his own country. Ideally, a meaningful conservation project should involve the local scientists, as well as make a positive impact on the local forests.

Our long-term goal was to foster conservation of African epiphytes through education. We proposed to train the local Pygmy villagers to use single-rope techniques, binoculars, and climbing to survey their epiphytes (predominantly orchids) and host trees around the villages. The objectives were (1) to compare the diversity of epiphytes between undisturbed and fragmented forests, (2) to identify the most abundant host-tree species, and (3) to collect specimens for museums (technically called herbaria) in Cameroon, Europe, and the United States. According to Bernard, who grew up in these villages, many locals incorrectly assumed that epiphytes were parasites on their trees and they sought to destroy their potentially valuable "canopy crops." We hoped to correct these misunderstandings.

One year after we submitted our grant proposal, the funding was awarded and we set out to organize conservation classes for local villagers at each of three villages. Bernard hoped passionately that villagers would learn about the diversity of epiphytes, become aware of their economic value, and perhaps seek ways to propagate and farm the orchids for sale in markets. Such epiphyte farming would result in sustainable use of their forests rather than sale of logging contracts, which was all too frequent.

We experienced some frustrating moments in the execution of our project. For example, buying the climbing gear and transporting it to Cameroon was a challenge. The African customs officials repeatedly opened Bernard's suitcases and removed the ropes and harnesses. He made two trips to the United States to ship ropes, hardware, and a second-hand computer necessary for fieldwork. Finally, we sent his equipment via a visiting American colleague, and it arrived untouched.

A second rather amusing challenge was persuading the villagers to attend our botany classes. Using the local schoolroom as a night school center, Bernard — with his charming smile and infectious hu-

The villagers in Cameroon where Bernard Nkongmeneck and Meg taught classes in identifying and understanding the value of local epiphytes (photograph by Bernard Nkongmeneck)

mor—had a great solution to enticing the older village men: he bought beer to serve at the first class. I called it the *international elixir of male bonding*. Attendance was enormous, with an average of fifty villagers in each class. Everyone had fun, learned to identify epiphytes, and promised to use their newly acquired knowledge to identify and preserve (not burn) their local orchids. They were thrilled at the notion of propagating and selling them instead of destroying them. The villagers requested follow-up classes, a true testimony of success. We felt convinced that the local host trees and their epiphytes would be better protected in the future. Bernard's knowledge of the village and the culture was indispensable to the success of our project. Despite the best of intentions, foreigners could not have garnered the trust of the villagers as effectively as a local botanist.

By the end of one year, we had accumulated an impressive list of epiphytes in three regions of Cameroon. Many villagers were amazed at the diversity of plants in their local trees. Climbing themselves, they discovered that most epiphytes lived midway up the canopy. Approximately 65 percent of epiphyte species were orchids, while 26 percent were pteridophytes (ferns). Only one species of bromeliad exists throughout the entire continent of Africa, and that one species was rare. Further, we found that the epiphytic flora was extremely diverse and differed significantly between undisturbed and disturbed forest fragments. In other words, the forest fragments supported a population of epiphytes that contained species totally different from those in the shady forest.

Villagers in the schoolhouse learning about epiphytes (photograph by Bernard Nkongmeneck)

In addition, the diversity of epiphytes was greater in open habitats than in intact forests, a fact that initially surprised us. On further thought, we realized that light was more available in small patches of fragmented forests than in large tracts of intact forests. For epiphytes, as for most plants in the short term, sunny conditions favor increased growth and lower herbivory over shaded situations. In my rainforest tree research I have found that foliage growing in the shade is softer, longer-lived, and more highly defoliated, compared to leaves in the sun, which are tougher, shorter-lived, and less extensively munched by herbivores.

A large number of sun-loving epiphytes may establish in small patches of forest habitats after recent clearing efforts, whereas the slower-growing, shade-loving epiphytes may take longer to regenerate and grow. This is only a hypothesis, however, and many years of observation and measurement are required to confirm the theory. We do not know if these epiphyte populations in the fragmented forests will persist over time following disturbances and clearing, since the harsh sun may eventually kill them. The sensible solution is to retain both disturbed and undisturbed forest stands, because together they will support a broader diversity than just one type of forest.

In addition to hosting epiphytes, some trees have important uses for the villagers: *Erythrophleum suaveolens* (family Leguminosae) as a truth serum; *Cola acuminata* (family Sterculiaceae) and *Uapaca guineensis* (family Euphorbiaceae) for a range of medicinal purposes; and *Alstonia boonei* (family Apocynaceae) and *Bombax buonopozense* (family Bombacaceae) as food. These applications provide further impetus for conservation. With appropriate economic incentives, a sound regional management plan for both trees and orchids in forest fragments and also in undisturbed forest tracts could greatly enhance the sustainable economy of this region. Our study showed that different-sized forest plots had varied levels of diversity, and each may support different species of epiphytes. All of these epiphytes collectively may create sustainable industries for the villagers. The edge effects of trees along the pasturelands foster sun-tolerant epiphytes, while the undisturbed forest canopies house shade-tolerant orchid species.

The next step in our joint American-Cameroonian epiphyte project will be to undertake farming programs for the orchid species that appeal to city markets. Pilot programs in orchid farming, undertaken in Costa Rica by Rolfe Oldeman, may someday create a solid economy for local people without logging, which invariably destroys the entire ecosystem. Experimental farming of epiphytes has included the creation of canopy platforms that are hoisted into the dappled light of the midcanopy to maximize orchid growth. The platforms can be lowered for watering or harvesting and are inspected regularly. Aerial platforms provide conditions that simulate epiphyte substrate in the perfect environment. Only time will tell if farming epiphytes succeeds in the tropics as a sustainable industry.

Conservation efforts that involve partnerships of local villagers and scientists will ensure practical outcomes. Field research that directly promotes habitat conservation is by far the most important action needed over the immediate future. On a global scale, forested lands have declined from 44 percent to 28 percent, according to a 1997 report by the Food and Agricultural Organization. Current studies estimate deforestation at 11 million acres per year. My own perspective has changed from twenty-five years ago, when I climbed my first tree in the rain forests of tropical Australia. Back then, I was curious to discover "what and why?" Now, first and foremost, I ask "how can we save it?" so that later I can return and ask "what and why?"

Postscript, 2006. As this book goes to press, several rain-forest species have already been cultivated or farmed for sustainable economies compatible with conserva-

tion of the local tropical forests. These include butterfly farms in Costa Rica and other Central American countries, and iguana in Belize. Let us hope that within the next decade orchids and perhaps other sustainable rain-forest products will be featured in stores such as Bloomingdale's, Harrods, and Neiman Marcus.

USING INSECT CANDIES TO FUND SCIENCE

By James, Memories from Age 6

As kids, Eddie and I always tried to help support our mom and her science — with varying degrees of success. For example, it is really quite difficult for a six-year-old and an eight-year-old in the rain forest of Belize to stop playing with the wolf spider on the wall or stop chasing the army ants and actually contribute to productive scientific work. Despite these challenges, we *have* been able to be helpful from time to time.

During the Second International Canopy Conference, Eddie and I did our best to help one of my mom's colleagues, Dr. Bernard Nkongmeneck from the University of Yaounde in Cameroon. Our mom had worked with Bernard on the canopy raft in 1991, and she had funded him to attend the conference. Bernard brought to America a fairly daunting list of medical supplies, scientific books, and equipment that he hoped to take home. Eddie and I devised a plan to assist him. We spent our time walking around the conference, handing out chocolate-covered ants and other insect candies. For an optional donation, we offered the conference attendees a healthy dose of protein and crunchy chitin, along with the understanding that they were helping Bernard to buy much-needed books to bring back to Africa for research and education. In addition to raising about $200, we met a lot of very cool scientists!

5 An Emmy Award for the Treetops: Ballooning in French Guiana

The dirigible was launched daily at 6:00 A.M., weather and health of crew permitting. A launch pad had been carved out in the forest and was covered with a plastic tarpaulin to cushion the huge balloon. Entry onto the tarp was permitted only with bare feet. The French have a wonderfully casual sense of organization; everything got done with nothing like the fuss or stress that might occur if Americans were shouting orders and organizational advice to one another. Two Africans held the ropes in front while Danny, the pilot, fired up a small flame just under the dirigible . . . Finally, liftoff! The colorful balloon sailed quietly over the tips of the umbrella trees (*Musanga cecropioides,* family Cecropiaeae) that edged the clearing, then ventured out over the vast sea of green.

— Margaret D. Lowman, *Life in the Treetops*

It is 1996 and I am back in my Army-surplus hammock. It is slightly skewed owing to hasty, late-night suspension upon arrival at our rain-forest camp, but its all-important mosquito netting provides a safe cocoon for sleeping without fear of malaria. Only thirty hammocks constitute the lineup for this expedition to French Guiana, as compared to fifty scientists in Cameroon. But the snoring brings back old memories, as my comrades break into a full symphony. I know all the occupants from our many years of fieldwork, so I do not hesitate to gently shake those who are vying to perform solos. The sounds ease back to a dull roar.

Out beyond our sleeping hut is the real concert: incredible night sounds of red-legged tinamous, bats' squeaking, crickets and cicadas of all shapes and sizes, laughing frogs, and many unidentifiable noises in the tropical rain forest of French Guiana. By day, the symphony continues but with different instruments: high-pitched squeaks of golden-footed tamarinds darting around like popcorn in the bushes, troops of shrieking spider monkeys, screaming pihas echoing across the fig trees, cotingas flying, rapid exchanges of researchers in French, German, Spanish, and English, to name but a few of the nationalities present.

After my 1991 expedition to Africa with the Radeau des Cimes (raft on the roof of the world), my nonscientist friends thought I must surely be mad to subject my body to the rigors of another balloon expedition in a remote location. Would I again endure two weeks in a hammock as the sole woman scientist on an international expedition without electricity or creature comforts? I guess everyone has a different definition of fun. In my view, it was a privilege and an honor to travel into the jungle with some of the world's top scientists, uncovering new secrets about the rain forest. The biting insects, venomous snakes, lack of facilities, and absence of cold drinks paled in comparison to the thrill of riding a hot-air balloon above the treetops.

Francis Hallé had again invited me as part of his international canopy-raft expedition. My focus was to be herbivory. Recall that this phenomenon creates a veritable pharmacy in the sky, since each species of plant produces its own chemical defense. And in response to this unique plant chemistry, many animals have adapted to store or sequester their own toxic compounds, so that they can feed on otherwise poisonous leaves.

Our 1996 Radeau des Cimes mission to French Guiana was funded in part by the Glaxo Pharmaceutical Company in Europe. Part of the agreement was that scientists would collect from the canopy as chemical prospectors — bark, leaves, flowers, scents, and even stems. Any new plant material could, in theory, produce a life-changing drug for the world. In addition to this support, National Geographic sent a film crew, headed by the world-renowned filmmaker Neil Rettig and film director Tim Scoones, to feature my scientific exploration of this chemical warfare in the canopy.

NOVEMBER 1996. I awoke at six in the morning, hearing the enormous swishing sound of the dirigible inflating about a mile away. The enthusiastic French team of engineers and dirigible experts had already started their busy day of launching scientists into the canopy. I was not part of today's lucky team, but instead looked forward to ground reconnaissance in this new flora. French Guiana was reputedly one of the last bastions of undisturbed tropical rain forest in all of South America. For political and physical reasons, its trees far from the coast had been relatively overlooked in the timber quests of the last twenty-five years. We were fortunate to be explorers in this green expanse, thanks to the political connections of my French botanical colleagues.

Much as I enjoyed working with the French botanists, I did not enjoy their breakfast — the traditional crusty loaf plus black coffee was never enough to fuel my tree-climbing activities. So I furtively opened and devoured a sweet bun, hoarded from the plane and hidden in my carry-on bags. Luckily I had beaten the ants to the sweets. In the 1991 balloon expedition, alas, my coveted supply of Oreos became a major banquet for tiny sugar ants that discovered my luggage during the first day in camp.

My scientific role on this international team of canopy scientists was to measure plant-insect interactions from the raft. My herbivory research team had some new faces for this expedition: Bruce Rinker, educator and novice canopy recruit, returning to test his newfound confidence in climbing, after his reluctant attempts in Africa some five years ago; Robin Foster, tropical botanist extraordinaire; film crew Neil Rettig, Kim Hayes, and Tim Scoones; and canopy climber Phil Wittman. Working together, Robin and I hoped to identify and quantify the herbivory of as many canopy trees, lianas, and epiphytes as was humanly possible during our two weeks.

Because this expedition was sponsored in part by a pharmaceutical company, I also wanted to correlate herbivory with plant defenses. Based on long-term data from other tropical rain forests, I hypothesized that leaves with lower herbivory might have a higher level of chemical or physical protection than leaves with high herbivory, which indicated a lack of defense. In Australia, some tropical rain-forest leaves had suffered up to 30 percent herbivory per year and lived only one to three years; other leaves had negligible herbivory and lived as long as nineteen years! These data have changed the way ecologists view foliage, especially in terms of its longevity as part of the energy budget of a forest.

My first day on the raft in French Guiana was similar to my fate in Cameroon: I descended from the treetops with a large dose of heat prostration. Symptoms included headache, red cheeks, dehydration, and body dripping with sweat. Once again, my trusty supply of Oreos nursed me back to health. I lay in my hammock vainly seeking any hint of a cool breeze, drinking water, and carefully consuming first the chocolate outer cookie and then the delectable white frosting within. The delicate art of savoring Oreo cookies did not lose its ceremony even in the remote jungles of French Guiana.

After an infusion of sugar, I was ready for more adventure. We climbed using slingshots and technical ropes during our first day, reacclimatizing ourselves to ascenders and harnesses. Lauren, a viva-

cious French climber, loaned me one of his newest quick-climbing ascenders from Paris. I felt like a canopy fashion plate, sporting his new
gadget. My ascent was twice as fast as before, and I felt just like "one
of the boys." But then, as the only woman, I had no choice.

On the second day, Bruce and I were scheduled to ride in the "sled"
to collect leaf samples for herbivory assessment from the uppermost
canopy. The sled, or luge, was a device developed after the last balloon
expedition in Africa. A triangular-shaped inflatable raft structure dan-
gled below the balloon, and was towed through the canopy as a mo-
torboat might tow a plankton-collecting device. In the sled, we would
collect leaves, flowers, and insects from our green ocean.

We arose at 4:30 A.M. with the balloon crew, feeling as excited as
children at Christmas. I donned harness, helmet, and wasp-mask (just
in case we encountered an angry swarm) and carefully stowed my insect nets, beating trays, plastic bags, vials, marking pens, notebooks,
clippers, aspirators, cameras, water, Oreos, and more. The enormous
balloon was swollen and glowing in the dark, its primary colors taking on a surreal image in the predawn light.

Just prior to launch, Danny, the balloon's engineer-driver, detected
some trouble in the fuel pump. In the final countdown, our mission
was aborted. We were sad, but grateful not to have experienced any
breakdowns high above the treetops. This was the first mechanical
mishap in 206 flights, an admirable track record when compared to
most airborne vehicles. The problem was diagnosed as water in the
fuel tank, although a more humorous rumor floated about, that the
driver had a case of hemorrhoids and elected not to fly. Regardless,
we postponed our launch until the following morning.

Robin and I wandered all that day in the understory, identifying
and collecting plants in this new forest. Like art lovers in a gallery, we
botanists enjoyed encountering familiar "faces" in the woods. To find
a known plant family in the forest is as reassuring as recognizing an

artist in a gallery. In science as in art, it is pleasant to be surrounded by good friends. We identified seventy-eight understory species, nine lianas, and thirteen canopy trees, and mapped the diversity of the understory to compare it with the canopy. Our hypothesis was that fewer species would dominate our foliage map at canopy level (95 feet), as compared to the visible stems in the understory (4–6 feet). We were correct: of eighty or ninety species encountered in the understory, only eight to ten made it to the top. In short, we found that the botanical map of the forest was so different high to low that it was impossible to link the two regions from species identification.

Such a "photograph" of the canopy produces a significantly different picture of biodiversity than does the forest floor. It is vital that scientists recognize this discrepancy, because we do not often have the luxury of a canopy raft to allow us to see the forest from the top down. What lived at the bottom was simply not visible (or even present in some cases) at the top. Our assessments may provide useful clues for interpretation of aerial photographs of tropical forests, as well as information about the distribution of the biomass from top to bottom. As we marveled at the wealth of floral diversity, Robin, in his admirable yet absent-minded habit of seeing the world as green foliage but nothing else, nearly backed into an eyelash viper curled up on a palm frond. I was relieved not to lose my botany partner to snakebite!

On the third day, we donned our canopy gear again. Liftoff was achieved. This time the National Geographic film crew accompanied the flight. Neil Rettig, heavy video camera in hand, daringly tethered himself to the side of the balloon so that he could film downward from the sled as I sampled leaves in the uppermost canopy. Neil proved to all of us that filmmakers have a much more dangerous career than canopy biologists! Once airborne, I felt like Dorothy in *The Wizard of Oz*. It was wonderful to be home again in the canopy. Dangling aloft

The newest canopy access tool, the sled, suspended under the hot-air balloon and traveling from treetop to treetop to sample leaves or other canopy inhabitants (photograph by author)

in the canopy sled under a colorful hot-air balloon was totally exhilarating.

We sampled nine canopy trees in an hour, an effort that would require several days using slingshots and ropes. Furthermore, we sampled the uppermost branches of the canopy as well as the midcanopy, making these sled samples more comprehensive than those obtained by single-rope techniques alone. Partway through our transect, the sled flew over the raft. Perched on top waving to us after sleeping in the canopy the previous night was Gilles Ebersoldt, the French engineer who had designed the raft and the sled. We hovered over him, because Francis Hallé had asked me to deliver a small surprise. From my pack emerged a long, crusty loaf of French bread. I shouted "Patisserie, monsieur" and dropped the bread on his head. To this day, he marvels at having room service delivered to him in the canopy.

Sailing gracefully onward to new green treetops, we left Gilles to enjoy his breakfast. My body glistened with sweat, mud, leafy bits, dew, petals, and chips of bark that had been stirred up by our fast-moving nets and clippers as we collected flowers, insects, and branch material. Fortunately, we encountered no ant nests, for ants are one of the biggest dangers of sled-sampling. The center of our sled quickly became a cornucopia of botanical booty.

When we landed, all the scientists scrambled into the center of the sled like sharks in a feeding frenzy, grabbing tidbits of botanical specimens that represented their specific requests. Francis Hallé wanted collections of woody branches to test his hypothesis about aerial roots. Patrick Blanc requested flowering branches for the herbarium in Montpellier, France. Bruce and I collected leaf samples from mature branches to measure herbivory levels. And Robin wanted vines, preferably in flower, for identification. Upon descent to base camp, Francis in his delightful broken English asked what I thought of the ride in the new sled. My response, using a word picked up from my children, was "Awesome!" *Awesome?* Francis mulled over this new word, asked me to spell it and to explain its meaning. "Awesome," he practiced several times in English and then smiled at me, "I like that new word."

To share my research with young people and families, I had contracted part of my expedition time to National Geographic. The film from this expedition would become part of a Sunday-night television special entitled *Heroes of the High Frontier.* As predicted, some of the scientists grew resentful of the film crew. They argued that the presence of its members diminished the sense of pure science, and that catering to the needs of media might create inefficiencies in the schedule to achieve real results. This attitude was not surprising, since many scientists still felt that communication to the public was a low priority.

Fortunately, Neil had anticipated this cold welcome. After three days of feeling ostracized at the dinner table and obtaining little cooperation in the canopy, he took matters into his own hands. Neil was in his own right an experienced canopy biologist, having filmed and published the first-ever documentary of harpy eagles in their nests. Perhaps because the scientists were so preoccupied, no one on the expedition recognized him as the famous National Geographic bird photographer. Akin to classic animal behavior where male dominance is determined by physical prowess, Neil challenged some of the French engineers to a climbing race. They laughed, since their years of experience had made them incredibly quick on the ascent. Neil, however, had his own secrets and had recently perfected a new ascender that was extremely fast. The French went first: sixteen seconds to climb a rope approximately 125 feet into the raft overhead. Neil went next: eight seconds. Everyone gasped, and Neil instantly made lifelong friends with the canopy crew. After that, Neil and Kim received all the respect and assistance needed to make their National Geographic film a big success.

Nothing quite describes sleeping in the canopy. For no reason other than my sense of wonder, I sleep in the canopies of every research site. Occasionally I have found nocturnal insects worthy of observation, but their discovery does not usually require sleeping at the top. It is simply fun to experience this lofty world by dark.

Four of us decided to sleep on the raft one clear, warm night. Without light, the climbing rope looked like a liana that disappeared into a black hole above our heads. Up through the dark understory, past the cathedral of the midcanopy, we eventually reached the raft and sprawled on the mesh. Myriad constellations blazed overhead. We were silenced by the beauty of this starry galaxy, and also by our appreciation of the diversity within the canopy roof beneath us in darkness. Phil had brought champagne in his backpack. We toasted the rain-forest canopy and fervently hoped that our research efforts would lead to better conservation. We discussed the potential of our National Geographic film to teach the public about the importance of this "eighth continent."

Dark clouds rolled in the distance. In no time, thunder clapped directly overhead. We scrambled, desperately trying to hide under the one tiny tarp that covered the extra ropes. The heavens let loose. I brought out my field umbrella and for a brief minute felt very smart as I finished my champagne in the pouring rain without getting wet. However, my joy was short-lived. In no time, my bottom was in a pool of water, as the rain pelted sideways onto every square inch of my body. There was nothing to do but laugh about our wet-canopy slumber party. We all dozed eventually, and awoke to a steamy sunrise, with our bodies soggy and smelly. As the only female, I had a secret success

story—my bladder lasted through the night. I had purposefully refrained from any liquids at dinner and barely sipped the champagne,
in hopes of minimizing any need for a toilet. Despite the recent downpour, the glorious sunrise more than made up for any discomfort.

We descended to a late breakfast of cold coffee and the crumbs of a
French loaf. I had to rely on my dwindling Oreo supply to survive until lunchtime. After our rainy slumber on the raft, even a cold shower
felt delightful. The shower stall at base camp left much to be desired,
with its trickle of icy cold water behind a sheet of filthy black plastic.
But nothing compared to the décor of our "outdoor bathroom." This
elegant setup consisted of a tree stump with a communal tube of
toothpaste, spigot of cold water, and shared tin cup plus minuscule
mirror for the men to shave.

The sequence was to fill the cup with water, bring it to the stump,
and brush, shave, wash, and dry in full public view. Because the outdoor ablutions stump was only 10 feet from the sleeping hut, users remained in the relative luxury of their hammock beds watching like
hawks for availability of the bathroom stump. I took a photo of myself sporting a Tommy Hilfiger sweatshirt in the salubrious base-camp
bathroom, to send to Tommy himself, who was a high school class-
mate of mine. I kept hoping that he might someday consider designing a line of khaki clothing for scientists. However, I imagine that the
market for rain-forest wardrobes is not very lucrative. Fortunately, my
role as chief plant-insect ecologist did not require high fashion.

During this expedition, Robin and I were fortunate enough to
sample four individuals of one canopy tree. In temperate forests, this
was a simple task because multiple individuals of one species were easy
to find. In tropical forests, it was daunting. To find four canopy trees
of relatively similar size of one species, and also obtain their foliage,
was nearly impossible. *Pradosia cochlea,* a member of the predominantly New World family Sapotaceae, was common enough to allow

for replicated sampling. Robin and I had encountered its "cousins" *Chrysophyllum* and *Manilkara* in Belize, and another cousin *Pouteria* in Peru, but never before this particular genus.

Think for a minute about life as a plant. You cannot escape from enemies because you are restricted to one spot, subject throughout your entire existence to being clipped or bitten or perhaps ripped by mobile creatures. You may or may not germinate with any of your own kind in the neighborhood. How do you survive? Why are you not eaten by enemies whose populations build up around you? Such a lifestyle has the makings of a horror film — with our protagonist, the unsuspecting green plant, the victim of all potential marauders that move in and threaten to devour it. No doubt all plants would have become extinct long ago but for their unique mechanisms of defense: chemicals, thorns, stinging hairs, and toughness.

Chemicals from nature are a major part of human culture as well as of the natural world. Indians in South America coat their blowgun arrows with toxins called curare from certain plants or from poison dart frogs, instantly poisoning the speared animals. The chemicals in quinine bark years ago provided a cure for malaria. Oak tannins not only prevent herbivores from eating their foliage, but also are used to preserve leather. In addition to oaks, many other plants contain specific chemicals that defend their tissues from predators. In the canopy, it is possible to identify plants with the most effective toxins or chemicals simply because nothing eats them. These chemicals in turn point to the global pharmacy that could be a source of important cures for human diseases. As field biologists studying the interactions of insects and plants, we will probably not make millions from our discoveries about plant defenses, but perhaps by partnering with pharmaceutical companies we may find that tropical plants create incentives for conservation.

Herbivory was the first order of business in my ecological prospecting of the canopy. To measure which leaves the insects avoid eating provided clues to which plants might contain effective toxins and thus potential medicines. When we found a plant in the tropical rain forest that was avoided by herbivores, we suspected chemical defense mechanisms. Although in some cases we observed obvious physical defenses such as thorns or spines, an effective chemical defense warranted investigation in a laboratory.

In French Guiana, the pharmaceutical representatives were keen to see my results and earmark the plants with low levels of herbivory for chemical analysis. On the last few days at our canopy base camp, a local scientist who studied herbivory, Gombouard Pascal, and the expedition coordinator, Guy Renault (leader of Pro Natura), joined us to survey leaves. During most of my nonclimbing hours, I measured leaf areas in an outdoor laboratory that consisted of a ramshackle table, a plastic chair, and the luxury of a generator to hook up my workhorse, a leaf-area meter that digitized surface areas.

We might have collected more leaves for chemical analysis except for the weather toward the end of our expedition. The rains began gently. Then, during the final balloon trip, enormous clouds gathered overhead. The balloon wafted into the trees and the entire operation nearly got caught in the canopy forever. Eventually, down came the balloon and down came the rain. Packing a wet balloon was no easy task. It weighed several times its normal weight after absorbing so much moisture. As we folded up all the wet fabric, waterfalls of rain gushed over the edges and by the end of the exercise we all looked like drowned agoutis.

It rained for the rest of the day. The film crew brought out rum and sugarcane as an after-dinner treat, so French conversations were overly animated at the hut that evening. That night, the heavens really opened. Lying in my hammock, I was thankful that this was my last night for a long time with knees bent backward in my swaying

Meg's field laboratory in an open-air shed in the tropical rain forest of French Guiana, with a board for a table and a generator to power her leaf-area meter (photograph by author)

"bed" with surround-sound snoring. The wall of rains approached like a tsunami roaring in the distance. The downpour was magnified on the tin roof, and the sounds of snoring were drowned by the rain, as were the transects Robin and I had created in the understory.

I chuckled when, on this last wet and miserable day, a reporter from the French *Vogue* arrived at the height of the storm. She wanted to do a story about me, the lone female scientist on the expedition, including photographs (rain or shine!) of me in the canopy. Enduring many jokes about wet T-shirt competitions, I trudged out to the raft site with her photographer. Up we climbed onto the raft during the brunt of the downpour, which was falling harder in the treetops than in the understory. To get to the rope connecting the ground to the raft, we literally waded through rivulets along the trails and two fairly large stream-crossings that had arisen during the night. The notion of even combing my hair for the photographs became ludicrous. I had brought my expensive Li-Cor area meter to illustrate some of our canopy leaf sampling, but I kept it safely inside its waterproof case. The writer insisted on having some photographs taken, which no doubt were not of the quality and glamour that *Vogue* requires; but at least readers in France saw a woman in the canopy exhibiting the rougher side of fashion in a water-logged tropical jungle!

As I luxuriated in my hammock on the morning of departure, I was thankful that my humid, mildewed, sagging green hammock-cocoon was still intact — no loose knots or rips had brought my bottom to the floor throughout our field expedition. All of us were thrilled at the prospect of lying prone on a mattress in a matter of twenty-four hours. On that final morning, a few stalwart biologists unpacked the balloon for its last flight. Francis and I stood by, watching and discussing the upcoming canopy conference that we would cochair. Like proud grandparents, we watched Robin Foster, Phil Wittman, and a Scottish scientist named Adrian Bell successfully achieve liftoff. In the heat and humidity after the monsoon-like rains, my entire body was one pool of perspiration. I could barely see, and clothing stuck like skin to my body. Francis was in the same condition, so we just laughed. Walking back to our last breakfast after the balloon was safely crated up, we were drenched yet again. Our wet clothes and equipment made our luggage bulkier and heavier than it had been when we arrived.

Much as I love the challenges of rain-forest fieldwork, this trip seemed particularly rough — extreme heat, high humidity, and heavy rains. I have never sweated so much or experienced such a sleep deficit. Nonetheless, the camaraderie of an international group, the challenge of filming canopy research for families, and the thrill of "sledding" in the treetops formed lifelong memories. The canopy is a global heritage, and I am honored to be one of its stewards. If indeed we can educate the public about this important region of the planet, and inspire new scientists through the power of National Geographic television, then the adversity of the expedition is more than justified. And if asked by Francis Hallé to go on another balloon expedition, I know my answer will be, "That would be *awesome!*"

November 23, 1996.

Postscript

On our departure, Francis took us to the capital city, Cayenne, to greet the beaujolais. I believe only French scientists keep accurate calendars that track the schedule of the vineyards as well as the seasonality of the forest. Was it a coincidence that our expedition ended on the exact day that this celebrated wine arrived via cargo ship from France, or was Francis Hallé just a genius at planning? Regardless, we toasted the canopy with the new beaujolais and paid tribute to grapes, one of the world's best fruits from a vine in the canopy.

Several years later, Tim Scoones produced his canopy film, Heroes of the High Frontier, *that included Neil Rettig's footage of me exploring in the upper canopy using balloons, raft, and sled. It premiered on National Geographic's Sunday-evening show and was awarded an Emmy for Best Documentary in 2001. This honor was a tribute to the canopy and its exploration. In 2004, the esteemed Explorers Club featured Tim's film in its one-hundredth anniversary celebration as an outstanding expedition documentary.*

JAMES AND HIS HORRIBLE HOBO HIKE

By James, Aged 16

Throughout the years I have always been left in wonder and fascination when hearing my mother's tales of living during her remote research expeditions outside the "normal" comforts of life in the United States. Like many teenagers, I often viewed creature comforts through a rose-colored lens and held them in some disdain. I secretly loved to hear stories of discomfort and of challenges such as finding basic amenities like food in the middle of the wilderness. I admire those intrepid Antarctic explorers and early American adventurers who trekked across the rugged Rocky Mountains in search of new settlements. My favorite tales include the story of how my mom, a penniless graduate student in freezing Scotland, lived off roadkill for many months in order to afford heating, or how she lived within feet of a deadly Gabon viper in her hammock amid the tropical jungles of Cameroon, Africa. And I loved reading her journal about the hot, humid, rough conditions of base camp in the jungles of French Guiana. I have always been engrossed by the real struggle to live in a difficult world, and consider it a personal goal to become self-reliant and independent of modern conveniences.

This is why I leapt at the opportunity to create a taste of physical suffering as part of my job on staff at a nature camp this summer. One of our most popular activities, offered during each two-week session, was a backpacking trip to Monongahela National Forest, West Virginia. Two staff members asked if I would help them lead a specialty trip dubbed the "Horrible Hike." We combined the tales of previous trips-gone-wrong, such as terribly uncomfortable backpacks or a broken camp stove, with our own ideas of quasi-torture which—while not actually life-threatening—would, we hoped, rival some of my mom's stories on Tantalus' scale of discomfort and pain. We also hoped to become more self-reliant by sacrificing some of the backpacking comforts on which we had all become dependent.

We advertised our theme to the campers as a Horrible Hobo Hike. We planned to rely on ourselves and on inexpensive supplies largely acquired from the Apple Blossom Market dumpster located along Route 50 in West Virginia. The idea of a trip fraught with soreness and discomfort, and of relying solely on cheap, self-made gear, immediately attracted a group of campers with similar mindsets and philosophy about experiencing self-induced physical distress. Perhaps it was the notion of shared hardship, or of creating a

James, with his makeshift backpack, teaching the Hobo Hike. On the trail, he and his campers utilized only recycled material and ate unidentified cold canned goods (self-photograph by James Burgess)

bond from our challenges, that appealed to them. Perhaps for kids, the opportunity to live for a brief interlude without the priorities of cleanliness, hygiene, or creature comforts seemed novel. Maybe it reminded us of Thoreau. Regardless of the reasons, the group was highly motivated to eliminate luxury items from our backpacks and experience a simple sojourn in the woods.

We began preparations for our hike by looking over a list of conventional supplies, omitting anything that was not directly essential to our health and replacing any quality items with a suitably uncomfortable or low-budget alternative. Rain gear was replaced with trash bags, an empty can substituted for a cooking pot, hygienic products and clean underwear were scratched off the list with such fervor that our pens tore holes in the paper. All of these changes, however, were not entirely unheard of in the backpacking history of the Burgundy Center for Wildlife Studies and were mere hors d'oeuvres to the true substance of the Hobo Hike.

Any backpacker of moderate experience will tell you that a pack not well fitted to the wearer or improperly padded can easily become a torture device after several days of hiking over rough terrain. A small protruding corner, initially a minor bother, can wear away the soft human flesh underneath until the spot becomes raw and bruised. With due respect for this potential pain, but with the romantic idea of modeling ourselves after the hobos of the early 1900s, we set out to *create* our packs. We foraged for wooden produce crates and scraped together rope, cardboard, and duct tape. Each pack was designed very simply: a crate to hold supplies, bolstered by cardboard, with a length of cord tied and taped on as a strap.

In addition to revamping our backpacks, we decided to alter our food supplies as well. The traditional campers' menu of lightweight, "just-add-water" carbohydrate foods was replaced with a random hodgepodge of inexpensive cans from the local grocer. We selected foods that were unconventional for an American teenager's diet: beans, beets, pie filling, yams, corn, and spinach. All these and more were immediately stripped of their labels and randomly mixed to preclude any attempts to identify their contents. We taped and tied these cans to our packs, and the seven hobos took to the woods.

Eating, sleeping, hiking, and breathing nature all day and night was truly tonic for the teenage soul. The memories were as meaningful with canned beets as with the finest steaks and s'mores. We returned from our sojourn in the mountains full of stories, sore shoulders, and smelly armpits, but also with a new sense of wonder for nature, accompanied by a degree of scorn for the plethora of material goods in this country. Western society has become dependent on creature comforts and has paid the price in terms of frenzy, stress, and complexity. Our simplistic experience as hobos reminded us that the value of living in harmony with nature superseded our requirement for material luxuries.

6 Canopy Walkways: Highways in the Florida Sky

To know the forest, we must study it in all aspects, as
birds soaring above its roof, as earth-bound bipeds
creeping slowly over its roots.
— Alexander F. Skutch, *A Naturalist in Costa Rica*

In our world of computers, artificial environments, and electronic gadgets, many people hardly go outside in their day-to-day lives. I ponder this dilemma, questioning the progress it allegedly represents. In my work as an educator and scientist, I have met thousands of students and observed that their knowledge of and hands-on kinship with the natural world are declining precipitously. This saddens me, perhaps more than any other issue on the planet. Our children need nature; they are enriched by links to their ecosystem.

Canopy walkways were originally designed and developed as a research and teaching tool. Although treetop walks were first piloted in Australian and Asian tropical rain forests, our team of builders developed a modular construction design for the first time in a temperate forest at Williams College, Williamstown, Massachusetts. The demand has been so heavy that we created a company called Canopy Construction Associates (CCA). Our bridges and platforms are units that can be combined in myriad designs to best suit each unique forest site. I did not anticipate that, beyond their research function, walkways would become such a major link between nature and the public. Today we build walkways for ecotourism to promote forest conservation, as well as for canopy exploration. Our treetop walk in Florida — my own backyard — is a relevant example.

1997–2000. A close friend in my hometown of Sarasota, Florida, was a businessman named Bob Richardson. Bob sold real estate, so it may seem incongruous that we would have anything in common. But Bob was also an ardent conservationist and gave back to the community for any parcel that he took. A naturalist, he enjoyed time outdoors. One Saturday morning Bob and I went bird-watching in nearby Oscar Scherer State Park. The scrub jay (*Aphelocoma coerulescens,* family Corvidae), one of Florida's most endangered species, was relatively common in this unique habitat. As we walked along the trail, jays actually landed on our heads, showing their apparent lack of fear even for a real estate developer. Statewide, the decline of scrub jays was attributed to loss of Florida scrub habitat (hence the bird's name), required for nesting and survival of this endangered species.

The Florida scrub is also desirable to developers, who clear it with ease to build suburban housing estates.

Between scrub jays, Bob turned to me and asked, "Meg, if I could wave a magic wand, what would be your dream?" I thought for a few more scrub-jay sightings and then answered, "I would love to build a canopy walkway here in Southwest Florida, so that our community could learn to love and appreciate our forests as much as the people I encounter in places like the Amazon or Western Samoa." He laughed.

I told him that no canopy walkway offering public access existed in all of North America, yet a group of us had built ten of these structures for ecotourism in tropical developing countries. Bob's interest was piqued. He turned to me and said, "Meg, if you can design and build this contraption, I will find the funds to build it." We shook hands on the spot, and our canopy walkway was born. That was the easy part, however — just talking about it. *Conversation* is much different from *conservation*. The hard work and hours of negotiation lay ahead.

I immediately went to the leadership team at the Marie Selby Botanical Gardens, where I worked. It seemed a dream come true to guarantee funding for a project in its infant stages, and I hoped the director would share my enthusiasm. A canopy walkway had been foremost in the strategic plan of the previous director, for the obvious reason that it would attract visitors and also educate the public about our mission of conserving epiphytes and their treetop habitats. When a new director took over, however, those plans were shelved. It seemed a wonderful time to complete an unfinished goal, with a signed pledge in hand for both the project and its endowment. Upon conferring with the comptroller, the director told me that the Gardens would have no part of this crazy idea; I had better take my notion elsewhere.

Sadly, I went home to commiserate with my children. Thank heaven for youth. They urged me not to admit defeat, but just go ahead and find a solution. With my family's recognition that large portions of my spare time would be committed to this new "hobby," I started the wheels turning. One of my guiding philosophies has been that scientists should contribute a portion of their research and professional time to the local community. This was my chance. With a partnership involving local businesspeople, the likelihood of success was high.

When the Gardens rejected any sort of partnership with the walkway, Bob Richardson was disappointed. He had hoped that the project's tax-deductible status would encourage our fund-raising. We were stumped on how to proceed. A conversation with another close business friend, Mike Pender (a certified public accountant and a closet explorer), solved our dilemma. Mike suggested that we start our own nonprofit; he would serve as its treasurer. He worked many hours to complete the necessary paperwork, contact Tallahassee, and help Bob and me create a board of directors. TREE Foundation (Tree Research, Exploration, and Education) was launched in 1997. Bob became so enthusiastic that he doubled his initial pledge and raised enough money to take local disadvantaged children to a real tropical rain-forest canopy in Peru. Why not? His enthusiasm was contagious, and I accepted his offer to serve as scientist-leader for the kids. Almost overnight we doubled the community spirit behind this project.

Once the TREE Foundation was established and a core of local leaders was backing the project, I initiated work on the site and design. Sweat and toil began in earnest. The mission behind the walkway was to educate local people about their trees and forests, so we needed a site accessible to the public. A downtown botanical garden would have been ideal, but instead we had to seek alternatives. The state park was an obvious second choice. Slightly less accessible than a downtown location, it nonetheless offered natural stands of trees and shared our mission of educating the public about the natural world, especially plants. As my first step in a quest that turned out to be as adventurous as Dorothy's search for the Wizard of Oz, I wrote a memo to the manager of the park:

TO: Robert Dye, Myakka River State Park   *November 12, 1997*
FROM: Meg Lowman
RE: Proposed canopy walkway for education and research in Florida hammocks

I propose an innovative education project for Myakka River State Park, for visitors and students to learn about the natural history of Florida trees, and to appreciate conservation and management efforts in natural areas of Florida. It entails building a canopy walkway to show visitors the wonders of the treetops. The proposed walkway would be approximately 125 feet in length, with curves in and among the canopy trees, and extend up to a height of 35 feet maximum. The purpose of the walkway would be to interpret the canopy environment, to allow visitors to see firsthand the biodiversity in the tree crowns (epiphytes, vines, insects, birds, etc.) and to educate them about this aerial environment above the forest floor.

A preliminary meeting with park staff indicated that this walkway would be best sited along the existing nature trail. This site has well-developed live oak and palm canopies, both important species that make up the Florida hammock ecosystem. The proposed walkway would be constructed from timber and ropes that blend in with the environment. The entire structure would not be attached to trees, but based on a pole construction for purposes of minimizing impact on the natural ecosystem. This design has been used successfully elsewhere.

Please note that it is my intent to find donors to support this project. Not only would the donors fund the construction and interpretive displays associated with this structure, but they would also contribute an endowment to fund the maintenance of the canopy walkway after it is constructed. In other situations (e.g., Australia, Lamington National Park) we have implemented a similar project, and thousands of tourists flock to this structure each year to see the wondrous forest canopy. The structure will be user friendly and safe, with no severe vertical inclines and with safe railings and mesh to prevent slipping or falling. Since

1990, I have had experience building these structures all over the world, and good safety protocols are now well developed.

As Florida continues to see a decline in its natural landscapes due to the pressures of human development, I think it is a priority to educate the public about the beauty and importance of conserving Florida trees.

Please let me know at your convenience if it would be feasible to go ahead and submit a design for construction. I have donations available to fund a survey of this nature. I look forward to hearing from you and hope that we can work together to share the wonders of tree canopies with the visitors of Myakka.

We were launched. Robert Dye, the park manager, approved a feasibility study. Bob Richardson came up with seed money of $2,000 to fly down an arborist from Canopy Construction Associates to exam-

A diagram of the Myakka River State Park canopy walkway, North America's first public treetop walk, showing its intersections with oak and palm canopies in the Florida hammock ecosystem (illustration by Barbara Harrison)

ine the potential site. We had built or designed walkways in Western Samoa, Peru, Ecuador, Massachusetts, New York State, and now Florida. In 1994, CCA had also worked with the Jason Project for Education to build a walkway in Belize. For some of our assignments, CCA resulted in an adventurous "vacation" to the tropics for the builders in the middle of their temperate winters. Although the Williams College walkway was the first treetop walk built in North America, our Florida structure would be the first such walk that was *public*.

Meanwhile, the year 1998 was busy beyond the walkway project. The boys and I spent several delightful weekends in Myakka exploring the oak-palm hammocks. In our free time, Time-Life filmed us as their hosts for a documentary on Florida mammals. Eddie studied decay of plant material in these Florida hammocks for his science-fair project. Among all these forest activities, a blind date yielded fruit. I met a man who was to feature in our family's future, but that tale is reserved for Chapter 9.

HOW QUICKLY DO BROMELIADS DECAY?

By Eddie, Aged 13, Seventh-Grade Science-Fair Project on Florida Epiphytes (Written Later)

In seventh grade I became fascinated with how things fall from trees and turn into dirt on the forest floor, otherwise known as decomposition. Decay is an important process in ecosystems because it creates nutrient cycling — the passing of nutrients from dead organisms into the soil and back into vegetation. Having grown up in Florida, I also knew that epiphytes (e.g., bromeliads such as Spanish moss) make up a relatively large portion of the canopy vegetation. By deduction, I figured that bromeliads must make up a significant part of nutrient cycling in these ecosystems. Much to my surprise, no studies had ever been conducted on the fall and decay of these bromeliads. It was hard to believe that science had so many undiscovered elements, even here in North American ecosystems. I decided to measure bromeliad decay for a class science project. Even as a kid, perhaps I could contribute something new about plants in the forest canopy.

For the study, my brother and I selected foliage from six different species of plants: two bromeliads (ball moss and Spanish moss), one additional epiphyte (butterfly orchid), one vine (passionflower), and two trees (live oak and orange tree). We hypothesized that the toughest leaves would be the slowest to decay. First, we measured the toughness of the leaves using a fancy device called a penetrometer, a gadget that gauges the relative toughness of the foliage. (My mom uses it to estimate how difficult it would be for an insect to chew through different kinds of foliage.) We made multiple measurements for each species, and averaged our results. Second, we put one ounce of dried leaves in mesh bags on the forest floor and harvested three bags each month for a year. We then graphed the decrease in weight as the leaves decayed.

Eddie with mesh bags to test the rates of leaf decay of various canopy leaves (photograph by author)

The passionflower vine had the softest leaves and was also the fastest to decay. Its delicate foliage was no match for the fast-working microbes in the soil, and over 95 percent of its leaf material decayed after only one month. In contrast, the epiphytes decayed less than 50 percent after four months, with approximately 25 percent still remaining after one year. As we hypothesized, the toughest epiphyte foliage was the slowest to decay. The tree species live oak also had tough leaves and slow decay. After one year, it had slightly slower decay than any other species in our survey.

The bromeliads, however, did not follow the regular decay pattern exhibited by the other plants. In fact they *gained* biomass initially rather than losing it! The mystery of bromeliad decay accompanied by weight gain became very intriguing. We had our theories about this mystery: perhaps epiphytes such as bromeliads could survive on the forest floor for a short period and actually gain weight through a burst of growth? As with many scientific investigations, our discovery led to more questions than we initially asked. Why did the bromeliads gain mass? How does such a growth spurt before decay affect the nutrient cycling process in the Florida forests? How long can a bromeliad survive after falling from its host tree?

This experiment has been indelibly in my mind as I continue to experience science in college and with my family. Not only did this bromeliad experiment represent my first publication in a scientific journal, but it also showed me that the natural world is full of new things to be discovered, even in our own backyards.

Once school was out and science projects completed, the boys and I took a nostalgic vacation in West Virginia. We returned to Coopers Cove, the mountain retreat where the Burgundy Center for Wildlife Studies was located. Long ago, when I was a teenager, this summer camp had provided me with a life-changing experience and I truly became committed to a career in field biology. I served for many years on the staff of the camp, and the directors, John and Lee Trott, were inspirational throughout my youth. Burgundy, the only camp of its kind, is devoted to rustic living and studies of the natural world. No phones, no archery, no movies on Friday night, but an abundance of bird songs, animal tracks, constellations, and pond biology provide endless entertainment.

Our trip to Burgundy that May was the second reunion of all campers and staff throughout the camp's thirty-year history. We had migrated to all corners of the world since our camp days; regardless of career choice, however, we still shared a love for nature and a strong affinity for the mountains of West Virginia. My old friend Bobby Kluttz from Charlotte, North Carolina, met us at Dulles Airport in Washington. With a southern accent thick enough to cut with a machete, Bobby regaled Eddie and James with birding stories and endeared himself forever by offering a limitless budget for candy at the Winchester grocery store (something their mother would never sanction). When we arrived at camp, the sun was setting, the whippoorwills were revving up, and a barred owl was announcing nightfall. We pitched our tents on the site of a rickety old sheep barn, which had served as a secret spot for staff meetings until it simply collapsed of old age.

After a great night's sleep overlooking Coopers Cove, we spent a morning reacquainting ourselves with favorite places. We first visited the loo (camp terminology for bathroom), perhaps not a "favorite place" but nonetheless an infamous place. In 1969 I initiated an idea that is still pursued today — putting scientific articles and information on the walls of the stalls. This loo literature rotates between boys' and girls' toilets, providing a cornucopia of knowledge throughout the summer. Some of the tattered articles were my originals, including how to tell air temperature by counting a cricket's chirps. Next, we

visited the pond and watched tadpoles. The boys were ecstatic to meet
with notables such as Don Weber from the U.S. Department of Agriculture and Nate Erwin, director of the Smithsonian Insect Zoo. To
have all these wonderful scientists acting like kids again was an unusual experience. We were all thrilled to see "old friends" — bobwhite
quail, viper's bugloss, timothy grass, Saint-John's-wort, and blue-
birds!

At the end of our weekend, we discussed the camp's future and how
we could collectively leave a legacy. My current project in Florida to
build a public canopy walkway for education and research piqued
everyone's curiosity. As a result, the Burgundy reunion group opted
to investigate the notion of a similar structure at the camp, to be
funded perhaps by alumni. Director Vini Schoene and I resolved to
keep in close touch about this exciting proposition.

In 1998, not only did Burgundy Center for Wildlife Studies construct its own canopy walkway, but also my original partner in walkways from Australia, Peter O'Reilly, came to visit on a global walkway
tour. Peter was the director of a well-known ecotourist lodge called
O'Reilly's Guesthouse in Queensland, the site of my original in-
volvement with canopy walkways back in the 1980s. I had led several
Earthwatch expeditions to O'Reilly's and hauled volunteers into the
canopy on ropes. Peter got nervous. He wanted to find a safer way to
pursue research in the treetops. On a paper napkin in the pub at the
guesthouse, he and I sketched a prototype of the first canopy walkway. We toasted the idea, and resolved that somehow this plan would
happen at O'Reilly's Guesthouse. When I returned the following year,
the Green Mountain Natural History Society had raised the funds and
built a treetop walk, true to our napkin design! It was a great moment
for canopy research, and for ecotourism as well. To this day, some of
my Australian colleagues attribute much of the pro-conservation

change in local attitudes toward rain forests to that walkway and the appreciation of forests that it generated.

Peter had recently lost his wife, Karma, to cancer. In the healing process, his family and I worked out a plan for Peter to visit me and tour the walkways on the other side of the globe. Since Peter had been the major energy behind that Australian walkway, he was enthusiastic to see designs in other forests. As the scientist who had taken this concept of walkways to places far from Australia, I was his obvious tour guide.

Peter's first destination was New England, where he toured the walkways we had built in Massachusetts and New York. Next he came to Florida to see the future site for our Myakka subtropical walkway. Then he flew with me and the boys to Costa Rica for the annual meeting of the Association of Tropical Biology and Conservation (ATBC). At the conference Peter was heralded as a hero for his pioneering canopy work, and he was thrilled to see so many field biologists in one room. Conferences are great venues not only for sharing ideas, but also for camaraderie.

In Costa Rica we took several day trips to important canopy projects. First, we glided through the canopy in camouflaged green gondola cars at the aerial tram built by Don Perry outside San José, viewing cecropia trees and admiring the layers of understory beneath. Sloughing through the muddy trails back to the lunchroom, the heavens let loose with a torrential downpour. We almost bumped bottoms with an eyelash viper curled up on a palm frond at waist height. It reminded me of a similar encounter by Robin Foster in French Guiana. Avoiding any snakebites, we next stopped at La Selva Biological Field Station, premier tropical rain-forest research station, where we discussed the possibility of a canopy walkway with the station manager.

At La Selva, Eddie became a true "birdo" (bird-watcher). We got up early each morning, and his young life-list doubled and tripled, perhaps because he was old enough to operate his binoculars effectively. Whatever the case, by the end of the trip Eddie was identifying bird calls almost as well as our host, Gary Hartshorn, then the executive director of the Organization for Tropical Studies, the consortium that operated the field station. New feathered friends included turquoise brown motmot, white-whiskered puffbird, bicolored ant bird, rufous-tailed jacamar, and orependula.

One of my memorable jungle moments was a sunset paddle along the local stream, where we watched a sun bittern take flight in the dappled light. As nocturnal creatures began to stir, we became casually acquainted with the notorious fer-de-lance, an aggressive but venomous snake that is featured in the adventures of most tropical biologists. A large female was lolling outside the dormitory door, not a great place for striking up a friendship (no pun intended). We gave it a wide berth. My herpetologist colleagues advise me that very few venomous snakes climb trees. I am not sure if that is true, but my only snake encounters have occurred at ground level.

Returning to the States, I worked doggedly on the Myakka walkway project. My partner Bob Richardson continued to raise funds for the walkway plus the Amazon trip planned for Thanksgiving week 1999. We called it the Peru-Myakka connection, since the young participants would experience both the tropical rain forest and the Florida tree canopies. In late summer, twenty-four youth from the local Boys and Girls Club and from Girls Incorporated were selected to participate. The kids worked hard to learn about the rain forest, and each also raised $100 toward airfare and another $100 for the local canopy walkway. It was a fine experience for them, and also for the community. After a naming competition, the director of the Boys and Girls Club, Mack Reid, proudly wrote to me announcing "Amazon Adventurers" as the winning title of the Expedition.

In no time, it seemed, the fateful week of Thanksgiving 1999 was upon us. Many of the mothers from Girls Incorporated had undergone trials and tribulations getting their daughters outfitted with passports, walking shoes, daypacks, and a few rugged outfits. They shed tears as their offspring departed from an urban jungle and ventured into the real jungle.

Twenty-four young people, eight community chaperones, Eddie, and I flew from Miami to Lima, and then up to Iquitos. This route was becoming a regular commute for Eddie and me, since my canopy research had focused on the Amazon for the past three years. Once in Iquitos, we were whisked through the city streets. The students' eyes popped as they observed the scarcity of automobiles, grocery stores, street lights, cell phones, and other American urban amenities. We boated down the Amazon for approximately two hours to reach our destination, Explorama Lodge. Dodging mud and leaf-cutter ant highways, the kids were relatively quiet on the walk into camp. Seeing their rooms with thatched roof and mosquito netting over each bunk, they were still fairly quiet. Then someone shrieked, "Snake in the rafters!" and total chaos ensued. The warning was a false alarm, but I guess the Amazon has that effect on everyone — first, silence and awe, then total sensory overload. We had no television, video games, or computers, yet everyone found entertainment through the natural world.

We separated the boys and girls into two base camps, so that each group would maximize his or her experience in the jungle rather than worry about interaction with the opposite sex. At dawn, I took the girls out on small boats. We heard an orependula chortling like a moog synthesizer. Its operatic songs were unlike anything in our North American forests. Willie, our Peruvian guide, brought fishing nets so that the girls could try to catch breakfast. We all laughed at each futile attempt, and some recognized that their families would have gone hungry if they had been the breadwinners on the Amazon. One young teenager named Tina caught eight fish, and we joked that her gene pool was sure to succeed.

Rumors filtered back to the girls' camp that the boys had wrestled anacondas (false) and encountered wasp nests (true). My coleader, DC Randle, an energetic scientist from Minneapolis who had partnered with me for many years of Amazon research, suffered seven stings. In his inimitable fashion, he laughed as if it were simply an everyday event.

The highlight of the entire week, though, was our excursion to the canopy walkway. Spanning approximately 1,200 feet, this treetop walk was at the time the largest in the world. It rose to 125 feet in the canopy of an emergent tree, providing views of the Amazon as well as untouched acres of tropical forest. I often wondered at sunset how many years would pass before that view would cease to be pristine. One of the teachers crawled along the walkway, hugging each and every slat in total fear. But she was jubilant at the end, having overcome her acrophobia!

Considering that our diet was quite different from that in the States, the students remained in surprisingly good health. One teenager named Jasmine threw up in her room. Another refrained from eating anything except the candy she had brought. But for the most part, everyone was adventurous. A tarantula appeared on the wall of one room and caused a near-riot. Another girl claimed that a vampire bat nipped her even though none had ever been recorded in that region. As I had done with the girls, I led the boys on a special night walk into the canopy. To their amazement we found a nutmeg canopy beetle, the new species of insect studied in the Jason Project earlier that year, which fed exclusively on one species of bromeliad. As we returned from this nocturnal exploration, a sudden thunder-and-lightning storm came up. I halted the group in the stairwell of the walkway access. In one of the most vivid memories of my entire career as a mentor for students, this group of twelve youths from predominantly disadvantaged homes, with very little worldly perspective, sat in total darkness — without talking — for over ten minutes. That is the litmus test of true naturalists. I was proud of them. Perhaps they were numb with fear, but none of them would ever admit to that. I prefer to believe they simply had developed a sincere respect for nature, manifested by the darkness, by the canopy, by the Amazon, and by the power of a storm.

Another insight for our Sarasota youth came when we visited a school in an extremely remote village. In disbelief, our group observed that no girls had dolls and that almost no children owned shoes. The one-room school taught math, history, science, language, and religion; everything was learned without textbooks, computers, or calculators. One of our students asked the students what they wanted for Christmas. A young Peruvian piped up, "*Postre*" (a cake). Our group marveled at desires so different from the American norms of Nintendo, Nike, and Nokia, most of which the Peruvians had probably never encountered. We also marveled at their shaman, who showed us the plants used for medicinal purposes that served as their local drug store.

In the village tradition, our boys were invited to play soccer against the local team. With an average height at least one foot shorter than our tall, gangly American teenagers, and with no shoes, the Peruvian youth beat their U.S. counterparts 7–6. Slightly embarrassed, our guys graciously admitted defeat to a better team. With these memories, we returned to America with changed attitudes. Bob Richardson, who had been unable to travel at the last minute despite being the chief fund-raiser, was presented upon our return with a hand-carved Amazon paddle, autographed by all the participants. He claims that it remains one of his most prized possessions.

Meg and Eddie with villagers along the Amazon River near Iquitos,
Peru (photograph by author)

One half of Bob's pledge was successfully fulfilled, but the walkway
still lay ahead. Many were the trials and tribulations between launching our walkway project and actually building it. As I tell tour groups
when leading canopy walks, it took two years to obtain permits for
construction in a Florida state park, and it took only two weeks to
build the walkway. Unlike our experience of building in remote tropical rain forests, where the construction process represents a huge
challenge, here in America the issues of permitting, insurance, and liability proved almost insurmountable. We hosted a design workshop,
bringing in the team from CCA to work with Myakka staff. Then we
vetted the design, and it went back and forth numerous times. In the

final hours, insurance reared its ugly head: CCA's out-of-state insurance was not acceptable in Florida. A local builder named Jon Swift kindly stepped in and offered to partner in construction of the project. His insurance covered the crew in Myakka, and his permitting was more acceptable to the powers-that-be in the state capital.

Our permitting process ran hot and cold, but the park staff was persistent. And our CCA crew doggedly kept revising the design as necessary, including a last-minute request by the Myakka Park staff to add a 75-foot tower to the walkway itself. This was a significant addition, but would enhance the educational value for visitors. From the top, the Florida hammocks, wetlands, and pine flatwoods that constituted the Myakka River region would be visible.

On December 17, 1999, a contract between the TREE Foundation and the builders was finalized, and the park staff granted official permission. Arriving just in time for my forty-sixth birthday, the signed contract was one of the best gifts I had ever received. With designs approved, we scrambled to complete the fund-raising. The TREE Foundation did the bulk of the work, calling on me for an occasional talk or grant-writing exercise. The Friends of Myakka Park, a volunteer group, assisted with all aspects of fund-raising and publicity. And park biologist Paula Benshoff became our expert grant writer.

Meanwhile, I juggled paperwork leading up to permits and funding, along with hardware requests from the construction team. Timber orders included 120 lengths of 2 × 10 × 12 feet, 200 lengths of 2 × 6 × 12 feet, and some 16 other lengths in specific amounts. Hardware ranged from 1,200 feet of 7 × 19 × ⅜-inch galvanized cable to 50 ⅜-inch heavy duty thimbles, 75 ⅝-inch forged cable clamps, 100 #16 hot-dipped ring shanks, and 300 ⅜-inch zinc-plated swages. My doctorate in botany was absolutely useless when it came to construction jargon.

Construction officially began on February 7, 2000. The builders, working with park volunteers, had pre-cut most of the timber so that everyone could maximize their field time to get the job done. Like a hive full of bees, the construction area was abuzz with activity. All the gear was carted to the site on a temporary trail, minimizing any disturbance on the permanent trail. Although this required extra time and energy, it was well worth the effort; today it is virtually impossible to tell where the timber was hauled in through the trees. Eight builders came from points across America, all experts in some technical aspect of canopy construction. They stayed in hand-hewn log cabins at the park, working long hours in the treetops, almost like a troop of monkeys! The weather held and on the eve of the last night, members of the TREE Foundation and I took champagne out to the team, where we quietly toasted their success. The walkway was constructed in ten days.

The first visitors to explore the canopy walkway in Myakka River State Park (photograph by author)

Subsequent to the major building activities, other tasks remained. Signage, parking, trail access, and park maps were required. Not surprisingly, we had a few more hiccups with the state park leadership in Tallahassee, which at one point questioned the engineering of the tower. It was difficult to resolve such issues where few architectural precedents existed. CCA was used to this type of dilemma, though, since our designs were in many cases the "first of a kind." However, the state required strict guidelines in order for the site to open officially. The construction team hastily did more calculations and changed some angles in the guy wires.

At long last, opening day came — almost four months after the structure was officially built. We amassed a group of dignitaries that included the young people who had gone to the Amazon, the ambassador from Peru, state park officials, local scientists, and philanthropists. On Thursday, June 15, 2000, the Myakka walkway was officially open to the public. Costing a total of $93,860.50 plus a $15,000 maintenance endowment, the walkway project logged over 1,220 volunteer hours in the construction phase alone. Donors included local philanthropists who gave as much as $25,000, as well as fifth-graders who sponsored brownie sales that netted $100. Each plank was marked with the name of the person or group who had sponsored it. The Year of the Canopy, complete with Amazon Adventurers and the Myakka Canopy Walkway, was over.

In the five years since the opening, hundreds of thousands of visitors have walked through the Florida treetops. The canopy walk has promoted an appreciation for our Florida forests far beyond any technical scientific findings, and far exceeding our expectations. For most visitors, the notion of epiphytes is new. These travelers from temperate forests have not previously realized that some plants in the tropics and subtropics live in the canopies of other plants. At Myakka the Spanish moss (*Tillandsia usneoides,* family Bromeliaceae), butterfly

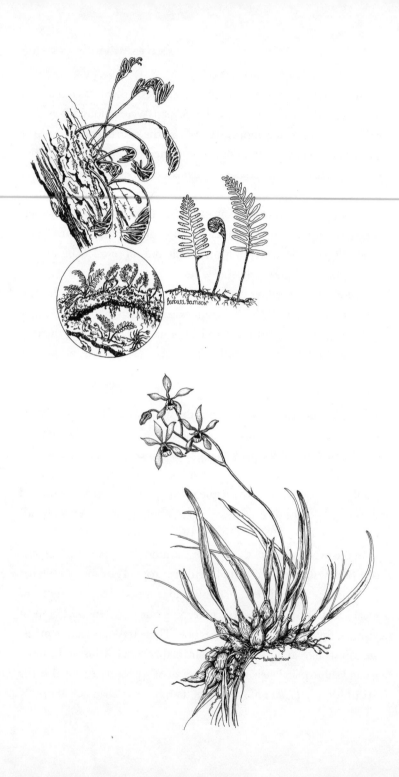

Four epiphytes grow-
ing in the oak-palm
hammock of the
Florida forest canopy:
(clockwise starting
with top left) resur-
rection fern, Spanish
moss, bromeliad, and
butterfly orchid, (il-
lustration by Barbara
Harrison)

orchid (*Encyclia tampensis,* family Orchidaceae), resurrection fern (*Polypodium polypodioides,* family Polypodiaceae), and bromeliad (*Tillandsia fasiculata,* family Bromeliaceae) form a dense foliage in the mid layers of the Florida hammocks. Such biodiversity provides a vivid introduction to the complex world in the treetops.

I have a thick folder of feature articles from newspapers throughout the country, encouraging tourists to visit Southwest Florida and experience this unique highway-in-the-sky. I have an equally large folder of letters from students and teachers, exclaiming about their field trips and the research projects conducted on the walkway. Best of all, I frequently visit the site and eavesdrop on visitor commentary. One of my favorite incidents occurred during the wet season, when the path to the stairs was approximately knee-deep in muddy water. Two children were hiking with their parents. The delight of the children, after their mom allowed them (grudgingly) to walk through the puddles, was infectious. Their laughter and joy rang throughout the trees. It reminded me how important it is in our antiseptic society to let our kids get muddy, at least once in a while.

CANOPY WALKWAYS — HIGHWAYS IN THE SKY

By James, Aged 16, Adapted from Essay in Forest Canopies *(Elsevier, 2004)*

Research in forest canopies has been limited by the challenges of access. During the 1980s, several relatively inexpensive solo techniques were developed: single ropes, ladders, and towers. In the early 1990s, collaborative canopy access techniques were developed, including canopy cranes, the raft and dirigible apparatus, and canopy walkways.

Walkways create permanent sites at moderate cost for long-term observations and data collection, allow collaborative research by a group of researchers within a region, and are the most effective compromise between inexpensive but inefficient access methods and those that are costly but productive. I recently completed a study of a herbivorous beetle in the bromeliads of the upper canopy of Amazonian Peru, where walkways provided canopy access throughout night and day, rain and sun, wind and calm, and over many seasons at the same site.

Structurally, walkways have a relatively simple modular design incorporating bridges and platforms that interconnect to form a network in the treetops. The network can have as many platforms and bridges as needed, the basic minimum module consisting of one platform or bridge. Walkways are usually supported by stainless steel cables with aluminum or rot-resistant wood treads.

Selection of sites depends on both engineering and biological factors. For engineering purposes, the site must contain healthy, mature trees with upper branching conducive to platform support. The trees must also be in close proximity to one another and away from edges and treefalls, which could create dangerous wind patterns. Biologically, the site should include a species diversity that is representative of the forest type. Platforms should be placed to maximize observation of the crown area but create minimal disturbance to the tree.

Walkways have been constructed in many different forest types, including temperate deciduous forests, tropical forests, and subtropical forests. In short, any area with a canopy is a potential candidate for walkway construction. Canopy Construction Associates (*www.canopyaccess.com*) has played a large (but not exclusive) role in development of a worldwide network of canopy walkways. CCA's sites include Upper Momon River, Peru (1990); Williams College, Massachusetts (1991); Hampshire College, Massachusetts (1992); Coweeta Hydrological Lab, North Carolina (1993); Blue Creek, Belize (1994); Mountain Equestrian Trails Lodge, Belize (1994);

Marie Selby Gardens, Florida (1994); Millbrook School, New York (1996); Batuampar, Indonesia (1998); Tiputini Biodiversity Station, Ecuador (1998); Grandfather Mountain, North Carolina (1999); Myakka River State Park, Florida (2000); University of the South, Tennessee (2001); Burgundy Center for Wildlife Studies, West Virginia (2001); and Inkaterra Association, Peru (2005).

This global walkway network facilitates comparative canopy research among all major forest types, utilizing a standardized access technique.

7 Of Tarantulas, Teenagers, and Turkey Basters: Distance Learning from the Treetops of Peru

A child's world is fresh and new and beautiful, full of wonder and excitement. It is our misfortune that for most of us that clear-eyed vision, that true instinct for what is beautiful and awe-inspiring, is dimmed and even lost before we reach adulthood. If I had influence with the good fairy who is supposed to preside over the christening of all children I should ask that her gift to each child in the world be a sense of wonder so indestructible that it would last throughout life, as an unfailing antidote against the boredom and disenchantments of later years, the sterile preoccupation with things that are artificial, the alienation from the sources of our strength.

—Rachel Carson, *The Sense of Wonder*

How do you blend two million teenagers, five hundred thousand leaves, twelve hundred feet of canopy walkway, one hundred one bromeliads, fifty-three tarantulas, twenty-four headlamps, five unknown brown beetles, and one turkey baster into a single story? The Jason Project for Education, of course.

In 1989 Robert Ballard started a unique distance-learning program to promote science education for students. When Bob discovered the ship Titanic in 1985, he arrived home to find some sixteen thousand letters on his desk from students asking to join him on his next undersea exploration. Obviously, Bob could not bring thousands of teenagers in one tiny Alvin submarine to find new archeological wonders in the deep sea. How, he mused, could he capture this energy and enthusiasm in young people who were eager to pursue science? The Jason Project in Education was born (it has recently been renamed the Jason Expedition). Teaming up with Electronic Data Systems (EDS), AT&T, National Geographic, and other partners, Bob devised technology to relay live broadcasts from remote locations via satellite into classrooms and museums. Today the Jason Project spans the world and in 2004 reached almost three million students and teachers in ten countries.

The first four Jason expeditions (1990–1993) featured Bob's undersea explorations only. To fulfill a broader mission, Bob sought different ecosystems to investigate. Thus Jason contacted me in 1993 about the possibility of exploring the rain-forest canopy, a region of the planet that rivaled the ocean floor for its remote and uncharted mysteries. I worked with Bob's team to produce Jason V in 1994. It featured the canopy ecology of Belize, using a treetop walkway we built specifically for the Jason broadcasts.

Jason V incorporated canopy research that I had adapted for middle-school students. Classroom activities included measurements of leaf toughness (using the penetrometer, a mechanized device that gauged relative leaf toughness, or how much effort was needed for an insect to chew a leaf); building a mock walkway from popsicle sticks; and leaf-area measurements for herbivory. Students who completed multiple leaf-area measurements automatically became members of my Leaf Lovers Club, a loosely organized society started back in 1983 to keep my Earthwatch team members on task. I found myself autographing lab notebooks when visiting schools with my trusty penetrometer; it was the closest I *had come to stardom as a scientist. The kids were excited to hear firsthand about this infamous gadget.*

Five years after the success of Jason V in Belize, the Jason staff called me once again and asked which rain forests might provide another appropriate venue for Jason. I needed only two seconds to answer: the Peruvian Amazon. Over the past five years, I had led teacher workshops as well as family trips to the Amazon. During that time I had carefully designed what I call quick-and-dirty sampling techniques that enabled even the youngest and oldest members of my ecotourist groups to engage in the thrill of canopy research. We had mapped the forest canopy at a Peruvian research station, counted epiphytes from a walkway, and studied herbivores on Inga trees (Inga sp. family Fabaceae) and on bromeliads.

Teeming with life and overflowing with exciting scientific questions, the Peruvian Amazon proved to be a great backdrop for Jason X. My newest project was to survey the biodiversity that inhabited the watery center of bromeliads, whose leaves formed rosettes that created tiny swimming pools in the canopy. Picture the scene: teams of teenagers counting tarantulas in the treetops and using turkey basters to survey the insects in bromeliad pools, while literally sitting among toucans high in the trees.

1999. Jason X was sweaty, leafy, buggy, and busy with student questions both live and via headphones. During March, at our remote research site in Amazonian Peru, two teams of twelve students plus four teachers worked in the canopy. In 1999 called ACEER (Amazon Center for Education and Environmental Research) but in 2000 renamed ACTS (Amazon Conservatory for Tropical Studies), this site housed the world's longest canopy walkway, designed by a colleague named Ilaar Muul. The walkway spanned twelve sections over one thousand feet, and I consider it one of the architectural wonders of the world. Canopy access was unprecedented here, and for several years I had been bringing groups of students and teachers to study bromeliad tank ecosystems, epiphytes, and herbivory from the relative comfort

of the canopy platforms. Throughout Jason X, I hurriedly made journal entries every morning in order to share my adventures with Eddie
and James when I returned home.

FEBRUARY 24 — Having arrived in Lima at one in the morning on
a delayed flight from Miami, I had time for only a quick catnap in my
hotel room. At four o'clock I was back on the bus to the airport to fly
Aero Peru to Iquitos, the river city of the upper Amazon nearest to the
base camp for Jason X. Iquitos was accessible only by boat or plane.
No roads traversed this dense, lowland tropical rain forest. I was anxious to reach the Amazon. This trip was a continuation of my love affair with Peru and its mighty river system. It was my sixth trip to this
special forest, a veritable treasure trove of biodiversity. (I flew to the
Amazon three times this year — each trip funded through different research programs, all of which combined science with public outreach
and youth education.)

Upon arrival in Iquitos, I had a joyous reunion with my luggage.
No shops existed in the rain forest, so any purchase of replacement
goods would have been out of the question. Twelve students, two
teachers, and I traveled via thatch-roofed boat to our base camp for
Jason X. There I had another reunion, this time with Bob Ballard,
founder of Jason. Since he explored undersea archeology and I studied the treetops, our paths rarely crossed at scientific conferences.
However, we both shared a passion for inspiring young people to
study science, and Bob had been a wonderful mentor to me.

Like a kid himself, Bob proudly showed me the barge constructed
for Jason that had traveled upriver to house the broadcast technology.
In one of the cabins on top, Bob had a private air-conditioned room.
I laughed. Bob loved his undersea career; he never complained about
spending many days cramped in a submarine studying the wonders
of hydrothermal vents or discovering old shipwrecks. However, he
felt uncomfortable in the rain forest with its high humidity, dense fo-

liage, and abundance of biting insects and snakes. (Staff later found a coral snake near Bob's room, and they respectfully decided not to tell him). Unlike Bob, I preferred the rain forest to a cramped submarine cabin. We loved to trade tall tales of our research adventures, two explorers of uncharted regions of Earth.

After lunch the students, teachers, and I continued downriver to our remote camp for Jason X, otherwise known as ACEER Camp. This location not only provided a safe sanctuary for the students, away from the rambunctious antics of the film crew, but also was the center of my research activities because of its proximity to the canopy walkway. After dragging my heavy baggage to my room, I hurried to take a quick shower. Scanning the walls for tarantulas, I was grateful to see none. The day was complete after a sunset stroll on the canopy walkway, where laughing frogs welcomed me "home" and a tinamou began its mournful call in the dark understory far below.

FEBRUARY 25. Happy Anniversary, Michael! Today we have been married one and a half years. I hope he will drink a tiny sip of champagne on my behalf. In camp we had no ice, so all drinks (limited to water and the occasional soda) were warm. Today I took the canopy film crew up for their first ascent into my research base camp, a platform at 125 feet. It was situated midway along the 1,200-foot-long canopy walkway at the highest point in the treetops. Our highway through the green heavens snaked among understory, midcanopy, canopy, and emergents—a biologist's paradise. Myron, the soundman, and Deb, the camerawoman, were both from Seattle, and they nearly expired with the heat, height, and humidity. Although the views were fabulous, we spent most of our time battling the sweat bees—tiny Hymenoptera that persistently sought our salty perspiration and seemed to invade all orifices. They sting only when squashed, so I have developed a very debonair swish to flick them off my body before they pierce the skin. (During one segment of the dress re-

James and Meg model their fashionable mosquito-netting hats in the tropical rain forests of the Amazon Basin (photograph by author)

hearsal for the telecast, Bob Ballard overheard me jokingly request DDT for the canopy to conquer the pesky sweat bees. Bob laughed and reminded me that there was now live footage to blackmail me for the rest of my scientific career!) I occasionally resorted to my head gear, a green camouflaged set of hoops with mosquito netting draped from head to shoulders. By no means a fashion statement, it was hot and sticky inside, but the insects stayed away from my face.

FEBRUARY 26. "Tropical tummy" hit me early this trip. I downed some Pepto-Bismol and prayed. Diarrhea in the canopy was no joke, and during live televised broadcasts it could be virtually intolerable. I tried to focus on my research instead of my stomach, while training the students to sample my artificial bromeliad experiments. Four years ago, Earthwatch volunteers had helped me map the walkway, identify the epiphytes, and create a guide along the 1,200-foot pathway. In subsequent years I published several papers with students on the taxonomy and ecology of the epiphytes. One of the bromeliads, however, was repeatedly chewed by some unknown beetle, and I was determined to find the culprit. Beetles were one of six common herbivores in forest canopies, leaving a fairly characteristic feeding pattern when compared to butterfly or moth caterpillars, walking sticks, leaf-cutter ants, grasshoppers, or katydids. Beetles were also abundant, perhaps representing nearly half of the insect biodiversity in forest canopies.

In addition, I was monitoring the diversity of organisms that relied on pools of water in the canopy. These water tanks existed in bromeliad rosettes, tree holes, curled leaves with pockets that collected rainfall, or any other container that held moisture. Believe it or not, the canopy was practically a desert except immediately after a rainfall. Most of the moisture flowed quickly to the understory, leaving the treetops dry most of the time. For this reason, many animals and plants in the canopy sought these water tanks for drinking, reproducing, seeking shelter, finding mates, and locating food.

With middle-school science in mind, I designed an experimental setup using green plastic cups that represented artificial bromeliads. Students could then manipulate the location of the cups and the length of time they remained in the canopy. The scientific hypothesis was that the water tanks, over time, would undergo a succession of different organisms settling in these tiny swimming pools in the sky, becoming more complex as the water tank aged. This simple design enabled students throughout the world to replicate our Jason experiment in Peru and compare the biodiversity of our tropical water tanks with their local ecosystems.

During the broadcasts, we checked the green cups that had been set up three months ago and compared them to newer water tanks placed during the live broadcasts. In ecology it was important to compare spatial scales (sites from Alaska to Peru, heights from understory to canopy) as well as temporal scales (three months versus three weeks versus three days old). Even after three months, which is a relatively short time in a rain forest, succession had occurred in nature and the water ecosystem had changed. Creatures that visited or moved in on day one were different from the creatures found three months later. As an example, we found mosquito larvae hatching during week one and poison dart frogs hatching after three months.

I got no sleep that night. Sunburn had rendered me feverish and sweaty.

WATER POLLUTION IN BROMELIAD TANKS:
AN EXPERIMENTAL APPROACH

By James, aged 14

(James's experiment on pollution in bromeliad tanks was also his science-fair project, based on ideas from Jason X and the green plastic cups with which students documented biodiversity in water tanks in the canopy. He used the same artificial water tanks, but experimentally applied differ-ent pollutants. James published a technical version of these results in the Journal of the Bromeliad Society.*)*

Epiphytes are a treetop specialty — they live in some canopies of tropical and subtropical forests. They do not parasitize their host trees, as many people erroneously believe. Bromeliads, an impor-tant type of epiphyte, play a critical role in these ecosystems; their rosette structure allows a tank of water to form in the center of the plant, creating a miniature swimming pool in the treetops. These tanks allow the survival of many tropical creatures including ants, beetles, mosquitoes, spiders, millipedes, centipedes, slugs, snails, frogs, salamanders, lizards, snakes, birds, rats, mice, and opossums.

Though the bromeliad ecosystems are fascinating, they are troublesome to biologists because there is no accurate way to survey them without destroying the bromeliads. As junior scientists, my brother and I did not allow this minor logistical detail stand in the way of our investigating the interactions of water tanks and organisms in forest canopies. Instead, we came up with an alternate solution: we created our own water tanks, or artificial bromeliads, with plastic cups. My mom found green plastic cups at the local supermarket, and they even vaguely resembled epiphytes (if you used your imagination). With our artificial containers, we were ready to design an experiment to investigate these mysterious ponds in the treetops.

As pollution in the environment continues to increase, bromeliad tanks will undoubtedly be contaminated, because airborne particles will land in the pools. We decided to look at how different contaminants might affect the diversity and abundance of the pool inhabitants. We placed forty-five cups in groups of five at random locations in the canopies of a Florida hammock. We built a small walkway in our own backyard and used our own hammock for this study. We compared five treatments: salt water, detergent, fertilizer, acid rain, and a control. The control, which was bottled water without any pollutant added, served as the reference point for the study. Each of the newly constructed artificial bromeliad tanks contained detergent, acid rain, fertilizer, salt, or just pure water. We hypothesized that the contaminants would decrease the abundance and diversity of life in the tanks.

We harvested three cups of each treatment after two, four, and six weeks, and surveyed what had settled into the bromeliad tanks. Diversity of species ranged from zero to eleven types, and abundance ranged as high as thirty-seven individuals in one cup. Much to our surprise, the control did not yield the highest number or diversity of organisms. Instead, the dish-detergent solution housed the greatest abundance. We were faced with one of the harsh realities of science: unexpected results. Our hypothesis had not been upheld, since the controls did not have the greatest abundance or diversity of invertebrates. Perhaps the time scale was too short? Perhaps the detergent attracted invertebrates because of its floral scent? Perhaps the scented detergent attracted insects that inadvertently fell into the pool and died, rather than taking up residence?

Although our results were unanticipated, they gave us some key insights. Perhaps some toxins do in fact attract certain organisms, or perhaps we needed more time for the bromeliad tanks to undergo the succession process of forming a stable tank community. In any event, as with most science, there is plenty of room for further investigation on this topic.

FEBRUARY 27. I awoke to lightning, thunder, and heavy rain. The storm delayed our dress-rehearsals. Furthermore, the downpour had washed away the ant colony scheduled for excavation on the live broadcast. Randy Morgan from the Cincinnati Insect Zoo, alias "Bug Man," hurriedly shifted his site to higher ground, since fortunately ant colonies were plentiful. After a day's practice, the students and I had our canopy "act" worked out — tree climbing, measuring leaf toughness using the penetrometers, checking the bromeliad experiments, and sampling insects in the foliage of an emergent tree. One teacher and three students shared my canopy research platform throughout. We were to complete fifty-five broadcasts over ten days, an almost impossible physical feat even in perfect weather and under ideal working conditions (which the canopy was not).

MARCH 1. I awoke to a blood-curdling scream. It may be safe to assume that every Amazon trip has a snake episode. In this case, a teacher discovered a fer-de-lance in the ladies' outhouse, not a pleasant way to start the day. And pity the poor snake — getting cornered in that smelly place with a shrieking human was probably a dreadful reptilian fate.

On canopy research trips, ablutions were always a challenge, but usually outhouses represented low-risk, almost stylish conditions.

The logistics of using the toilet while working in the treetops was a huge challenge. This topic never failed to be a source of giggling at every school lecture I presented. Our Jason X toilet situation was no exception. The crew had placed an outhouse discreetly in the forest, under the canopy walkway, for us to use between broadcasts. On the first day, we simply could not find it; the green metal structure was too well camouflaged. When we finally located it on day two, by 11:00 A.M. it overflowed because no one knew how to "flush" it. On day three, army ants found it and we could not safely get within 10 feet. I soon learned how to balance water intake with perspiration and thus entirely omit the need for a toilet. I imagine that over the long haul my body would have slowly dehydrated with this pattern of marginal drinking, but I managed to survive the rigorous broadcast schedule. Five shows aired today — only fifty to go!

MARCH 2. One of the teachers spotted three brown beetles on *Aechmea nallyi* (family Bromeliaceae), the bromeliad species under study for high levels of herbivory. Their description matched that of our herbivore. Oh joy! We continued our nocturnal searches each night, heading into the treetops with headlamps and notebooks, determined to make observations of this herbivore. The bromeliad's leafy rosettes were notoriously tough, and it was hard to believe that any beetle would manage to bite through its tissue. Still, it was fairly safe to assume that every plant in the tropical rain forest had at least one insect that fed upon it. Bromeliads were no exception.

Today it was 99.1° F in the canopy, with 60 percent humidity. On the broadcast I came very close to losing the contents of my breakfast. So we discussed biodiversity in our guts as well as in the canopy, just in case my student co-broadcasters needed to explain "Why Dr. Lowman was sprinting on the walkway out of camera view!"

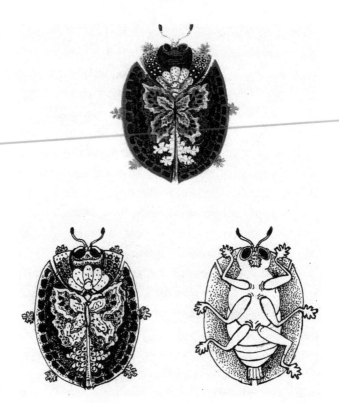

The nutmeg canopy beetle, a herbivore on a bromeliad in the rain-forest canopies of Amazonian Peru. The two views from the top show pattern variations in the shell. (illustration by Roohee Mirbaha)

MARCH 3. Today was known as "the big melt!" (This was closely related to our previous Jason experience defined as "the big sweat.") The canopy nearly wilted at a record 112° F. We were issued tiny battery-operated fans that served to deter the sweat bees, but only if held about an inch from our faces. It was a small consolation in this tree-top lifestyle. My respect for roofers grew with each day of exposure, as I imagined their conditions were quite similar. Nonetheless, it was a gorgeous place to spend the day, hot or otherwise, and we managed to collect data despite the big melt. Our bromeliad observations were going well, and students found the herbivorous beetle in its bromeliad home. I asked the producer if we could allow the Jason students in our global audience to help me name our alleged new species of beetle. We circulated photos and drawings via the Internet and created a naming competition. After just one week, approximately nine hundred schools had submitted names.

In conjunction with our observations of the beetles on the bromeliads, we examined the biodiversity that lived inside the water tanks. This study not only provided additional information about the habitat of our herbivore, but also served to link the water tank of a bromeliad with the artificial green cups used for our experiments.

To sample the water column from a live bromeliad was a challenge. It was not possible to pluck the plant from its host tree and turn it upside down to empty the water, without killing the plant; scientists simply cannot destroy the very subjects of their research. So I brought along a handy tool for sucking up a subsample of the bromeliad's water. It was a good ole' turkey baster. To my surprise, the middle-school students had never seen such a device. Their families cooked self-basting turkeys for Thanksgiving, so the baster proved to be an artifact of my childhood. I later bought three at my local grocery store, stocking up on this useful sampling tool before manufacturers ceased producing them. Examining the water tank inside a bromeliad, we found creatures ranging in size from tiny mosquitoes to enormous tarantulas. With patient observation, the students also saw larger animals such as hummingbirds drink water from the bromeliad tanks. Most likely sloths and other canopy creatures may rely on these treetop pools, because it is so dry between rainfalls.

MARCH 4. Happy Birthday to my mother (back in my hometown of Elmira, New York)! Today was also the twentieth anniversary of my first tree-climbing adventure in a coachwood tree (*Ceratopetalum*

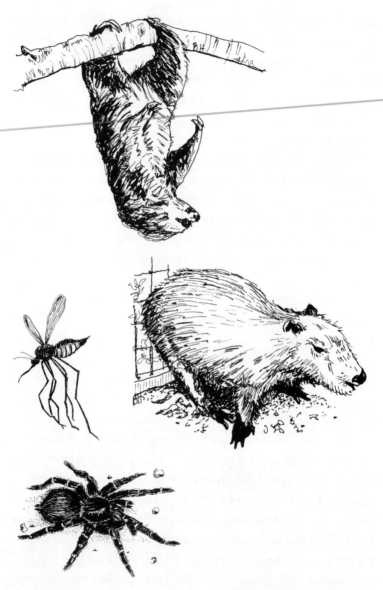

A compendium of Amazon animals: sloth (top), tarantula (bottom), capybara (middle right), and mosquito (middle left). Sizes not to scale (illustration by Barbara Harrison)

apetalum, family Cunoniaceae) near Sydney, Australia. I thought nostalgically about my first harness, made on a borrowed sewing machine from seatbelt webbing. And I mused about the Sydney caving club that taught me to go up instead of down, as cavers are used to doing. I took an anniversary climb up our Amazon emergent, *Cedralinga cateniformis* (family Meliaceae), which has distant cousins in the Australian rain forest as well as throughout Central and South America. I pondered my situation: out on a limb, in the middle of the remotest Peru, fighting hordes of sweat bees, avoiding fer-de-lance snakes in the outhouse, getting bugs in my stomach, but having the time of my life broadcasting tropical science to millions of teenagers around the world. I could never have envisioned this scenario at the time of my first climb. To celebrate this anniversary, we identified a new creature that inhabited the artificial bromeliad tanks. *Dendrobates ventrimaculatus* (family Dendrobatadae), a species of poison dart frog, had laid its eggs inside a green cup. Evidently our artificial water tanks had passed muster with the native fauna.

Lunch was delivered by Cleever, a Peruvian guide who was invited back to the States with the film crew. I asked him what he hoped to see in America, and he answered, "Mega-grocery stores and highways." I felt slightly embarrassed — were these our significant contributions to global stewardship?

Twenty-five broadcasts completed by Friday night, with thirty remaining . . . almost halfway.

MARCH 6. Tomorrow was our day off, so Bob Ballard and I and some of the other talent flew into town for a night off. This was likely the first and last time I will ever be referred to as "talent" — the crew's term for anyone who was on the air. From our seaplane, we looked down on the canopy walkway with its magnificent spans, and I could see platform 6, which had been my home all week. Canoes on the Amazon resembled tiny floating leaves on the surface of a vast waterway, as we flew high above the airstreams of harpy eagles. In Iquitos, I luxuriated in a hot shower, enjoyed clean sheets without the requisite mosquito netting, and read by electric lamp. The price to pay for this "privilege" was the loud noise of cars honking and people shouting, the constant drone of air-conditioners invading my quiet thoughts, a glimpse of television preoccupied with news of war and terrorism, and a cement wall outside my window instead of a green verdant jungle. We dined with Gilbert (Gil) Grosvenor, long-time leader of National Geographic, who had brought along his teenage son to experience Jason in the jungle. Bob had a way of attracting VIPs to our insalubrious Jason broadcast sites; no doubt, their experiences had a significant impact on their support of future Jason education expeditions.

MARCH 7. Our quick getaway to Iquitos was over in twenty-four hours. Wandering back to a rickety dock in late afternoon, we boarded a small boat to meet our seaplane. It was crowded sitting amid crates of oranges, an order of T-bone steaks (for the film producer), many boxes of electrical gear and miscellaneous supplies, cartons of water, Gatorade, and muesli bars. No one came except the no-see-ums, which were fierce. Finally, a messenger arrived via another small boat and announced that the pilot did not wish to fly so close to sunset, but that we should return at 5:00 A.M. for a sunrise flight instead.

March 8. We arrived back at the dock by five in the morning. More no-see-ums greeted us, but they faded away as soon as the blazing sun began to heat up the dock and the tin-roofed shed. On this beautiful Amazon morning, river people were quietly active — fishing, washing clothes, paddling canoes, eating breakfast, and tending to the day's chores. By 7:45 we were really hot and recognized that the Amazon working day was almost over. Dawn and dusk provided the coolest hours for labor. Our pilot arrived, but now the seaplane radio was broken. Approximately eight men conferred and then began to work on the broken parts. It was a team activity, but very few people actually put their hands on the materials; instead, they served as cheerleaders. Finally, everyone clapped and it was fixed.

Luggage, people, apples, T-bone steaks (in questionable condition?), oranges, and other supply boxes miraculously were loaded back onto the tiny seaplane. The pilot made two noble efforts to taxi and lift off, but with no success. All of us lurched forward in synchrony to assist the lift efforts of the plane. The plane's load was simply too heavy. We offloaded apples and muesli bars and tried again. Still no success. The pilot brought us back to the dock, and we overheard heated radio conversations in Spanish. Eventually a boat picked us up, to return via water instead of by air.

At this snail's pace, we had missed participating in the first of Monday's broadcasts. The crew used some pretaped segments, and fortunately few schools watching around the world noticed the difference. Bob and I disembarked partway up the river and were whisked onto the backs of small motorbikes. We whizzed along a small cement trail that turned out to be a shortcut bisecting a river bend. Another boat waited on the opposite side, and in no time we were back at camp. I scrambled into the treetops just in time for the afternoon broadcasts.

Whew — more record-breaking heat in the canopy, 112° F again. Memories of air-conditioning and cool clean sheets made it difficult to adjust. That evening, exhausted from the day's transition from city to river and from camp to treetops, I nevertheless felt cozy under my mosquito netting. The tinamou serenaded me to sleep, its lonely cry piercing the dark, humid rain-forest night. After the breakdowns of machines and technology, it was comforting to be reminded of the constancy of natural cycles.

MARCH 9. What a great day! My lost laundry was found. Now I will no longer need to wear yesterday's smelly shirt. Somehow, in the canoe trip upriver to the washing site, my plastic bag had been offloaded at another village. Today I have clean shirts for the broadcasts. The small pleasures of life are often the best.

National news ricochets through the camp. Aero Peru, the national airline, has declared bankruptcy, and our flights home have all been canceled. While some of the team grabbed phones and quickly made other arrangements, those of us in the canopy needed to be "on air" with the sad realization that our stay in Peru might be indefinitely extended. We hardly had time to think about flights, arguably because the temperature in our canopy platform hit a new record high of 117° F. We heard howler monkeys in the distance, but otherwise not even the resident lizards ventured out into the desert-like conditions of the upper canopy.

MARCH 11. Only ten shows to go. We ascended into the treetops with renewed vigor. The end was in sight! At midday a huge thundercloud rolled in, and the canopy crew raced down to the forest floor, barely escaping a deadly thunder-and-lightning show. Our treetop gang got a bit giddy by the end of the afternoon: Donna Krabill, the day's teacher assistant, pretended to net some Oreos in the canopy instead of insects, to the delight of all of us who ate them afterward.

Our last evening was devoted to the long-awaited culmination of the beetle-naming competition. A committee of scientists was to select the winner from all the Internet submissions. Some names were fairly silly, such as BOB ("big ole' beetle" or Bob Ballard), bromeliad ripper, megabeetle, or beastly beetle. Others, such as kaleidoscope or butterfly beetle (because of its coloration), were extremely clever. After sifting through all the emails, our committee voted. The winner was Mrs. Baisch's fifth-grade class at the Orangewood Elementary School in Fort Myers, Florida, with "nutmeg canopy beetle." The name incorporated three factors: the nutmeg coloration of the beetle, the fact that this bromeliad often grows in the nutmeg tree (*Myristica* sp., family Myristacaceae), and the cryptic inclusion of my nick-

A

B

A, Mrs. Baisch's fifth-grade class at the Orangewood Elementary School in Fort Myers, Florida, which won the beetle-naming competition with the name "nutmeg canopy beetle"; B, students look closely at the beetle with Meg (photographs by author)

name. (I actually visited Mrs. Baisch's class after returning from Peru, and I met the next generation of scientists, as I called them, who had achieved immortality by naming the new beetle.)

I gave the privilege of announcing the winner on the last broadcast to Pamela Montero from Iquitos. Pam was a local student, but she had never in her thirteen years traveled 25 miles upriver to study the rain forest. Jason provided her with a scholarship, and she became an enthusiastic canopy research assistant. To this day, we continue to correspond as she studies biology in college. Her first trip away from Peru was to work with me at New College, Florida, in 2005.

During the last show, both scientists and students engaged in entomophagy (the culinary art of eating insects). Some of us munched on termites, which have a fairly benign taste, while Randy "Bug Man" Morgan impressed all of us by eating suri. These large maggots or larvae, also called palm grubs, are soft and soggy with a crunchy exterior. I confess to having tried one on a previous trip, but never again. The local Indians considered them a delicacy because they were only found in the unlikely habitat of decaying palm trunks.

Our final evening was somber, since no one knew if it would be possible to fly home the next day. In dinnertable conversation, Aero Peru was downgraded to Aero Perhaps and then to Aero Never Never.

MARCH 13. Bags and bodies were loaded onto boats in the pouring rain. I was relieved to know that a luxurious hotel bed awaited me at the end of this last dugout journey, plane or no plane. The journey to or from the Amazon involved many legs, including canoe, ferry, small plane, bus, taxi, and international jet. On this expedition, a dugout canoe proved more reliable than an international jet. Once we arrived in Lima, the news was not good. It was rumored that at most ten seats remained on the next American Airlines flight to Miami, and we were advised to arrive at the airport at least four hours prior to the departure. Our last meal of ceviche (raw fish marinated in lemon) was delicious, but no one was optimistic that it was indeed our last meal. We might have the unwanted privilege of eating ceviche for days to come.

MARCH 14. Up at 3:00 A.M. to get to the airport. We arrived to find the lines winding up and down and around and out the doors of the international terminal. Everyone shrugged and sighed. Some of the team returned to the hotel, admitting defeat. But I was so anxious to see Eddie and James that I stayed with the others in the long snake-like queue. James was entering the science fair next week; Eddie had another track meet at school that I badly wanted to see. I had already missed so much in their youthful lives that it broke my heart not to be able to return at the soonest possible moment.

We stood for three hours. When the American Airlines counters finally opened, there were literally fistfights as tourists and nationals competed to be first. We were so far behind that it didn't matter; no amount of aggression would improve our chances.

Suddenly I heard a loud voice from far away; "Meg . . . Meg, get up here!" It was Bob Ballard, who no doubt had arrived at the airport by two in the morning. With two young children awaiting him, he too felt a strong urgency to return home. He was at the front of the first-class line, holding two seats. Bless you, Bob! I rushed up and for an astronomical price was able to join him in this one-way ride home to our respective children. The additional cost was well worth it — to see the boys instead of ceviche in Lima would be truly a blessing. Battling crowds and security, and collapsing in our seats some three hours later, we knew Florida would be a welcome sight.

DIARY OF JAMES

Aged 13, grade 7 (almost)

To many Americans the Amazon rain forest is about as far away as the moon. I, however, have had a different experience. I have been there twice and had a wonderful time on both occasions. Many things about Peru are different from America. For instance, in the Amazon region of Peru, outside of the few major cities there are no roads — the river provides all the transportation that is necessary.

August 8. I woke up this morning without an alarm clock; I realized my mom was still asleep. Gosh, she must have been really tired getting all three of us packed, on the plane, and into the jungle. She had just been to Peru three months ago as part of the Jason X expedition, and now we were back as a family while she taught a summer workshop. I slowly got out of my bed surrounded by mosquito netting, and wondered how anyone could sleep through the noisy calls of the macaws and toucans.

Probably the most exciting part about the Amazon is the fact that all around you are millions of species of plants, mammals, insects, birds, and other types of creatures. Some of these have extremely colorful patterns or strange forms. Others have exotic names, beautiful calls, or special physiological features. One thing I learned in the Amazon is that the name does not always indicate how a bird looks. An ornithologist told me about a bird with the longest Latin name in the world — Griseotyrannus aurantioatrocristatus. I have been trying to memorize it, but it is tricky. When I went on a bird-watching trip, we saw this bird, and to my dismay it was gray with a slight yellow patch on its head.

August 9. I went into the canopy for sunrise with my buddy DC Randle. It was nearly dark on the forest floor, but when we climbed up all the steps into the canopy, the first rays of morning sun dazzled us. The birds and monkeys up there were also awake and active. Mist was rising from the river in the distance. I wondered if boys my age were out fishing in their dugout canoes, getting breakfast for their families. How different our lifestyles: they had canoes, blowguns, and soccer balls; we had computers, cell phones, and Nintendo. It might be fun to trade places.

August 10. We found out that an anaconda had been sighted and went

Eddie and James trade for blowguns in the Amazon (photograph by author)

quickly to the river to see it. Its magnificent bright yellow spots and huge girth made this one an impressive specimen. One of the most awesome sights in the rain forest is the anaconda. However, not everyone gets to see it. Fortunately for me, I saw one on my second trip to the Amazon. This enormous snake was draped on a bush 3 feet above the edge of the river. We were told that it had just eaten (the cause for its laziness?) and had to wait three days to digest its meal. The snake had a big bulge and I wondered what it had eaten — maybe a sloth? or an agouti?

In the Amazon, people are different from those in America. In some American cities, it is hard to trust people and to find kindness, but in the jungle everyone is kind and generous. When we visited people in the Amazon, sometimes we traded things. Peruvians had many handmade crafts like knives, blowguns, baskets, masks, necklaces, bracelets, and decorations. The villagers liked to trade for my soccer shoes, T-shirts, or serving spoons, which were not easy to get along the river.

I have written here only a few of the things that separate Peru from America. If I were to list them all, this diary would be several hundred pages long. However, you should now have a feel for what a wonderful place the Amazon is. It is my favorite place on Earth.

8 International Powwows: The Indian Connection

Never doubt that a small group of thoughtful committed citizens can change the world. Indeed, it's the only thing that ever has.

— Margaret Mead

The conference scene for field biologists was both a positive and a negative experience. Professional meetings required time and energy to conduct research, write a seminar, enroll for the conference, travel and attend, and subsequently summarize proceedings. They detracted from time available to collect data. Over time, many scientists learned to avoid conferences in deference to spending more time in the field. I once knew a famous scientist who only attended conferences that synchronized with games in the World Series.

Still, conferences brought intellectual rewards to one's fieldwork by providing an opportunity to develop collaborations, obtain feedback about a research idea, and share new methods. For tropical biologists, conferences are the best opportunity to interact with colleagues after spending months in remote jungles. For my career track in tropical rain forests and canopy biology, I rated meetings of the Association for Tropical Biology and Conservation and the Ecological Society of America (and occasional International Canopy Conferences) as "must attend," whereas other conferences were ranked "attend if possible."

I was very proud my sons at ages 15 and 13 when they sat through Egbert Leigh's technical talk about tropical tree diversity at a conference in Panama; and when they dined with Tom Lovejoy and held their own on subjects as diverse as tropical canopy birds or the Catskill Mountains watershed. My children were indoctrinated early on to interact with scientists. Whereas I would have been tongue-tied, James at age 14 presented a talk to ecotourists in Peru about the rain forests of Belize; and Eddie gave a series of lectures on science and religion for our local church, attracting classes of more than a hundred people. Together the boys and I have published their findings on herbivory in bromeliads and decay of Florida epiphytes. Needless to say, they have accompanied me to many lectures, tours, and research trips around the world. Although they may ultimately choose careers as bankers or builders, it is heartening to have shared my career with them while they were growing up, and to have had the benefit of their young minds to contemplate scientific hypotheses.

During July 2001 the Association for Tropical Biology and Conservation (ATBC) held its conference in Bangalore, India. Both of my sons were working their first summer jobs as camp counselors so did not accompany me for this long trek. Bangalore was reputedly the technology capital of India, where Indian women with perfect American accents answer toll-free numbers for American computer-help lines. As treasurer of the association, I was proud to have computerized the accounts for the first time in the group's history, and also set up its first endowment.

Accompanying me on this sojourn was ATBC's tax accountant, who was approximately 6′4″ and had never traveled overseas before. Mike Pender (also founding accountant of the TREE Foundation, which had built the Myakka walkway) had faithfully served ATBC for many years but had never witnessed the kind of scientific passion that was so obvious at a conference.

As part of the delegation, Mike and I booked economy seats on Delta Airlines for this trans-Atlantic and trans–Indian Ocean flight. Scientists, unlike many other professionals, rarely travel business or first class, instead allocating their hard-won grant funds to bug-counting gadgets, new raincoats, or Swiss Army knives with all the extras. Poor Mike's legs would not even fit into our economy row. The flight attendants graciously invited Mike to dine in the back with them, since his tray could not stay level atop his protruding knees.

We arrived in Bombay at 12:30 A.M., excited yet exhausted from the eighteen hours of flying (or standing, in Mike's case). Even at this late hour, the airport was busy with tourists as well as Indians. In every corner and hallway, men were sleeping with their turbans serving as pillows. We were given incorrect directions to locate the transfer bus to the domestic terminal and walked the entire perimeter of the international airport. When we finally found the bus, to our horror the queue was approximately seventy-five people long, and our connecting flight was only an hour from departure.

A taxi driver targeted us at the end of this long line, illegally offering us a ride for only $10. Signs were posted warning passengers not to use taxis for airport transit, but in our exhaustion and relief we followed the driver to a dark, isolated parking lot. Hopping into his van, we left the international airport. At one dark intersection, a crowd of men huddled around a burning oil vat along a dirty roadside, and the driver stopped until we paid another $10 for gas. At another crossroads, he requested extra money for our luggage. Some $25 later, we finally reached the domestic terminal just in time for our 3:00 A.M. flight to Bangalore. We had learned an unfortunate international lesson: don't be tempted by "bargain taxis."

Upon arrival in Bangalore at 5:00 A.M., we squeezed fifteen scientists and their gear into two small minivans headed to the Hotel Ashok. For a five-star hotel, it offered some surprises. My first room assignment had a Vesuvius-like eruption of mud from the toilet. Back to the desk for another room. My second room smelled strongly of a combination of rancid beer stains on the carpet and mildew that hinted of Legionnaire's Disease from a dysfunctional air-conditioner. Nonetheless, I collapsed on the bed.

Some three hours later, Mike and I met for breakfast in the hotel, excited and eager to take advantage of our "free day" to see India. The restaurant steward, Mr. Vaharadavan, greeted us warmly and suggested that we obtain a competent driver for a day tour. Even better, he claimed to know just the person, his friend Vasu. His idea sounded wonderful to our jet-lagged ears, but we lived to regret the tale. Vasu toured us in his clunky white cab, which threatened to die at every intersection. He was courteous and knowledgeable, although we suspected he was in cahoots with the shopkeepers after we were swarmed at each cottage industry we visited. First, Persian carpets, then cashmere shawls, followed by jewelry, sandalwood carvings, and traditional saris.

We also visited the 240-acre Lalbagh Botanical Garden, to stroll through their rose garden, glass house, and other displays where families were enjoying their weekend. My first experience with an Indian public toilet was sobering: a hole in the ground with a water jug to rinse my private parts, followed by a donation of coins for the privilege of using the cubicle. Groups of teenagers and middle-aged men loitered in the gardens. Some spat in our path, probably their emotional response toward "rich Americans." In this country of abject poverty, we empathized with their sentiments.

With over 5 million citizens and a salubrious climate (called Pensioners Paradise by the locals), Bangalore was India's fastest-growing city. It was famous both for its centers of technology and for its gardens. Like many parts of Asia, India was undergoing a rocky transition from rural to urban living. The roads exploded with old and new transportation: bullock carts next to sleek Mercedes taxis. Modern hotels were under construction next to fields of rice with workers living in simple shacks. I read in the newspaper about a family that had found 3,500 cobras living underneath their floorboards in a suburban neighborhood. (A snake charmer was called in to remove them and boasted of grabbing several hundred babies in his teeth and hands.) In contrast, another article depicted the city's epidemic of wife abuse, although this injustice was not limited to southern India. The hospitals of Bangalore had been highlighted in several articles and newscasts featuring women burned by their spouses for domestic unrest. In most cases, the women had no rights and no ability to protest or seek legal justice.

From the hotel, we saw occasional signs of enormous wealth: fancy cars, cell phones, mansions. But close by, we saw beggars, children bringing crops to town via horse cart, makeshift shacks along the roadside where homeless people lived, and men sweeping large sidewalks with inefficient hand-made twig brooms. One scene burned in my memory was a line of women pounding large white rocks with primitive hammers; a second line of women pounding the medium

The Indian snake charmer pictured in an Asian newspaper who removed 3,500 snakes from an urban home, using his hands and mouth to hold baby cobras (illustration by Barbara Harrison)

pieces of rocks into small stones; and a third group of women crushing the small stones into powder. By hand, they were making cement to create curbs, to control drainage, and to improve sanitation. The guilt-ridden vision of their manual labor haunts those of us who simply drive to Home Depot and buy such commodities with ease.

Although we were spellbound by the cultural aspects of our visit to India, our mission was the business of ATBC. At the annual meeting of the council we mulled over the budget, made changes to *Biotropica* (the association's international publication), and mapped out some improvements to the group's mission in these changing times. As secretary/treasurer of the organization, I obediently took the minutes. My laptop sputtered and groaned when the electrical outlet surged and even created visible sparks. Needless to say, my computer died permanently after its visit to India.

Meg boarding a taxi, amid the intersection of old and new on the streets of India: bullock carts, little three-wheeled taxis, and automobiles (illustration by Barbara Harrison)

Like the other attendees, we spent the week juggling sightseeing and conference sessions. One afternoon, Mike and I visited the historical city of Mysore. A quick exit from our hotel produced our driver Vasu as if by magic, waiting with his rundown white cab. Even more coincidental, his wife was standing on a street corner, so she came with us.

Driving both within and outside Bangalore was a suicidal art. Cars used all lanes plus the shoulder and sidewalk when available, passed on either the right or the left, and *constantly* honked. Bicyclists, bullock carts, motor scooters, and pedestrians put their lives in the hands of the gods. Vasu himself was a serious honker; we later realized that it was because his brakes were not functional. His "beep beep beep" warned other drivers that he was charging through, and "beeeeeeeeeeeeeeeep" meant that everyone's life was in grave danger if the other drivers did not yield to him.

The drive was nauseating. Bumps, screeching halts, terrible fumes with the windows open, and claustrophobic heat if the windows were closed, punctuated the trip. Our engine overheated twice and starter problems were commonplace. Even the doors did not open or close properly. Poor Mike was once again wedged in the back seat, knees bumping the front seat and head smashing against the ceiling.

We stopped for a roadside breakfast: tea in tiny cups (with an overdose of sugar and milk), fried bread, and unknown spicy objects. The meal was incredible at the price of 62 rupees (approximately US $1.25) for four people. At the end of our meal, the waiter brought out a small piece of newspaper (approximately 8″ × 8″) and placed it on the table — a napkin for all of us to share. One simply cannot fathom the chronic shortage of resources in this country without experiencing it firsthand, or perhaps it is more appropriately viewed as an overabundance of resources in other regions of the world.

Stomachs full of mysterious new substances, we rejoined the chaotic traffic scene. I will never forget careening toward a big knot of traffic at a red light. Vasu drove in the left gutter right in front of a bus that was stopped and letting off people. Swerving around a large tree on the sidewalk, Vasu sped into the intersection just as the oxygen-masked traffic cop waved to our lane to advance. Our intrepid driver grinned and said, "You see, Vasu is first car!!!"

We toured the Mysore palace, residence of the former royal family. Their descendant, Prince Jayachamaraja Srikandatta Wodeyar, was appointed first governor of Karnataka. The palace had precious artifacts, including gold, silver, historical murals, and beautiful antiques, but no sophisticated security measures.

In the parking lot, a magician performed tricks in exchange for a few rupees. When I jokingly asked if he had a cobra, he immediately whisked a box out of the bushes, and pulled out a large snake. He then asked Mike to hold it by the tail. Frozen in fear, Mike bravely followed instructions. Later, Vasu explained that the poison glands had been removed from these snakes. Mike laughed nervously and fervently hoped it was true. Driving back to Bangalore, I tried to doze but the incessant horn reminded me that our lives were in constant jeopardy. It was an anxious return journey.

Our conference continued its hectic pace with a banquet, tours, keynote talks, and biological sessions. I presented a talk in the Canopy Ecosystems session and had some stimulating discussions with my international colleagues. New projects were born, such as a planned India collaboration at the Western Ghats Forest, a possible botanical garden exchange, and a new canopy crane project to compare herbivory among forests. Collaborations that take months of written exchange can mature in one evening of face-to-face conversation.

Several young Indian scientists respectfully introduced themselves to ecologist Joe Connell and me, explaining that they were devoting their research to a hypothesis from one of our earlier publications. That was heartening, as we all hope to pass the torch as we age. In 1987 Joe and I had published our premise that perhaps mycorrhizae create a competitive advantage for certain tree species. Now this idea was being tested by students in different forests around the world. The story behind the theory is perhaps as unique as the hypothesis itself and warrants digression.

Joe and I had worked for almost ten years in Australia on a rain-forest seedling recruitment project. We spent hours collecting data along transects in rainy and muddy conditions (with leeches crawling up our legs to body parts there is no need to mention). Throughout these long field days, we mused on the causes of diversity in tropical forests. Joe's intermediate disturbance theory postulated that low levels of disturbance create ideal conditions to foster diversity in tropical ecosystems. I countered with a different question: then why were there so many low-diversity forests in the tropics?

My perspective was slightly different from his. Joe had come to Australia purposely to select high-diversity sites in rain forests and coral reefs, whereas I had come to compare herbivory between high-and low-diversity forest stands. I was particularly puzzled by the cloud forests where one species of tree, the Antarctic beech or *Nothofagus moorei* (family Fagaceae) dominated, and by the Australian dry forests where eucalypts grew almost exclusively. Joe and I sparred, discussed, and debated this high-diversity versus low-diversity issue, and the one commonality we observed with single-species-dominant forest stands was their relationship with specific mycorrhizal partners.

Our debates ceased when I became pregnant. Eddie was born in 1985, and my ability to participate in rigorous fieldwork was in jeopardy. As a housewife on a sheep ranch, I not only had an infant to tend, but also many domestic duties. Joe, however, was not just brilliant about ecology, was also a creative thinker. As a lover of astronomy, he was mindful that 1986 was the year of Halley's comet. He suggested coming to our sheep farm to work on a theoretical paper explaining low-diversity forests. His presence allowed me to pursue science despite the limitations of housewifery and motherhood in a rural setting. It also allowed Joe to see Halley's comet, since our outback Australian sky was hundreds of miles from any city lights.

The end result was a theory postulating that mycorrhizae may lend a competitive advantage to certain tree species, facilitating dominance in certain forest types and conditions. This paper was a by-product of both Eddie's birth and Joe's flexibility, demonstrating that science can indeed integrate with parenting. Perhaps that is why Joe Connell has been one of my lifelong colleagues and a wonderful role model. While meeting young scientists at the conference in India, I enjoyed sharing this tale of juggling family and career.

Two Indian scientist-friends, Soubadra Devy and her husband, Ganesh, took Mike and me carpet shopping after our debacle earlier in the week with Vasu. (On a personal note, I had funded Soubadra and Ganesh to attend the Second International Canopy Conference in Sarasota in 1998, at which they courted and subsequently married.) They directed us to a store off the tourist path, where the owner brought out some silk rugs. We gasped — finally, true artistry. Mike and I left, clutching our magic carpets despite almost having an anxiety attack. The shop owners had wrapped our carpets in the "back room" into one brown paper package. Fearful that our rugs might not be inside, our hosts opened the package to confirm that it did indeed contain our purchases.

At last we reached our final night of curry. (I must confess to longing for salad and fresh vegetables.) The conference field trip into the Western Ghats region was canceled because of a sandalwood smuggler and bandit named Koose Muniswamy Veerappan who frequented that remote region. In India, a natural ecosystem created the perfect hiding place for one of the country's most notorious outlaws. Field biologists and poachers worked the same habitat, but in this instance we graciously declined to share the same hillside.

Instead of risking our lives in the Western Ghats, Mike and I stopped in Delhi overnight to see the Taj Mahal. Having by now proudly mastered the complex taxi system at the airport, we were thrilled to find the kind of hotel with hot showers, clean towels, and functional plumbing that had been lacking in Bangalore. The Taj Mahal, much to our surprise, was approximately 100 miles south of Delhi and it was already noon. In haste, we booked a taxi (actually air-conditioned) and a picnic lunch to devour en route, because the Taj closed at sunset.

The guidebook called the drive "harrowing" and that was accurate. Our driver was excellent, but spoke no English. From the window, along the extensive outskirts of Delhi we glimpsed cows, bullock carts, hundreds of trucks, cyclists, walkers, motor scooters, congested markets spilling onto the road, homeless camps, and towns. Whenever we stopped, beggars came to the car windows, including a man with two monkeys that leapt onto the car and tried to pry open the windows. We felt really frightened in this sea of people, all of whom needed money, clothes, food, and shelter.

With pollution degrading its delicate marble walls, the Taj was now enclosed in a car-free zone. Just as we captured our first photo of this amazing site, it began to rain. Never mind—we inched our way up the steps to pay homage to this seventh architectural wonder of the world. The marble was dangerously slippery in the rain. Back in the United States, such steep, slick steps without a handrail would no doubt force the closure of a monument owing to liability risks. But in India, weather does not seem to curtail tourism. I witnessed an octogenarian woman on her pilgrimage navigating more gracefully than I, who relied on my posterior and slowly "bottomed" my way down the slippery steps.

We left Agra at seven that evening, our driver careening through the hustle and bustle of this city of several million just before dark. Once back on the highway, our honking was reduced to approximately ten toots per minute rather than the earlier twenty-five (my scientific counts were probably conservative). We arrived at our hotel by midnight, exhausted but thrilled to have seen this magnificent edifice. At the Bombay airport we waited more than four hours for the Delta counter to open up for our 2:00 A.M. flight. I disposed of my last 50-rupee note in the ladies' room; the attendant was thrilled with her generous tip.

Much as I love adventure, I was anxious to go home and rediscover the luxury of a flush toilet with paper. After breakfast in Frankfurt and dinner in Atlanta, almost miraculous in terms of physical and cultural distances, we arrived home twenty hours later—clutching our magic carpets, science projects, new collaborations, and budget notes. India taught us an important lesson, beyond the confines of the conference itself. It reminded us that most Americans are unaware of our over-consumption of resources. Sound science needs to develop creative solutions for this imbalance. Conferences are one effective way to communicate new ideas and solve environmental challenges.

A DINNER OF ADVENTURE (2001)

By Eddie and James, aged 16 and 15 respectively

The Waldorf-Astoria radiated its splendor as we arrived by cab. Our family strutted to the hotel entrance in the formal attire required for the occasion. Neither of us had ever worn a tuxedo before, so we looked like conventional party-penguins. We were attending the Explorers Club annual banquet, a gathering of prestigious scientists and adventurers known throughout the world. Although this was their annual meeting, it was different from the more somber science-laden conferences that we usually attended with our mom. The club had invited our mother to become a member because she is a pioneer in rain-forest canopy research. [James was later accepted as a student member because of his penchant for exploration to places like Peru, Nicaragua, and Antarctica.] We had high hopes of meeting some of the important members such as Sir Edmund Hillary, the first to scale Mount Everest, or Buzz Aldrin, famous astronaut.

We entered the banquet hall to discover that the Explorers Club had transformed this sophisticated New York venue into a madhouse. Exotic plants and stuffed animals decorated the rooms. Eccentric scientists filled the reception area. They darted in and out of the crowd with intent looks on their faces, as if on a dangerous expedition. Some carried walking sticks. Others wore round spectacles and long mustaches in the fashion of Teddy Roosevelt. We made a beeline for the exotic hors d'oeuvres. A global feast of indigenous ingredients greeted our palates:

West Virginia cave crickets, with pepper jelly and cream cheese on celery and baby corn

Mealworms, rising from escargot butter in a delicious puff pastry

Korean spring rolls with roasted, herbed mealworms, termites, and crickets on pink radishes

Roasted tarantula tempura, with sweet chili dipping sauce

Succulent North American beaver, oven roasted, herbed and glazed

Poached bovine brain, with remoulade

Roasted termite, on cherry tomatoes

Brandy-spiced Madagascar hissing cockroaches

Braised earthworms, sandwiched in snow peas

Ostrich tartare

Feral hogs, rubbed with garlic, lemon, paprika, and chili pepper

Succulent rattlesnake, roasted and stewed with chipotle peppers

Eddie eats hissing cockroach and James ingests tarantula tempura at the Explorers Club centennial anniversary banquet (photograph by author)

Along the walls, some explorers displayed information about their recent trek to Antarctica. Others showed artifacts from their journey to the Sahara. This truly was an adventuresome crowd.

Finally, waiters herded us into the grand ballroom for dinner. Dazzled by the colorful flags strewn over the balconies, we recognized the true diversity of people within this organization. The grand feast began with a ptarmigan salad, and ended with ice cream volcanoes erupting with chocolate lava. Speakers included the head of astrophysics at the Smithsonian, who spoke about the structure of the universe. The audience did not seem to miss a word of his speech, despite its fairly tedious technicalities. From the hush, we sensed the passion that explorers felt to learn about one another's discoveries. An award was given to the first man to circumnavigate the earth in a hot-air balloon. Jim Fowler entertained the crowd with a small menagerie of mountain goats, anteaters, and even a rare marmoset up on stage. A rebellious snowy owl flew to the top of the Waldorf-Astoria's finest chandelier and refused to come down. Doubtless, no other organization would dare to release wild animals into the elegant ballroom of a five-star hotel. Their absurdly adventurous instincts are what drive the Explorers Club members to achieve unimaginable feats. We left the banquet hall that night with an eagerness for discovery that continues to nourish us to this day.

9 Colorful Bodies: Home to the Black Waters of the Amazon

*T*o be poor and be without trees, is to be the most starved human being in the world. To be poor and to have trees, is to be completely rich in ways that money can never buy.

— Clarissa Pinkola Estés, *The Faithful Gardener*

When I was a child, we used to travel each summer to the Finger Lakes in up-state New York. That was my home away from home, representing nature, con-tentment, and the halcyon days of a New England summer. Our lake cottage was a cozy cocoon without phone, dishwasher, television, or videos. Many subtle aspects of nature came alive for me during those childhood summers. My senti-mental parents reluctantly sold the lake cottage because they needed to budget for retirement. As an adult, I find the same contentment in Amazonian Peru. This is my tenth trip, and my sons also appreciate this special sensation of "com-ing home to nature."

After a decade of leading hundreds of ecotourists into the Amazon, I am happy to report that most travelers have had a life-changing experience. (Only one gentleman, sad to say, boasted that the casino in Lima was the highlight of his trip.) Tom Lovejoy, a distinguished tropical conservationist, taught me a very important lesson when he explained that it might be a more valuable use of a scientist's time to take politicians to the Amazon for two days to observe it first-hand, than to devote two hundred days writing technical documents to describe it on paper.

Why write a chapter on the "oohs and ahs" of the tropical jungle in this vol-ume, which centers on research? The boys and I debated this issue. We have no scientific justification, but we hope that reinforcing the importance of ecotourism as a tool for education and conservation, and the need for support of these activ-ities, are reason enough.

2001. Overnight, our boat steadily motored through the confluence of two rivers that make up the mighty Amazon — the Rio Ucayali and the Rio Maranon. The Ucayali represents water from southwest Peru; the Maranon, from northeast Peru. About 60 miles west of Iquitos they converge and the Amazon begins, some 2,400 miles from its eastern mouth in Brazil, where it meets the Atlantic Ocean.

Throughout its long journey east from Iquitos, the Amazon drops only 300 feet. The complete river system, originating in the Andes in southernmost Peru, spans 4,200 miles in its entirety. The momentum of its initial descent from steep snow-capped peaks creates a strong muddy current that pushes logs, old huts, entire villages, timber, roofing, and other flotsam and jetsam from the Andes all the way into the Atlantic Ocean. Because of the relatively small elevation change in the last 2,400 miles of its journey, the Amazon meanders across eastern Peru and throughout Brazil, forming snaky patterns and oxbow lakes in its vast floodplain. With its transient banks, the river is dynamic and always changing. It shifts seasonally with floods, causing the *ribereños* (river people) to become seasonally nomadic when the waters flood their banks. The rains delineate the only form of seasons in the rain forest, and plants and wildlife take their cues from the amount of moisture. Even the night sounds fluctuate with temporal shifts in humidity and rainfall.

No cities existed along our route. The only habitation of any size was the village of Nauta. The population of six thousand, we were told, would soon escalate because of the proposed construction of a road to Iquitos, scheduled for completion in 2006. After the tranquil blanket of darkness along the riverbanks for many hundreds of miles, it was a shock to view the streetlights of Nauta at the edge of the dark Rio Maranon. A jungle metropolis, Nauta even had generators and its own electricity. No doubt in years to come many more villages would be lighted at night as the jungle continued its modernization.

Expeditions to remote jungles change people. For participants, these trips provide a living laboratory of conservation education. As a biologist, I have witnessed firsthand the effectiveness of Tom Lovejoy's theory that exposing influential citizens to the tropics may be one of the most effective ways to save it. In addition to its professional role in my career, Peru was also the backdrop for a highlight in my personal life.

I met Michael Brown on a blind date. I wrote in my calendar "Dinner," he wrote "Golf." He came to Sarasota from the nearby town of Saint Petersburg to play golf with a mutual friend and then meet the friend's fiancée for dinner. I was invited along as the fourth. Not wanting to be too hopeful, I at least relished the notion of a delicious dinner at one of my favorite local restaurants, the Bijou. When Michael came to our house and saw the blowgun on the living room wall, he knew this household was different from those of other women he had dated. He sensed the special bond between mother and children that had been nurtured by our mutual experiences in nature, as the boys spoke enthusiastically of our pet tarantula or our recent trip to Peru.

On our next date, I invited Michael to dinner in the canopy; he passed the test by climbing his first tree with enthusiasm. Deciding that he wanted to know more, he signed up for my upcoming ecotourist expedition to the Amazon. Casting our fates to the wind, we listened to jaguars at two in the morning, found a dracula orchid flowering on a mahogany tree, witnessed sunrise in the canopy, stalked a cock-of-the-rock with our cameras, and were mystified by the stonework of Machu Picchu.

We returned from this magical experience in Peru and were married soon afterward. I always say to people that traveling up the Amazon for one week is equivalent to experiencing life together for one year. Since marrying Michael, I have returned to Peru at least five times, and, like my ecotravelers, been blessed by my experiences there. One couple became engaged, others were motivated to significantly simplify their lifestyles, several became significant donors to botanical research, and almost everyone who visits the Amazon becomes committed to a conservation ethic that includes rain-forest conservation.

A week on the Amazon could be characterized as overwhelming sensory overload — stimulating smell, sight, sound, touch, and taste. After trekking on foot through the Amazon with previous ecotourist groups (including Michael), I switched to boat tours, to better serve the elder members of Selby Gardens. When we boarded our boat, *La Amatista,* in Iquitos, my American guests from the sterile, temperate-zone world of electronics and sound bytes were delighted to rekindle their senses of smell to the odors of the jungle. Rich aromas of leaves, flowers, decay, and heavy humidity hung in the air. We felt invigorated, as if the photosynthesis of the forest were infused directly into our veins. This first exposure to the Amazon was at sunset, when our lack of vision enhanced our sense of smell in compensation. For most Americans, total darkness is an unusual phenomenon. We searched for tiny eyeballs of insects and animals reflecting along the riverbank, but soon weakened to the call of wine and pisco sours, which our guides teased would promote visions of jaguars. The sad truth is that in recent times this may be the only way to "see" a jaguar.

After a deep sleep on board with visions of jaguars in our dreams, we awoke at six to a dawn chorus of bird songs. Sunrise on the Amazon, one of my very favorite moments, illuminated subtle signs of life everywhere. Wisps of mist hung over cannonball trees, where the orependula were waking in their hanging nests. Quiet canoes paddled deliberately yet peacefully to a favorite fishing hole in hopes of hooking the morning breakfast. Even the logs floating along the river seemed to slow their pace as if celebrating the tranquillity of a new day. We cruised along small tributaries that merged with the mighty Amazon at regular intervals; each one piqued my curiosity. What life lurked there? What new birds were nesting?

Between tributaries, the Amazon banks spanned long and green. Tall canes of cecropia (*Cecropia* sp., family Cecropiaceae) leaned precariously into the river, perhaps in their final days of photosynthesizing before rising waters claimed still more vegetation to join the floating mats of river flotsam. Many trees would soon realize similar fates, because during the rainy season the river rose over 30 feet in some places. As this happened, the fast-growing or early-successional plants that had established along the edges during the year became part of the vegetation drifting in floating mats headed to the Atlantic. Sometimes an older tree also succumbed to the rigors of a windstorm or a logjam that pushed against the silty bank and loosened its root system. Life and death were part of the healthy cycle of nature along the Amazon. Like trees living and dying, the ribereños embraced and accepted the cycles of survival, in stark contrast to our Western attitudes that embrace life but fear death.

On our first morning, we spotted thirty-two species of birds before breakfast. It was hard to conceive that so many colorful bodies co-existed in tiny pockets of this jungle paradise. We motored in a small dingy up a tributary called the Sapote River into a marshland. Ribereños quietly fished for their morning breakfast of piranha, and the smell of cooking fires wafted in the breeze. Do these people have the same notion we do of their day ahead? Do they eat a quick breakfast on busy days? What is their idea of a successful day? (Or were such concepts the product of our more stressful technological world?) We passed tiny thatched huts along the shoreline, where children played while their mothers performed daily chores. What a contrast from our American mornings with rattling newspapers at the breakfast table, televisions blaring, last-minute neglected homework, husbands and/or wives grabbing cell phones and briefcases in a mass exodus from megahomes into gas-guzzling big cars. Some late risers in our American society neglect to eat breakfast at all, much less hunt and cook it over an open fire.

The differences in our two cultures are simply so great that I sometimes wonder if humans are evolving toward two subspecies, one that lives with nature and sustains itself in the forest while a second relies on technology and artificial environments. In this dichotomy, some people have adapted to respond to cell phones and others to toucans.

Those of us in "developed" countries are caught up in a maelstrom of technology, but at what cost in terms of limiting our understanding of nature?

Our boat driver cut the engine, and we floated through the marsh, gazing in wonder. More darting colorful bodies took shape in the morning mist, revealing themselves first by song amid the fog-enshrouded marsh grasses. Velvet-fronted grackle, roadside hawk, pygmy kingfisher, red-capped cardinal, oriole blackbird — all of these birds sound similar to species in the United States, but their tropical counterparts boast more colorful plumage. And for each species of kingfisher in the temperate zone, five or more additional species exist in the tropics. My ecotourists see firsthand that the biodiversity of most plant and animal families is more abundant in tropical than in temperate latitudes. Birds, like plants, are no exception to this rule of increasing diversity toward the equator. (Current knowledge indicates that two groups of organisms follow a converse tendency: lichens and salamanders are less diverse in tropical latitudes.)

More colorful bodies came into view . . . "Wow." "Holy cow." "Good grief." Everyone gasped at a bright orange ball perched on a dead cecropia branch. "An orange-backed troupial," our guide exclaimed joyfully. Now we began to learn birds that have no close relatives in America — wonders of evolution that we could not have begun to invent even if we possessed unlimited artist palates and imaginations. New species appeared in front of our binoculars: wattled jacana, yellow-headed caracara, Pacific hornero, and white-eared jacamar, to name but a few. My five senses rarely received such a workout in America, where they lay dormant between television and computer screens. Only here on the Amazon in the absence of technology could I reinvigorate my senses.

Farther up the Rio Ucayali we turned into a tributary called Rio Pacaya. Looking at our rough map, I wondered how the ribereños ever navigated, with no cell phones, no GPS (global positional system), no topographical maps, not even a simple compass. But they had explored every square inch of the Amazon and knew exactly where to build a hut and where to find the best catfish. The Rio Pacaya flowed through a new national park, Parque Natural Amazonico, that comprised 22,000 acres. Established by the Peruvian government in 1995, this biodiversity preserve was bordered by the rivers Maranon and Ucayali. The villagers who patrolled the park borders on behalf of the government allowed no hunting in the reserve, except for their own local sustainable fishing. What a brilliant system. No one knew the region better than the local people, so prohibiting local hunting would be impossible. But empowering the inhabitants as stewards of this preserve, to maintain their sustainable lifestyle by limiting outside poachers, seemed a perfect way to achieve the conservation of both wildlife and culture in this region.

Along the riverbanks where the village patrollers quietly paddled, the spindly cecropia was the most distinctive tree species. A secondary species or colonizer, cecropia grew rapidly after disturbance. Its large compound leaves were palmate, forming enormous green hands in the canopy with starkly contrasting white undersides. The leaves often died and dried without breaking away from the branch, so the cecropia canopy formed quilted patchworks of green and silvery gray and brown that crackled and rustled above our heads. The retention of dead leaves created a unique food supply in the treetops; some small birds were specialized to glean the tiny insects from these dead leaves, forming an unusual partnership in this competitive jungle world.

Cecropia also reputedly enjoyed a mutualistic relationship with several species of ants that lived in their canopies and fed on the sweet nectaries at the base of the leaves. In return for food and shelter, the ants protected the tree by keeping their leaf surfaces from hungry herbivores that would otherwise devour the foliage. Even with this protection, I have yet to observe a cecropia that was not riddled with holes in this region of the Amazon — the apparent result of many voracious and successful herbivores. Or could it be that perhaps the relationship simply did not operate in this particular region of the tropics? The ant-cecropia mutualism is cited in almost every ecology textbook, having first been observed in Costa Rica. But perhaps the phenomenon is geographically limited to a few forests in Costa Rica? Such anomalies are typical of tropical ecology: just when scientists postulate a new theory, observations in the next valley refute the hypothesis.

Cecropia is also called the sloth tree, because sloths allegedly prefer its leaves for consumption to other choices. However, in my ten years of research and experience in the Amazon, less than one quarter of the sloths I have been privileged to observe resided in cecropia. Again, generalizations in tropical biology are often disproved soon after publication. Obviously the taste buds of a sloth are partial to a range of species, not just cecropia. The jungles are so complex that it seems impossible to generalize about anything without many decades of observation. Yet urgent conservation pressures demand that researchers attempt to unravel the mysteries of this complex ecosystem rapidly before the participants disappear.

During our visit to the Ucayali-Pacaya reserve, we motored up a tributary to Ranger Station No. 3 for lunch and a hike. On the river banks, horned screamers (*Anhima cornuta,* family Anhimidae) shrieked from the tops of great kapok trees (*Ceiba pentandra,* family Bombacaceae). Hundreds of egrets, roosting along the river edges, created commotions of white wings when they flew in front of our boat, in stark contrast to the flocks of cormorants that blackened the sky when they flew from adjacent roosts. Blue and yellow macaws created their cacophony from the tops of cannonball trees. Roadside hawks perched at evenly dispersed 300-foot intervals served as the res-

Anhima cornuta

The horned screamer, which has one of the unique songs in the upper regions of the Amazon (illustration by Barbara Harrison)

ident fishermen. Myriad other colorful bodies delighted us with their sights, sounds, and names: plum-throated cotingas, scarlet-crowned barbet, blue dacnis, golden-headed manakin, black-tailed tityra, yellow-rumped cacique, russet-backed orependula, and silver-beaked tanager. I wondered if such abundance of bird life had greeted visitors to the Florida Everglades before it was altered by human activities. Next, we watched with delight as red howler monkeys navigated with their young from tree to tree. As if on cue, the next canopy featured a monk saki monkey, allowing us to compare its thick, fuzzy fur to the coat of its howler cousins. Sloths, capybara, and iguana lounged in many tree crotches or on banks of the tributary, overloading our senses with sights and sounds beyond our wildest dreams.

Disembarking at the ranger station, we donned mosquito repellent and hiked into the terra firma forest (forest located on firm ground that does not flood). Our group was anxious for a walk. Some went full gallop, joyfully stretching their legs after being boat-bound for two full days in the Amazon. As soon as we got into the shady understory, however, our gait changed. Because of heavy rains the previous evening, mosquitoes were both plentiful and starving. These clever diptera descended on us in the thousands. No one's skin was safe from the female mosquitoes' hunger. (Only females seek a blood meal.) Even through layers of clothing and generous applications of Off! repellent, each aggressive proboscis penetrated our veins.

A hundred feet into the forest, several of our most intrepid explorers sprinted abruptly back to the screened ranger station. Only the bravest, most determined hikers sprayed a second dose of repellent and donned silly-looking but functional mosquito-netting hats to protect their faces. One brazen traveler jeopardized all friendships by declaring that he had no mosquito bites. Someone retorted that he would have to sit alone at lunch — or, better yet, become food for the piranhas. The mosquitoes sucked not only our blood but also our stamina. After a short hike to hug a majestic great kapok tree, we struggled back to the insect refuge to seek shelter behind the screens of the ranger station.

In addition to the discomfort of mosquitoes in the tropics, there was the legendary Vampire fish or candiru (*Vandellia cirrhosa,* family Trichomyoteridae), a tiny catfish. This aggressive creature is renowned for swimming into human urethral openings and lodging there, via its sharp spines. Personal vampire fish stories abound, although I have heard that many have been embellished by vivid imagination. Tall tales about mosquitoes, leeches, and other more noxious creatures run rampant in biologists' memoirs. But after our first-hand encounter with one swarm of mosquitoes, our group had new respect for scientists who worked in tropical jungles, no matter how fanciful their stories.

Another legendary creature in the Amazon is the anaconda (*Eunectes murinus,* family Boidae). During a previous Amazon trip on which I had convinced my mother to accompany me, a villager dove into the water and wrestled a juvenile anaconda ashore. Even my mom was awed by the beauty of the smooth patterned skin. I imag-

Meg and her mother reluctantly help to hold two anacondas (illustration by Barbara Harrison)

ine that our boatful of ecotourists went home after that trip proudly boasting of holding an anaconda. I know my mom will never forget her terrifying feat of touching the 12-foot tail of that large constrictor, still only a juvenile.

Why bother to bring tourists to the Amazon, an experience often overwhelmed by complaints about bugs and snakes, when my time could be spent more productively working in solitude on a personal research question? I am often asked that question by scientific colleagues who are mystified by my unconventional behavior. Remembering the wise advice of Tom Lovejoy, I explain to them that ecotourism in rain forests plays an increasing role in conservation. If local people can profit by leaving their forests intact, and if leaders from temperate regions begin to understand the importance of the tropical rain forest, then perhaps we can reverse some of the current trends toward deforestation.

From many years of experience with tourists in the rain forest, I have learned some of the obvious fallacies that exist about the Amazon. Here is a list of must-know factoids:

1. Tropical rain-forest organisms are not necessarily bigger than their temperate counterparts; most tropical species are tiny and smaller than their temperate relatives (insects, for example). Because they are so small, some of them have never been observed or identified.

2. Tall trees and lush vegetation are not a consequence of rich soils; conversely, the Amazon is renowned for poor soils. Trees and their canopies are lush because the nutrients accumulate in the above-ground biomass of the vegetation. Many investors clear land for agriculture, only to discover that most of the nutrients have been lost by clearing or burning. The remaining soil will not support cash crops for many seasons because it is nutrient poor.

3. Despite their relatively vast expanse around the equator, rain forests may not last indefinitely. With current deforestation rates, many tracts will disappear in our lifetimes. It is heartening, however, to know that half of the remaining forests in Brazil are currently under protection.

4. It is impossible to predict accurately the success of tropical forest regeneration, even with satellite imagery. Given current levels of clearing, it is also impossible to predict whether the remaining fragmented forest tracts will survive over the long haul or eventually die.

5. Scientists have identified only about 1.5 million of the estimated 30 million species (or more) that probably exist. It is predicted that many species are becoming extinct before being discovered.

6. Almost half of the planet's biodiversity is estimated to live in the rain-

forest canopy, yet only a handful of research sites foster research in the treetops, and even fewer scientists are trained to explore this "roof of the world."

Ecotourists always appreciate the opportunity to visit a village and observe the lifestyle of people along the Amazon. Though the natural world is the best lifelong teacher in the Peruvian Amazon, in the villages formal school attendance is mandatory through the elementary grades. A teacher is assigned from the nearest city; depending on the size of the village, perhaps two or three are employed. Teacher salaries average about $250 per month on the government payroll. Most villagers do not need money except for a few important staples: mosquito netting, kerosene, sugar, salt, and school expenses.

In the hierarchy of village life, teachers and shamans are among the most highly respected individuals. Shamans, or jungle doctors, use special plants to waft over patients as part of their noninvasive diagnosis, and they then administer cures from plant concoctions. Amazonian plants create an entire apothecary, or so it seems. One particular species with many medicinal properties is dragon's blood (*Croton lechleri,* family Euphorbiaceae), also called sangre del grado. Growing as a large shrub or medium-sized tree, dragon's blood exudes red latex when the trunk is lacerated. Applied to wounds, this latex both heals the cut and serves as an antiseptic. If vigorously massaged onto a wound, the sticky substance forms a rubbery coating similar to a Band-Aid. The same plant is also used as a purgative, for healing abortions, as a douche in childbirth, and for treating tuberculosis and bone cancer. Every shaman I have encountered cultivates a dragon's blood shrub in his medicinal garden.

Annatto (*Bixa orellana,* family Bixaceae) is another multipurpose plant. This shrub produces red fruit capsules whose pigment makes body paint for ceremonies. Additionally, it is employed to treat dysentery, venereal disease, tonsillitis, rash, conjunctivitis, fever, hepatitis, and dermatitis, and as an insect repellent. Only the shaman determines the dose and specifies the plant parts to make concoctions for different ailments. This botanical heritage has been handed down from shaman to shaman over many generations.

My respect for the shaman grew when I encountered the cat's claw vine (*Uncaria* sp., family Rubiaceae). Cat's claw, or una de gato, is a common tropical vine covered with sharp recurved spines about an inch long. Like many other tropical plants, the medicinal value of cat's claw is not limited to one malady. Cancer, internal wounds, stomach ulcers, urinary infections, prostate and kidney problems, tumors, ulcers, and even the prevention of AIDS are associated with different parts of the vine. Village markets abound with either liquid doses or small bundles of twigs from this miracle plant. Cat's claw is marketed internationally to cure rheumatism and arthritis.

As important as curing physical ailments is the shaman's role in treating mental and spiritual health. In Samoa, the kava shrub provides a hallucinogenic drink used in ceremonies and for seeking spiritual advice. In the Amazon, the soul vine (*Banisteriopsis caapi*, family Malpighiaceae) or ayahuasca is its counterpart. A tea extracted from the bark of the vine has hallucinogenic properties. (The same plant also cures digestive problems and other ailments.) Under the influence of ayahuasca, the shaman communicates with the spirit world and is able to diagnose a patient. The Harvard ethnobotanist Richard Schultes spent a large part of his career sampling and studying the use of *Banisteriopsis* sp. throughout South America. He was probably one of the few tenured professors who publicly experimented with hallucinogenic plants as part of his scientific career.

To round out my list of favorite medicinal plants in Peru, I would add *Ficus* sp., otherwise known as the fig. Used for food and timber, and as an attractant for monkeys and birds, the medicinal fig (*Ficus in-*

sipida, family Moraceae) or oje is nicknamed the children's tree, which helps my botany students appreciate its life-saving qualities. Whenever we visit a remote village, oje occupies a central location accessible to the entire village. This tree produces milky latex, like all members of the Moraceae family, and its juice is a purgative. Intestinal parasites are a major cause of mortality among children in tropical countries, so the monthly dose of oje juice is a lifesaver for village families. Again, the shaman carefully prescribes the dosage, since excessive amounts harm one's intestines.

These few species constitute a small sample of a shaman's knowledge, which in turn represents the collective wisdom of many generations and perhaps thousands of years of botanical experience in the Amazon. This cultural knowledge of the tropical rain plants requires careful conservation. Research support to identify the chemical components of tropical plants may reverse the current tendency of the younger Peruvian generation to seek artificial drugs instead of retaining knowledge of their botanical traditions.

Of special interest to the women in our group was the fact that shamans are usually not required for childbirth. In the village of Yaralpa, we greeted a young man with a toddler on his lap. He sat peacefully enjoying the view of his papaya trees. When asked where his wife was, he smiled and replied that she had had a new son the night before and the two of them were sleeping. Amazing events come and go every day. No giant blue balloons hung from his mailbox; no bottles of champagne popped; no relatives celebrated in his living room; no bassinette and layette of blue clothes were purchased for the new arrival. One of our travelers hastily found a Spanish children's book in her backpack and left it with the proud father as a gift for his newborn son. The dogs barked. The chickens gobbled. It was just another quiet day for a river family that was now 33 percent larger.

We moved on to another village called Vista Allegre. Here we were privileged to hold a baby sloth. Its mother had died and the young sloth was rescued in the forest. The sloth hugged our necks in a grip similar to its hold on the branch of cecropia. Like a young movie star, this sloth was no doubt the most-photographed individual of our entire Amazon voyage. Other pets for village children include boas, parrots, and even capybaras — all members of the natural environment of the Amazon.

Back on the boat, our eyes scanned the cecropia trees, hoping to see a sloth in its natural element. We nearly lost our balance as the boat veered sharply to avoid a large, mostly submerged log that threatened to lacerate our hull. The captain finessed his path brilliantly, negotiating all the bounty contributed from hundreds of miles upriver. The heavy tropical rains had caused both soil and vegetation to slip into the river, becoming collectibles for fencing or hut-building many miles downriver. Here was recycling at its best, with nature and people reusing the vegetation that was rescued from the currents. Occasionally we heard a telltale thud as one of the heavy logs collided with our underpinnings. No wonder the Ucayali River translated into "canoe-breaker."

A river taxi churned upriver, motoring several hundred villagers back home again. After taking their bananas, rice, and perhaps some crafts to sell in the market, they returned with kerosene, sugar, possibly some kitchenware and a few new clothes for the children. In many cases, ribereños sold the river rafts they had used to drift downriver to pay the fare to return home on the ferry. That was expensive (almost six dollars) but certainly faster and more reliable than trying to paddle upstream in a homemade raft.

For each villager who traded in town, a tug-of-war developed between returning home to the traditional ways of the village and seeking a fortune in the fast life of a modern world. Will the modern backdrop of Iquitos tempt yet another young person to relocate there and seek his fortune? Iquitos has grown from one hundred fifty thousand to over one million in just a decade, as the ambition for urban life captivates many villagers. In most cases, their quality of life declines in the city; but the opportunity captures their imaginations and the one-way migration continues.

When we reluctantly departed the Amazon, my mind was full of tropical memories generated over a week of sensory reawakening. I wondered if the horned screamers were calling to their mates back into the great kapok canopy. I wondered if the new father at the last village had caught extra fish this morning for his expanded family. My questions, however, did not weigh anxiously on my mind as do the daily issues in our technological world. Instead, my thoughts were reflective and as fleeting as the flight of green kingfishers seeking fresh fish for breakfast. I felt comforted to use all five senses, and use them perhaps as nature intended.

BEETLES BY NIGHT

By James, aged 14

July 2001. We stood at the head of the trail, the last of the oil lanterns scattered about the complex just in back of us. Behind us stood the lodge, filled with humanity and light; in front of us was uncertainty, a forest filled with darkness and strange creatures. Our imaginations sparked with anticipation of a new species. We had work to do. We stared into the void and then, setting our resolve, we snapped on our flashlights and trekked into the woods in search of discovery.

All around us, the noise of the nighttime jungle echoed out of the darkness, but we never saw the players in this eerie symphony except for an occasional glimpse of some outlandish, metallic, crazy-colored arthropod body. To the right and left, our headlamps illumined a darkened cathedral filled with massive, woody columns that seemed to extend forever upward into the darkness. My mind drifted off, lulled by the visual monotony of darkness, until I nearly lost my footing as the world suddenly appeared upended with tiny, glimmering pinpoints of starlight at my feet. I soon discovered that these "stars" were actually tiny bioluminescent fungi living off the dead plant matter underfoot.

A misplaced wooden staircase reared itself from the forest floor and climbed up into the dark ceiling with the gargantuan trees. The ground below us quickly disappeared into the darkness. As we climbed the final flight of stairs, we burst upon a perfect, unobstructed dome of sky sparkled with stars, unrivaled in beauty by any modern contrivances. Our wonder lasted only momentarily, however. We were detectives in the night, on bug assignment.

I found myself stationed on a platform connected to a complex network of bridges 100 feet above the ground. Up here in the highest level of the treetops, bromeliads thrive. Physically supported by the thick branches, the plants find nutrients in the dust and sediment brought by rain and wind. The leaves of bromeliads form a watertight rosette that holds tiny reservoirs and supports microecosystems. My job was to search these bromeliads for a recently discovered species of beetle that is nocturnally active. Although scientists had classified the beetle, no information existed on its behavior and no specimens were alive in captivity. Unfortunately for me, though, there are more than three hundred thousand species of beetles, and this particular species is brown, nondescript, and about the size of the nail on my pinky finger. Sightings of the beetle, though, had proved that it did inhabit this area, so I was on a mission to find it.

Standing on my platform, I could reach about twenty-five bromeliad plants and rifled through them all in entomological anticipation. My first discovery was that the tanks of bromeliads hold myriad creatures, including thirty-something species of cockroaches and even an occasional tarantula. Working on through the night, I catalogued each plant and marked it on my list, but saw no sign of the nondescript beetle.

Then, just as dawn was peeking over the horizon, a small brown spot on a final bromeliad caught my attention. Feeling a rush of elation, I hurried to catch it. In my haste, I upset the plant and, as its hard shell glinted in the new morning light, the beetle tumbled off its leaf and fell into the inky blackness below. For a moment I felt sadness and frustration. Perhaps it was a small consolation to know that my beetle had such strong survival instincts. As I descended into the wakening forest below, I realized that science is not accomplished in one night, and that many nights of collecting lay ahead. But now I knew where to look.

A TREETOP WALK

By Eddie, aged 16

July 2001. I walked quickly down the dark trail anxious to see what the Peruvian jungle had to offer. I nearly slipped off the narrow log bridge, as my thoughts drifted to blue morpho butterflies and rare hoatzin birds. The air was moist and the ground saturated after a newly fallen rain. Leaf-cutter ants paraded up and down the trunk of a nearby tree. Finally, I reached my destination, Platform No. 1. In all, fourteen treetop platforms connected the trees with a series of swaying walkways. As I climbed into the canopy, my surroundings brightened. On the ground, foliage blocks most of the light, but up high, objects are illuminated and alive. The rain forest's complexity always amazes me. I could have stood there for years without seeing every detail of those few trees.

Despite the urge to linger for a while, I kept moving so that I could enjoy the walkway alone before a tour group arrived. Solitary observation always generates better results than observation with a noisy group. I was hoping to add a few more tropical birds to my life-list, but I had not seen any ornithological activity that day. Rain-forest birds are shy during the lull of the late afternoon. Suddenly a peculiar brown shape glided over my head and landed on a mossy branch. The bird itself was not so extraordinary — its average size and drab coat were not uncommon — but it had the longest bill I had ever seen! The narrow bill curved so sharply that the bird could have easily scratched its belly. I fumbled for my field guide as the curious animal crept along the limb. Unfortunately, the bird noticed my commotion. When I looked up, the creature had taken flight and left me once again alone. I thought hard to remember exactly what it looked like for identification. Finally, I settled on red-billed scythebill, a new discovery for my life-list.

After that sighting, I noticed more activity. Parakeets of all colors chattered in another tree. Endless numbers of insects darted past my face. The clicking of castanet frogs resonated through the understory beneath me. Hummingbirds sipped nectar while suspended by their ghostlike wings. I saw a variety of exotic species that morning, but for some reason the scythebill amazed me most. I could not stop thinking about its bill. What purpose did that unique apparatus serve? The bridge swayed in the slight breeze. I was so lucky to be in the canopy at that moment. If I had not been right there at that exact instant, would I have seen the bird? How many other birds was I missing right then? Those questions would not be answered. Soon I heard shouts from a tour group on the trail below. The abundance of life dissipated as the crowd drew nearer. The noisy group would certainly not experience the excitement I had during silence. I felt sad for people who don't appreciate the wonders of nature. They are missing one of life's best treasures.

A RARE BEETLE FEEDING ON BROMELIADS IN THE CANOPY

By Eddie and James, aged 17 and 15

Herbivory, defined as insects eating plants, is a fascinating topic that often demonstrates the complexity of the delicate web of interaction between plants and animals in an ecosystem. The perfect example of this complexity was our family's observations of a beetle herbivore in Peru. A bromeliad ecologist named David Benzing claimed that bromeliads, with their tough leaves, experienced little or no herbivory. What would want to eat such a dry and tough old leaf? But the scientist who made that claim had perhaps never climbed into the canopy and looked closely. Thus we were delighted to discover a beetle that did in fact make its dinner from the foliage of *Aechmea nallyi* (family Bromeliaceae), a rare bromeliad growing in patches of the canopy near our field camp along the Amazon River. We were stationed at the Amazon Center for Education and Environmental Research (ACEER), a rustic research and ecotourist camp with a canopy walkway. We used the entire 1,200-foot span to observe this epiphyte and its herbivory.

For almost five years we returned periodically to the Amazon and worked on different projects at ACEER (now called ACTS, Amazon Center for Tropical Studies). My mom was very happy to have such a long, extensive canopy walkway for her research. It saved a lot of time and sweat, and she did not need her conventional tools of ropes and climbing hardware. She led education workshops, conducted the Jason Project, raised funds to bring a group of disadvantaged kids to experience the Amazon, and also brought donors from the botanical garden to this exquisite site, where nature is so complex that we get sensory overload just standing still.

During these years, we measured the herbivory of our special bromeliad species, *Aechmea nallyi,* because one herbivore appeared specialized to eat it. On each visit, we found the same characteristic racing stripes along its tough green leaves, where the unknown insect had chomped between the leaf veins, feasting on the softer intervein tissue. The amount eaten by the mysterious chewer was fairly consistent: 10.4 percent in year 1, 9.0 percent in year 2, 10.4 percent in year 3, 8.7 percent in year 4, and 11.8 percent in year 5. (Percentages represent the amount of leaf surface eaten, measured by tracing the leaves and calculating with graph paper.)

As is so often the case, the unexpected elements of field biology surprised us. We were not prepared for the extreme circumstances surrounding this insect-plant interaction. After 560 hours of bromeliad observation, only eight beetles were sighted. The herbivores were observed feeding at night. It was mind-boggling to think that the organism responsible for this important transfer of

Eddie and James use headlamps at night to search for nutmeg canopy beetles in the canopy of Amazonian Peru (illustration by Barbara Harrison)

nutrients was in fact so rare. It took human beings approximately 70 hours of observations to locate one beetle, not a very efficient process. Yet this relatively rare beetle had chewed at least one brown stripe through almost every leaf of each bromeliad rosette. This cryptic chewer sure got around, yet was too well camouflaged for our visual senses to detect it easily. In field biology, rare species are often overlooked in research simply because the time and effort to find them are enormous. This probably creates a gap in our true understanding of ecosystems. We hope our family sojourns in the canopies of Peru have contributed one tiny data point of information about the likelihood of finding rare species in forests.

10 Down from the Treetops: Life in the Padded Chair

One of the most meaningful insights that I have acquired along my life's journey is that it takes the same amount of energy to complain as it does to exclaim — but the results are incredibly different. Learning to exclaim instead of complain has been my most valuable lesson.

— Margaret D. Lowman, *Life in the Treetops*

In midcareer, after careful contemplation, I literally climbed down from the treetops to occupy the padded chair as executive director of a botanical garden. This decision stemmed from my passion to serve plant conservation. My first three years as director were blessed with a great team who grew the gardens and expanded botanical programs with unprecedented community support. However, an incident occurred while I was away on vacation in June 2002 that ultimately turned the gardens upside down. Surely, I tell myself in amazement, small botanical institutions do not generate tales of dubious and lustful behavior when their mission is all about plants. Or do they?

This is a true story of smuggling, intrigue, threats, federal investigation, and international treaties. More aptly stated, this is the saga of one tiny flower and some enthusiastic but misguided efforts to identify it. Underlying the drama, but an issue that never surfaced, is the aborted effort to conserve it — which, alas, should have been the orchid world's major concern from the outset. Sometimes emotions cause the judgments of well-intended people to become distorted. One pink flower catapulted our eleven-acre botanical institution into a federal grand jury debacle and all kinds of questionable behavior: clandestine meetings, defamatory accusations, theft, hiring and firing, board resignations, staff terminations, and false statements. Albert Einstein once said, "Great spirits have always encountered violent opposition from mediocre minds." I came to understand what he meant.

NOVEMBER 1999–JULY 2003. Although the board chair did not know it, I was in a bubble bath at the Beverly Hills Wiltshire Hotel when he called to offer me the directorship of the Marie Selby Botanical Gardens. I had just flown in from Australia, after groveling for two weeks in the tropical mud of Queensland to survey seedlings as part of a long-term project on rain-forest diversity. Ironically, some agents in Hollywood had suggested meeting on my way home to consider making a movie from my book, *Life in the Treetops.* Intrigued by the notion of giving rain-forest conservation such prominent media attention, and cheered on by the staff at Yale University Press, I found myself stepping from a leech-infested rain forest into the elegance of Beverly Hills. Upon arrival at this palatial hotel, I quickly bought shoes and an outfit more appropriate than my dirty khakis and muddy boots. The bubble bath was a much-needed scrubdown of ticks, leeches, leftover bloodstains, thorns, seeds, and ground-in dirt from the Australian rain forest.

Still jet-lagged, I returned home from my brief stay in Hollywood to take over the directorship of Selby Gardens. Back in 1992 I had made a five-year plan to work as a scientist in a botanical garden, with the intent of later returning to a university setting to share with students my experiences of tropical exploration. I remain convinced that education is the most important cog in the wheel of conservation. The responsibility of scientists to educate students, leaders, and citizens about ecosystems and how they work is a critical priority in today's world of dwindling resources. By 1998, when my five-year plan expired, I had started making inquiries. The network in science and research was vast and intertwined, so it was not difficult to seek new employment. As I contemplated a return to academia, some Gardens board members approached me with a new idea. The last executive director had experienced personality conflicts with donors; his budget had been in the red; deferred maintenance was at a critical stage; and perhaps most important but difficult to measure, the Gardens' message to the larger community had not been nurtured. The board sought a visionary leader who could speak passionately to local as well as international audiences — a cheerleader for plants!

I debated long and hard about a shift from swinging in the vines, literally, to occupying the padded chair of an administration office. I was candid with the search committee about my lack of a business degree, but they appreciated my unusual combination of a botany degree plus entrepreneurial experience. Having started a successful ecotourist operation in Australia and helped manage a large sheep and cattle operation, I had faced business challenges (such as weather, budgets, and marketing) akin to those of a botanical garden. Their feeling was that most day-to-day operations could be handled by an associate director, but it was difficult to find a CEO with scientific credibility who could articulate a botanical mission to donors. I did some homework of my own and found that garden directors came in all shapes and sizes, but the most successful ones tended to have botanical training and a passion for their mission. The search committee did its homework, too — advertising nationally, checking references, and interviewing candidates from across the country. I was offered the job, and the board of trustees charged me with revitalizing Selby Gardens and moving it into national and international prominence.

My first challenge as director was to raise the institution's level of professionalism and reactivate languishing programs. I had the benefit of a wonderful support group through a network called Leadership Florida. I was the only international botanist in this group of bankers, executives, real estate developers, and entrepreneurs. We shared the common bond of seeking excellence in our careers to improve the quality of life in our state. Various leaders advised me about marketing, fund-raising, facilities, and accounting. One by one, like building a wall one stone at a time, I hired a fine team with experience, pride, and potential. This group of enthusiastic, dedicated workers, collectively calling themselves "the dream team," undertook to make the Gardens' dreams come true.

In any business, newly hired professional staff and their inevitable aura of change may threaten older staff members who are uncomfortable with innovative practices and ambitious goals. Selby Gardens was no exception. I hired the first-ever marketing director to professionally promote the message of the Gardens. The research staff grumbled and was reluctant to cooperate. To them it may have felt like prostitution to "sell" a botanical message to the public in a way they had never experienced. I hired an enthusiastic professional fund-raiser with a successful track record who prioritized making the gardens all-inclusive, with events and memberships to suit all walks of life. Some of the horticulture staff protested that increased visitorship might trample the grounds. Growth had some trade-offs. I hired the first-ever facilities director, because physical improvements were imperative to enhance the visitor experience.

We all worked hard. I almost lost track of my children for several years — missing Eddie's crew regattas, skipping parent-teacher association meetings at school, giving up hobbies, devoting daytime hours to staff and operations, and dedicating weekends plus evenings to "friend-raising" (a precursor to fund-raising, because it is important to make friends first) and donor cultivation. In the eyes of my family, the Gardens owned me; but I was driven to carry out the board's direction and the vision it had mandated. I attended the Tuck School of Executive Management at Dartmouth College to bone up on administrative issues, even though the board had not hired me for hands-on administration but rather as a visionary spokesperson for the mission.

Through the good old-fashioned hard work of dedicated people, the Gardens flowered. We completed property acquisition for a master site plan, raised annual donations over 100 percent and membership by 46 percent, tripled the number of fund-raising events, added new gardens, completed the groundwork for a capital campaign, and penetrated new markets with our message. I relished the new knowledge that my experience in the padded chair taught me, ranging from the finesse of hiring and firing, to fund-raising, to wearing many hats to represent the Gardens throughout the community. One week I spoke at Rotary, the next week at the Ivy League Club, and the following week at a high school convocation. Adopting the wall-building theory, we created solid relationships one by one so that our community and its philanthropists would embrace the importance of our botanical mission.

September 11, 2001, was as dreadful at the Gardens as it was all over our country. I released most of the staff early to be with their families. For many days the tenor of operations was somber. It was a testament to our leadership team, however, that admissions actually increased after that tragic event, whereas most regional tourism dropped precipitously. We created special activities such as interdenominational services under the trees, free days for dads or moms with children, outdoor music concerts, horticultural therapy classes, and special community lectures to remind our public of the natural world and its healing powers.

Most of America was unaware that three days after 9/11 Southwest Florida was hit by tropical storm Gabrielle, which brought much of the Gardens' canopy to the ground. We spontaneously hosted a public work bee to clean up the debris, which brought the community together during those difficult days. Although we did not welcome that storm, the act of gardening provided important therapy for many.

The volatility of the stock market after September 11 was another cause of sleepless nights. In the long run, however, it catalyzed our board to examine the investment portfolio carefully for the first time in many years. The members discovered that some of the assets were being managed poorly. After many hours of intense meetings the board revised the old policies, again a positive step forward after many years without careful scrutiny of investments.

The Gardens flourished professionally, scientifically, financially, horticulturally, and aesthetically. It became a place of recognition and pride locally, nationally, and internationally. In 2002 it was designated one of the top ten botanical gardens in the United States, despite its relatively small size. The development director and I cultivated generous new donors, and identified three separate million-dollar donors for leadership gifts, unheard of in previous years. We had excellent grant success for the first time in the Gardens' history: a half million dollars to create perimeter delineation (modern term for fence!) to protect our collections and also to announce our presence to visitors; another large grant to renovate our historical mansion as a centerpiece for events; a half million dollars in federal funds for canopy research; smaller grants for specific education projects; local grants for music performances in the Gardens; and a museum grant to assess our collections. Community members were generous with new gifts: a major conservation exhibit; a rain-forest poison-dart frog display for kids; a gesneriad research collection; donations to expand our global internship program; a pledge for a new sprinkler system; gifts to endow orchid displays; and a major donation to upgrade our wedding pavilion, thereby creating a long-term revenue stream. Such increases in revenue would in turn support expanded research, education, and horticulture.

Despite September 11, the Gardens underwent unprecedented growth. Many of my executive colleagues elsewhere were envious. I attributed our successes to an ability to prioritize friend-raising as much as fund-raising, thereby creating a sense of confidence and trust with donors, members, and the world at large. With this philosophy, Selby was laying the groundwork to do far more than just display pretty plants; it aimed to have a lasting legacy in the world of botany.

In the summer of 2002, the board honored me with a diamond necklace for extraordinary achievement during my three years of leadership and ten years of service. I was promised a significant raise in six months' time. But along with this positive team effort, two significant events occurred. The composition of the board changed under new leadership; and a new orchid was described by our orchid staff.

The incoming board chair was a relative newcomer to our community, with no cadre of colleagues to tap for fund-raising. A cloud of controversy had surrounded his first appearance at the Gardens, including accusations in writing by the previous director that he had harassed female staff and had agitated to be executive director. My staff was mystified at his sudden rise to power, but the board welcomed his credentials as a retired commercial orchid buyer and seller. He had the time and inclination to take charge, whereas most other board members were primarily committed to jobs or families. He was as passionate about cultivating beautiful orchids in a pot as I was about saving them in their habitat. As chief executive officer, I too praised his commercial experience with orchids.

I soon found I was dancing to a different drummer. My development director grew anxious when our new chair's mannerisms irritated some larger donors. Over time, a dangerously large number of board members resigned in protest of his leadership style, citing his overt micromanagement of the day-to-day operations as inappropriate. Concerns were voiced from within the staff as well as the community, even from around the world, that Selby's new board leadership was "about orchids and nothing else."

Before long, the performance of some staff members started to wane and divisive alliances formed. A member of my senior staff began covertly manipulating facts among staff and board, taking actions that were revealed to me only in the aftermath of what would follow. The board chair suspiciously prohibited my terminating her when I determined it was necessary. Suddenly the padded chair was becoming rife with politics, power struggles, and philosophical clashes that were emanating from the very top — the board itself.

Under a cloud of negativity generated by a small minority, the institution witnessed a drift into turf wars, personal agendas, and divisiveness that I was informed I had no authority to quash. I observed that when truth fails to be paramount and when prejudice overrules fair hiring, the end result is catastrophe. More board members quit, and I found myself standing up, with eroded authority, for my own values and ethics.

The last in a series of portentous power plays revolved around an orchid. Now, orchids are beautiful; I like them, but I do not lust after them as some do. I value them as a major component of a forest eco-system. Orchidophiles, orchidoholics, orchidologists, orchid mani-acs — these people breathe, smell, think, grow, eat, work, live, and perhaps die for orchids. How can such a relatively innocuous blossom imbue human behavior with such emotion?

I always knew that my scientific career took me into real jungles, where I was tangled in vines, threatened by dehydration and disease, and assailed by leeches, brown snakes, and spines. Having sat in the padded chair of a nonprofit institution, today I recognize another jun-gle. I had never before imagined that the story of a botanical garden, espousing a mission of plant conservation, could read as if it were the drama of a pulp crime novel.

Like cocaine or potato chips, orchids are addictive to those whom they seduce. Susan Orlean's 1998 book *The Orchid Thief* abounds with adjectives such as obsessive, passionate, delirious, smitten, envious, seduced, and lusting. For orchid lovers, the passion of collecting can drive hobbyists to extremes. As Orlean aptly describes it, "Nothing in science can account for the way people feel about orchids. Orchids seem to drive people crazy. Those who love them love them madly. Orchids arouse passion more than romance." She estimated the value of the orchid-collecting industry at $10 billion per year, so perhaps this is not surprising. According to many, her book actually contributed to the damage wrought by illegal collectors in south Florida. For it exposed the location of remaining rare orchids and romanticized several unsavory collectors, indirectly justifying their unethical behavior. Throughout botanical history, no other group of plants has generated such a subculture of characters involved in their collection, identification, and obsessive ownership.

Selby Gardens' notorious orchid episode actually occurred while I was away. In early May 2002, sixteen-year-old Eddie came home bursting with the news that his crew team was heading to the national championship regatta in Cincinnati, Ohio. His boat had won all its races to date, and the crew of eight rowers was now preparing for the biggest race of all. It was a proud moment for him. In Eddie's four years of rowing, I had yet to attend even one regatta, owing in large measure to the demands of my job. I felt guilty and quickly resolved to attend his final, all-important event. I put a big black line through my calendar for the first week of June and worked even harder throughout May to clear those five days to honor our family sports hero.

Eddie and I spent an expectant Wednesday in June packing and preparing for the races: new socks, pressed shirts for the dinners, bottles of water, snacks, and all the rest. We left for Cincinnati early Thursday morning. Upon arrival we ate at a chain steakhouse, and I promptly returned to my room and threw up. It is ironic that after eating unidentified foods in remote jungles of the world with few stomach mishaps, I succumbed to food poisoning at a suburban eatery in the Midwest. I spent a long and traumatic night hugging "Percy the porcelain" (as we called toilet bowls in the Australian outback).

A quick glance at my emails the next day revealed a glowing message from the Gardens' board chair, congratulating the orchid staff on a recently arrived magnificent specimen that appeared to be a new species. It sounded like the Rosetta stone of orchids. No stranger to the trade as a retired professional orchid buyer and seller, he kept close tabs on his orchid boys (as the nonorchid staff called them). This special interest fostered skeptical anxiety among some of the other staff members.

As the chair's email conveyed, this new specimen was sufficiently notable to provide a long-sought spotlight for orchids at Selby. I was relieved, hoping it would ease a sense of growing jealousy and tension directed toward the successes of canopy ecology, rain-forest poison-dart frogs, canopy walkways, music events, and other Garden activities. After reading the note, I hoped this discovery would prompt new initiatives by the orchid staff for increased funding, productive science, and public support.

Another (short) email from the orchid identification director mentioned that the research staff was going to meet that Friday to determine a plan of action for their windfall. Knowing that the board chair would be maintaining close oversight on this find, and that our associate director was overseeing the day-to-day operations, I felt elation, not anxiety. I spoke briefly to the orchid director from my cell phone and was told that the orchid was spectacular. He also said the collector's permits were in order. The only hiccup mentioned was a potential threat from a rival orchid taxonomist who lived four blocks from the Gardens. This disgruntled former employee had, over the past fifteen years, written scandalous letters to the staff at Selby as well as at other botanical institutions. The research staff seemed concerned he might exhibit violent behavior if Selby Gardens identified and published a description of this fabulous new plant before he did.

Apparently, the anxiety of the orchid staff had been short-lived: both the board chair and the orchid identification director eagerly supported Selby's opportunity. By the time they communicated with me, Selby's publication announcing the new species had already been written. Two orchid staff members had stayed up all Wednesday night to write, illustrate, and complete a scientific description. I was way out of this loop, but congratulated them and returned to my bathroom vigil as food poisoning continued to take its toll.

Over the weekend, I had a lakeside seat for the regatta, as I watched my son's boat come in ninth in the nation. Simultaneously, the editor of the Gardens' journal, *Selbyana,* was making a Herculean effort to distribute a special edition (in the newspaper business it would be an EXTRA!) announcing the name of this orchid. In taxonomy, the grand prize is not gold or money but the satisfaction (no doubt with some ego attached) of naming a plant that will exist in perpetuity. Ironically, ecologists tend to care far less about names or naming opportunities. In contrast, taxonomists spend lifetimes naming new species and sometimes even renaming them if the classification is initially flawed. Taxonomists themselves are sometimes classified, either as lumpers (taxonomists who wish to group many similar items together in one category) or splitters (those who emphasize the differences more than the similarities). A name is but the beginning for an ecologist. Current conservation policies have shifted over time from the starting point over a century ago of a checklist of names to the current practice of understanding ecosystem dynamics in order to best conserve species. Orchids in pots remain a popular pastime, but the activity alone does not satisfy the needs of twenty-first-century global conservation.

One more email came during the weekend. My incoming director of research confirmed that the orchid boys had all the required permits but repeated their fear of repercussions from the antagonist down the street. He also mentioned that the herbarium curator had agreed to return the plant immediately to Peru, as a gesture of good will to the orchid's country of origin. (Frequently the first described specimen, technically called the type specimen, is retained by the institution that names it.) Thus, I would never see this orchid, but since I was not an aficionado I never gave it a second thought. According to the research staff, by the time I returned on Monday the publication was in press and the orchid was en route to Peru.

Many orchids, including the entire genus *Phragmipedium* (to which this new species belonged), are protected under a 1973 international treaty called CITES (the Convention on International Trade in Endangered Species of Wild Fauna and Flora). CITES is enforced in the United States by a federal criminal law, the Endangered Species Act, violation of which can lead to prison terms of up to one year per violation and fines of up to $50,000 per violation. It is a violation to carry a *Phragmipedium* from Peru to the United States without a CITES permit; likewise, it would be a violation for Selby Gardens to ship a *Phragmipedium* to Peru unless the sender and the recipient organization were CITES-approved repositories of protected plants. Selby Gardens was such a repository. Its research staff was responsible for assuring that the Gardens exchanged CITES-protected plants only between institutions (or collectors representing institutions) that held appropriate CITES permits. The herbarium curator and the orchid staff were officially charged with keeping careful track of these exchanges.

On Monday the orchid identification director was jubilant, reporting that this identification would put Selby on the proverbial orchid map. The board chair was beaming. The marketing director orchestrated a media blitz on this scientific find, giving credit to the Gardens' orchid staff and journal editor for naming and publishing this extraordinary plant in record time. The world of orchids seemed thrilled with the new discovery. Yet, as I look back, the orchid staff was surprisingly vague about who actually had seen the orchid. Later, none of them could even agree on whether or not the type specimen had been exhibited at their Friday research meeting, although this famous plant sat in a drying oven in the very room where the meeting was held.

The recently appointed director of research, already on staff, was an ecologist like me. As the nightmare unfolded, he and I would later mull over his staff's allegedly weak sense of recollection. We were especially amazed that our orchid-loving board chair, who had been present that fateful week, never provided his own account of this fabulous specimen. If an archaeologist had the Rosetta stone brought to the doorstep, presumably that moment would be locked in his or her memory forever.

The orchid came from a hillside near a truck stop in Moyobamba, north central Peru, a jungle province halfway between the Amazon rain forest and the frozen peaks of the Andes. As I came to discover months later, this "*Phrag*" was the worst-kept secret in the American orchid world. Although it would be a crime for anyone to pluck a specimen of the unnamed *Phrag* in Moyobamba and bring it to the United States without a CITES permit, rumors were rampant about earlier sightings of it in Florida. Some of the Selby orchid staff later mentioned that this orchid species had been present at a recent orchid show they attended in Miami, but even though these illegal plants were the talk of the show, none of the staff could remember actually laying eyes on it.

The orchid collector who brought the *Phrag* to Selby, Michael Kovach, returned home to Virginia the same day. The research staff completed its professional identification in approximately twenty-four hours, naming the species *Phragmipedium kovachii* in his honor. The ability to quickly describe a new species seemed to me almost as important as the new plant discovery. One of the huge impediments to conservation is the relatively slow speed of species identification and inventory. In some habitats, species are disappearing faster than scientists can classify them. New methods of rapid assessment are desperately needed, and our journal editor received praise for his speedy review and publishing process. The apparent dedication of the research staff was timely, since salary reviews were only a month away. The orchid identification director reminded me at our brief Monday meeting that in his opinion the processing of this major new orchid warranted a big raise (for him).

Press releases came and went. I devoted my time to the upcoming fiscal year budget, which would be presented to the board in two weeks' time, and to time-consuming negotiations with our largest donor about his gift for renovations to our wedding pavilion facilities. Soon August was upon us and my sons returned to school. Sitting in my office writing thank-you notes to donors late in the month, I was surprised by an unannounced visit from a special agent of the U.S. Fish and Wildlife Service, claiming to seek an illegal orchid housed at Selby Gardens. I was as cooperative as possible, and stated that to my knowledge there were no illegal orchids at Selby. Moreover, as I had been informed, I told him that the staff had immediately returned the orchid in question to Peru. He said he thought otherwise, but thanked me for my information.

He walked to the research building to speak with the staff members who had been present when the orchid arrived at the Gardens. The research department was fondly referred to as "the Far Side" because it was housed a block away from the Gardens' main campus. That location was in part why my recent selection of research director had been critical. The new director had to be a leader who was excellent in communication as well as in science and organization, because he was essentially supervising a staff housed off-site.

A week later, the U.S. Fish and Wildlife Service made another visit. This time the agents brought a subpoena from a federal grand jury for documents and samples relating to *Phragmipedium kovachii*. I was shocked, but eager to comply and resolve their questions. I knew of nothing to hide. Musing over this second surprise visit, I became suspicious about the circumstances of the orchid's arrival at Selby during that fateful week in June when I was away. I determined to compile a specific chronology of the events surrounding the orchid's arrival and related staff activities during my absence.

I emailed all the research staff involved with the orchid (plus a few orchid lovers who had reportedly visited Selby's research department on that exact day) and asked each one to write a detailed report of what had transpired. At about four the next morning (not unusual timing, since I lived and breathed the Gardens' business throughout a twenty-four-hour day) I remembered that a part-time orchid contractor for the Gardens not only had been present that week but had even coauthored the published orchid description. I stumbled out of bed to my home computer and copied the same request to him at his home in Vermont.

Seven versions of the orchid event were submitted to me: those of the bromeliad curator, four orchid staff, one herbarium manager, and the director of research — not one of them altogether consistent with the others. My suspicions were now fully aroused. Even the board chair remained vague in his recall of events surrounding this stupendous arrival at the Gardens. The only issue that the staff seemed to agree on was that they considered this the most exciting orchid discovery in over a century. Some claimed this large, showy flower could be worth millions of dollars in the world of horticulture.

To summarize a long and convoluted saga, it took the combined efforts of the director of research, a highly paid law firm, the board chair, and me more than six months to piece together a quasi-reliable account of this ultimately (in)famous orchid and its presence at Selby Gardens. The Gardens hired an expert and expensive legal counsel, an unpopular decision recommended by me but formally approved by the board; hence the legal counsel was accountable to the chair, not to me.

I was assigned the legwork of compiling emails and trying to piece together the staff accounts. Complying with the strategy determined by the legal counsel, I vigorously defended the Gardens throughout an ensuing federal investigation. Months later I discovered that my loyal actions, hard work, and position as CEO of the Gardens had placed me directly in the line of fire from the perspective of a federal prosecutor, along with the institution and the orchid identification director. I found myself the third subject of the investigation, while culpable members of the research staff were granted immunity for their testimony. My colleagues at other larger gardens gasped in dread, realizing that any of them could have a similar situation arise without their knowledge.

As conflicting reports from the staff emerged, egos and strategies invariably clouded the facts. The board chair, perhaps anxious to vindicate the orchid boys, took complete control of the legal case and even held board meetings without my knowledge. At one point, he falsely accused me of lying about the facts, which infuriated me, since I had no firsthand knowledge of the orchid but was relying solely on the reports of those present while I had been away. Several more board members resigned over his handling of the issue. He never seemed to question the inconsistencies of the orchid staff reports about that fateful week. I wondered whether he knew something that I did not.

After countless hours of digging through emails and asking many questions, I found that some critical facts had been undisclosed, even concealed, until unearthed months later. Despite these discrepancies, the legal counsel and board chair continued to advocate not terminating any staff responsible for the oversights, to avoid undermining the Gardens' designated defense strategy. To me, the research staff's conflicting reports and omissions of fact, however, were of grave concern:

• The orchid did not in fact arrive at the Gardens with proper CITES permits, but research staff failed to disclose this until months later.

- Few admitted to a positive recollection of seeing the orchid(s), and it was never definitively confirmed how many plants were brought to the Gardens.
- The herbarium curator did not immediately mail the specimen back to Peru as he had agreed to do; rather, he instructed his assistant to mail this all-important package (which she did weeks later after he went on vacation).
- The orchid was returned to a non-CITES-approved institution in Peru. (Actually, there was no CITES-accredited institution in Peru.)
- At least one research staff member knew at the time that the Peruvian institution did not have CITES permits to accept the specimen from Selby Gardens, but neglected to tell the herbarium curator responsible for mailing it.
- A photograph of the dried type specimen returned to Peru revealed later that it was suspiciously incomplete and missing its root stock, which was not botanically appropriate for the type specimen of an important new species.
- The orchid staff's permit file for this orchid, containing agricultural permits but with the glaring omission of CITES permits, had been "lost" in the research department, although rumors circulated that it was "borrowed" by one of the staff.
- Selby's orchid contractor, who coauthored the identification, took a re-productive piece of the orchid back to his home in Vermont, saying he wanted to ensure its preservation and propagation, but failed to tell any of the appropriate supervisors that he was doing so.
- Although other staff members later claimed not to have known about the contractor's actions, he insisted that all of the research staff knew except their director.
- A DNA specimen from the orchid was taken by the orchid identification director, then "lost," then found several months later; no one mentioned these mishaps until questioned a year later.
- Almost two years later, the orchid identification director admitted publicly that he had been pressured to sign a federal document falsely stating that he had told me about the lack of any CITES permit (when indeed he had not). His delayed admission suggested to many that I had

apparently been chosen by someone as the intended scapegoat for Selby's orchid fiasco.

All of these selective oversights and omissions cost the Gardens a tidy sum in legal fees, since the lawyers familiar with CITES and the Endangered Species Act were located in Washington, D.C. Some of the research staff treated this incident as merely another chapter in the world of orchid lust and passion, akin to a movie script. At least one took to writing book manuscripts, hoping to one day make big money from the intrigue of the entire affair. One boasted that he intended to sleep with the (female) prosecutor before it was all over. The idea that their institution and perhaps several individuals might be indicted by a federal grand jury on felony smuggling charges did not seem threatening. They may have felt insulated because the lawyers advised the board chair and me at the outset to take no action against the perpetrators throughout the proceedings, and we followed the advice of our highly paid expert counsel.

I had no choice but to dedicate hundreds of hours to trying to ascertain the truth from the conflicting staff reports. This enormous task detracted from my other duties. Meanwhile, the board chair increasingly intervened with a take-charge, dictatorial approach, subjectively controlling the information transmitted to the board. In the end, his orchid triumph turned into a disaster.

Or did it? Ultimately, the orchid staff retained their jobs, but the ecology and conservation professionals departed under pressure. To this day, I wonder what happened to the remaining orchid(s?) and the missing pieces of the pressed type specimen. Will this prized species someday soon reappear in the orchid world as if by magic and create a hefty profit for someone? Could the costly case have been averted if the legal counsel had sanctioned the termination of staff responsible for the illegal activities?

Federal regulations involving permits and endangered species require strict compliance. It is imperative for scientific researchers to work professionally within the confines of the law. It is not acceptable to mask the truth or conveniently shift the blame, which in this case led to undermining the integrity of a respected organization. When professionals fail to be truthful, they invariably jeopardize not only themselves but the very institutions that support them. Many scientists, including myself, feel that CITES would benefit from more stringent regulation to include the protection of habitat as well as of individual species.

Eventually, the Gardens' board became so frustrated by the bleeding of resources to pay endless legal fees that it accepted an offer for the institution to plead guilty to a federal misdemeanor. The orchid identification director was persuaded to submit to a similar humiliation. The Gardens' decision could have long-term ramifications, affecting relationships with sister institutions and its reputation for sound conservation. Ironically, some of the staff directly involved with the orchid never admitted any culpability and remained invisible to the federal radar screen.

As the legal costs mounted, I was pressured to accept a proposed guilty plea, stating that I had committed a misdemeanor, thereby satisfying the prosecutor's relentless quest to identify a scapegoat. I refused, because to have capitulated would have condoned a lie.

This and other notable clashes of will inevitably led to my forced resignation from leadership of the Gardens. Though the issues were broader than one mishandled orchid, the physical and emotional costs of dealing with *Phragmipedium kovachii* may forever taint my view of those beautiful plants. I doubt I will ever know the whole truth about that fateful week in June when I was away watching my son's regatta.

As the orchid fracas was winding down, I was informed that the hillside in Peru where *Phragmipedium kovachii* grew had been totally denuded by outlaw orchid collectors. Because of their insatiable appetite, the orchidophyles may have committed the biggest crime of this entire debacle: irreversible destruction of the natural habitat of a rare and extraordinary species.

Throughout that orchid episode, board turmoil resulted in the resignation of many trustees, most in protest of the chair's behavior. A greatly reduced board voted to return to a narrower mission of prioritizing pretty displays and identifying plants, with less emphasis on ecology and habitat conservation. That was their prerogative, although for many it was breathtakingly fast, furious, and secretive. Overnight our global conservation mission was decimated by the actions of a few, akin to a military coup. There was no discussion, no warning, no severance, no attempt to seek consensus; the door was not just closed, it was slammed shut on many staff, board, and volunteers. Unpaid legal bills were left in my lap; disenfranchised donors were fuming.

Within months of my departure, the Gardens' mission statement was revised; a successful international internship program was curtailed; the Center for Canopy Ecology was closed; classes on ecology were axed; a distinguished advisory council was terminated; the professional staff with doctorates (except for one under house arrest) sought employment elsewhere; and the community lecture series was canceled.

I grieved over the carnage but, as in the natural world, organisms must adapt when the tsunami hits. I was fortunate to receive other offers and enthusiastically joined the science faculty and became director of environmental initiatives at New College of Florida, where twenty-first century plant ecology was respected and embraced. The global Center for Canopy Ecology happily relocated from Selby Gardens to the New College campus.

In private nonprofit institutions run by a board of trustees, the board rules and its chemistry is critical. One group hired me and, four years later, board turnover and turmoil led to a shift in priorities. During those last tumultuous months, my staff sensed this dramatic upheaval. In a noble attempt to thwart a growing perception of board negativity, they created an admirable list of their professional achievements over the past three years of service and distributed it to each member of the board. Only one board member noted or praised their efforts, and he resigned soon afterward.

The remaining board operated with vastly different principles, process, and style. Sadly, the orchid may have altered the institution's trajectory; ironically, the central participants are still employed.

When the world around me changed so rapidly in twenty-four hours, I packed up my children and headed for the New England forests of my childhood. My flabbergasted but intrepid husband stayed behind to pick up the pieces that invariably result from such sudden change. My sons and I sought shelter in the natural world. We needed the sanctuary of the woods during this period of chaos. We spent three precious days in the Adirondacks avoiding the shrapnel of board turmoil and press misinformation, observing nature and remembering what we truly valued. I have watched animals in nature demonstrate the same kind of parental behavior: mother birds take their nestlings under their wings and hide in the nest during periods of danger; lizards use camouflage to avoid predation; kangaroos tuck their joeys back into the pouch for safety and hide behind a thicket.

The Adirondacks were inspiring. Summer was waning, and we could smell the scents of autumn as we embarked on a quiet woodland trail to Hour Lake. Like the mother bird that gathers her babies under her wings when threatened, I surrounded myself with my genetic offspring in a safe sanctuary during this period of change and uncertainty. It was a delight to be hiking with my two (almost) grown-up boys. Our last hike in a New England forest had been twelve years before, when they were toddlers. We had spent hours, days, and many seasons in the maple-beech forests around Williams College, where I taught biology and built the first canopy walkway in North America.

Now, at ages 16 and 17, my offspring were looking after me. James carried my lunch; Eddie brought our ponchos and the bird guide. James read the map and navigated with his compass. Eddie casually lectured about the edible plants and we sampled them as we walked. James waxed lyrical about the emetic russula mushrooms and how they were used as a purgative in ancient cultures. Eddie sighted a black-throated blue warbler and identified the song of a hermit thrush. I smiled to myself: I had recited nature lore to the two of them throughout their youth and now it was coming full circle. It filled me with pride that they had become such competent naturalists and that they too cherished the solace and wonder of nature. One memorable sight was an amazingly tall spruce that grew atop a boulder. We marveled at the tenacious roots that had managed to reach the moist soil many feet below, where it had germinated decades ago. Like humans, trees survive insurmountable challenges. Eddie no sooner turned from admiring the spruce tree when a dozen grouse thundered around him as they simultaneously vaulted their fat bodies into the air. He looked up, enthralled. I watched his face rather than the birds, and I shared his joy in this natural event.

We lunched beside a pristine mountain lake. No people, roads, phones, faxes, or televisions were visible for miles. Loons called mournfully across the water. The edges of the lake were speckled with brilliant red bunchberries, growing among the green pincushion forms of alpine mosses and lichens. We picnicked, spellbound, and felt blessed to have such beauty to allay our anxieties about jobs, college, mortgages, and other realities of the suburban world back home. Careers, houses, schools, even spouses sometimes change, but our indelible legacy in this world is our children. Having attained what is euphemistically called middle age, I am conscious of passing the torch to them and giving them center stage in this drama we call life.

Looking back, my time in the padded chair provided several positive life lessons. First and foremost, an inspired team of dedicated volunteers and workers can achieve near-impossible dreams in a short time. In a heartbeat, we said good-bye to mediocrity and raised the bar. Over three short years Selby Gardens advanced as a global center of botanical leadership in both epiphytes and their forest canopy habitats, in taxonomy and ecology, and in collections and conservation, which is what we set out to accomplish. I utilized a personal network amassed over twenty-five years of professional science to assist that process, and my staff set aggressive goals and achieved them. We improved the Gardens on all fronts: marketing, development, events, facilities, budget, staff professional training, horticulture, research, conservation, and displays. Most satisfying to me, we did it with respect and compassion for people and with the highest standard of ethics. We were not finished; but when those professional standards came under the influence of a different style of leadership, our trajectory veered off course.

My second lesson is a reminder that life is not always the proverbial bowl of cherries. I remind my children that we must accept the fact that life brings challenges that we cannot always control. Despite a successful professional career with a supportive network of international colleagues I still fell victim to some unavoidable, albeit temporary, land mines. I don't think I will ever forget the pain.

The third lesson learned — of remarkable personal solace — is that under duress I gained strength from my love of nature and from my convictions about the importance of people and plants. Advancing plant conservation via public outreach ultimately proved more important to me than compromising that priority in order to keep my paycheck. Holding fast to my personal beliefs, with the blessing of my family, provided inner strength.

REFLECTIONS IN THE NATURAL WORLD

By Eddie, aged 17

Being alone in nature is, in my opinion, the best chance to reflect. At summer camp, where I worked as a science teacher, we would set aside half an hour each day simply to be by ourselves in the forest. Sometimes I would bring a book with the intention of reading it but would end up entertaining myself with my own musings for the full thirty minutes. Such opportunities to be alone in nature are missing from the lifestyles of most of my friends.

Although I was with my family in late July 2003, hiking in the Adirondacks brought a similar feeling. Sometimes I would speed ahead until I could no longer see the others, with only my thoughts and the surrounding wilderness to keep me company. These opportunities are rare, with the Internet and cell phones to keep us busy all day back in civilization. I am no exception: last month I overspent my allotted minutes on the cell phone. Unlike many, however, I have not lost the ability to get back to where it all started and appreciate the drama of a frog catching a damselfly in midair. Noticing these minor tragedies and triumphs of the natural world, I am reminded of what it is to be alive. My mind is alert, searching for chimney swifts on the horizon. Perhaps that is why nature yields such meaningful reflections. The senses are heightened. The brain is active. Thoughts stream easily.

I took advantage of the situation on that Adirondack trail to consider my most important subject right now: college. I am at perhaps the most crucial turning point in my seventeen years of life.

Similarly, my mother is at a turning point as she searches for a new job, but there is a major difference: she has already decided who she is, and I have not. Going to college is stepping into a new world. All anybody knows about me thus far is statistics such as my SAT scores and GPA. For the first time in my life I can decide who I really want to be. Until now I have been more or less the product of my friends and family. Now I get to call the shots. I think a friend of mine said it best: "High school is where you came from and college is who you have decided to be."

That hike in the Adirondacks is one I will remember. Although I never came to a definite conclusion, as is so often true when reflecting, I certainly had a good time wrestling with the ideas of where I came from and where I am going.

LIFE: ALWAYS AN ADVENTURE

By James, aged 15

When my mother became the executive director of the Marie Selby Botanical Gardens, it seemed a joyous occasion. A substantially boosted paycheck would allow us to live for the first time with fewer constraints, perhaps indulging in pleasures we had never dreamed of before. However, the novelty of wealth soon faded as the reality of the new job was apparent. It was the end of our excursions into the jungle, a moratorium on her lifetime devoted to solving the questions of the tropics, and the beginning of long forays into a more dangerous jungle than any previously encountered: nonprofit institutional politics.

Board power struggles, negotiations, and research turf wars sent my mother home many days drained of energy and devoid of time. The politics of orchids exceeded most other issues, and many of her many leadership colleagues had their own tales of intrigue regarding this plant family. The stress of dancing among egos instead of focusing on the mission of conservation began to build up, until it all came crashing down and she finally reconciled with her values. I was very proud of her.

When resignation discussions began, we escaped into the Adirondacks, returning to the natural world. Our greatest sadness was the imminent decline of her conservation voice in our community. As we gazed across an untainted mountain lake into pure wilderness, the loss of a job seemed less threatening and the question of how we would pay the bills did not dominate our thoughts. To me, the forthcoming change seemed a blessing. No longer would my mom need to debate the merits of floor tiles for weeks on end, spend hours Band-Aiding battles among board members, or calculate how to finance long-overdue building repairs. Now she could return to advocating conservation or studying the science of herbivorous insects and their immobile but devious herbaceous prey. The predators in nature seemed more worthy of time and attention than the predators in the boardroom.

11 Billions of Needles: Calculating the Consumption of Conifers

I t was architect Mies van der Rohe who said, "God dwells in the details." Scientists study fractals to find the order hidden within the chaos, the details of our world. Fractals — those things that reveal ever more detail as they are subjected to magnification; we are discovering that they suggest an underlying order in things as diverse as stock market fluctuations, flooding, evolutionary leaps, animal behavior, and the order hidden within the chaos of a running stream of water. I catch hints and whispers of a beneficent universe . . . Our familiar, intimate environment is a universe in itself — and one full of delightful relevations.

— Cathy Johnson, *On Becoming Lost: A Naturalist's Search for Meaning*

With the onset of high school, the boys' schedules became almost as hectic as their mother's. As a consequence, our family research efforts were frequently disjointed. We were overjoyed when our schedules overlapped and we could share a scientific problem, at the dinner table or in the field. The canopy crane was one of the boys' favorite research tools. It allows a small team of two or three researchers access to almost every leaf within a two-acre plot. At the time of our expeditions to the cranes in Panama and the Pacific Northwest, ten cranes were operable worldwide. We were fortunate to spend time with colleague Yves Basset, conducting rapid assessments of herbivory in the wet lowland tropical rain forest at the Fort Sherman (Panama) crane site.

Subsequently, I worked on rapid herbivory assessments in conifer forests using the Wind River Crane in Washington State. Eddie had just started his senior year in high school and had three hours of crew practice daily, as well as a smorgasbord of social events before college. James, a sophomore, was locked into precalculus and Advanced Placement computer science. He also juggled a busy schedule of crew and activities outside of school hours. So I joined a team of adult colleagues for canopy adventures in the Pacific Northwest.

SEPTEMBER 2002. Over twenty-seven years of botanical research I have avoided conifers. Their long, skinny needles seemed virtually impossible for any leaf detective to measure. It is also difficult to examine their tiny surfaces for damage or, even worse, to follow the growth, survival, and death of a single needle among the millions bundled in one tree. Their lush green needles were displayed collectively in a skimpy, lollipop-shaped canopy many feet overhead — on thin, brittle branches outside the reach of any researcher dangling on a rope. In a nutshell, conifers represented a challenge beyond my ability to design a creative solution. Foresters often used binoculars to estimate damage to conifers by insects, but they usually "guesstimated" with categories ranging from 1 (low) to 5 (high) levels of damage. These eyeball estimates did not have a high degree of scientific accuracy.

Eddie and James, in the canopy crane, assist with rapid herbivory measurements of the wet lowland forests of Panama (photograph by author)

In 2002, I joined a consortium called the Global Canopy Programme (GCP), headed by a visionary named Andrew Mitchell. As long ago as 1978, Andrew led an expedition into Borneo called Operation Drake; there he and his colleagues built a canopy bridge to explore the tropical rain forest. In addition to the normal infestations of parasites on that adventurous trip, Andrew was infected by a passion for canopy biology that has remained with him ever since. Andrew's lifelong mission was to create international funding and research projects in canopy biology. He hoped someday to create a rain-forest think tank that would be the equivalent of NASA in space research or of the Scripps Institution in California in marine research. Why shouldn't land-based ecology be considered equivalent to interplanetary space travel or marine studies? Andrew argued. Why should our terrestrial ecosystems be underfunded in comparison to systems located millions of miles away on other planets? The GCP awarded me and three other colleagues a small grant to develop a rapid technique to measure herbivory, including conifers, from canopy cranes. If successful, we could shortcut the long process for assessing leaf surface area and provide a quick method to quantify herbivory in forests, thereby reducing the temptation to guesstimate.

Three of us traveled from balmy Florida across the continent, to Portland, Oregon, to join our western partners for phase one of our project. It is awe-inspiring to view the United States from a height of 37,000 feet. The vast central plains enclosed by the western mountains cannot help but evoke a true appreciation of our terrestrial ecosystems. If all voters were able to view our planet from above, perhaps they would insist that policymakers prioritize conservation of some of our remaining natural areas.

This vast sense of earth from space also tugged at my heartstrings with the realization that I was now many miles away from my children. Such distances were inconceivable to mothers one hundred years ago. Our notion of distance has altered drastically with air travel. Work-related travel creates a huge chasm between parents and children, an unenviable element of many careers. Other cultures place a much higher value on the importance of staying within close proximity of family, as I witnessed enviously in Western Samoa. Upon arrival in Portland, we drove into the fast-approaching darkness. Barely visible were distant "views" (mostly clouds) of Mount Hood and Mount Saint Helens along the Columbia River. Under cover of night, we slipped between clean sheets at a country inn somewhere near Carson, Washington. Surrounded by the vast spaces and fresh air of the western mountains and forests, we came under the magical spell of the natural world. Many Americans now migrate west to live, eager to appreciate some of the last remaining wild spaces on our continent.

NATURE AND NURTURE: COLLEGE KIDS TAKE TO THE WOODS

By Eddie, aged 18

Anyone who has spent time in an undeveloped environment knows that such an experience can have a significant effect on a person's disposition. I came to understand this during a weeklong backpacking trip on the Appalachian Trail in Connecticut with friends from Princeton University. Trips like this reduce any connection to material concerns, worldly pressures, and social constructions.

At Princeton the freshman class is encouraged to sign up for a prefreshman year backpacking trip. Students invariably bond with each other in the natural world, without the trappings of technology. There is something magical and lasting about the friendships formed from such experiences in nature, and colleges — as well as businesses and other groups — increasingly offer group exposure to nature. I not only participated during my prefreshman summer, but also trained as a trip leader for the following year.

Rarely do I release my cares and experience life in the pure, unfiltered way I do when immersed in the natural world. Nature is a calming experience, helping me to escape the hustle and bustle of the day to day. After becoming accustomed to the outdoor environment, I find that nature becomes a revitalizing force. New excitement is revealed in simple pleasures such as listening to the wind blow through the trees or watching a woodpecker probe for insects. The sense of adventure gained by surviving in the wilderness is invigorating. Nature has the incredible power to make us enthused about life itself. I fear that our lives are becoming increasingly sterile and devoid of interaction with living things. We must make the effort to seek nature. As Henry David Thoreau said:

We need the tonic of wildness, to wade sometimes in marshes where the bittern and the meadow-hen lurk, and hear the booming of the snipe; to smell the whispering sedge where only some wilder and more solitary fowl builds

> *her nest, and the mink crawls with its belly close to the ground. At the same*
> *time that we are earnest to explore and learn all things, we require that*
> *all things be mysterious and unexplorable, that land and sea be infinitely*
> *wild, unsurveyed and unfathomed by us because unfathomable. We can*
> *never have enough of nature. We must be refreshed by the sight of inex-*
> *haustible vigor, vast and titanic features, the sea-coast with its wrecks, the*
> *wilderness with its living and its decaying trees, the thunder cloud, and*
> *the rain which lasts three weeks and produces freshets.*

Our research destination was Wind River, Washington (easily con-fused with Wind River, Wyoming). The canopy crane, the most re-cent and sophisticated tool for treetop research, is expensive: ap-proximately one million dollars to purchase and erect, and up to several hundred thousand dollars per year to operate. Wind River crane, situated amid a natural evergreen forest ecosystem, is still the only crane dedicated to eliciting the secrets of coniferous canopies.

Construction cranes are relatively new tools for forest biologists. First pioneered by the late Andrew Smith in 1990 in Panama, cranes number ten worldwide, plus one that has been decommissioned (Table 2). The Wind River canopy structure was the only crane located in North America and also the only one based in old-fir forest. Its jib load was 279 feet long with a diameter of 558 feet, and a height of 250 feet (approximately 22 stories).

Cranes are limiting in the sense that they are affixed to one site, but are limitless in offering access to almost every leaf within a forest plot. The intended site for this particular crane, proposed by program di-rector Jerry Franklin at the University of Washington, was originally on the Olympic Peninsula in Washington. However, in the early 1990s clashes between loggers and conservationists became so heated that it was considered dangerous for researchers to undertake long-term research in that area. As a compromise, the crane moved south

Table 2. CONSTRUCTION CRANES AROUND THE WORLD

Temperate Forests
1. Basel, Switzerland
2. KROCO (Kranzberg ozone canopy observation by crane), Freising, Germany
3. Leipzig Canopy Crane Project (LAK), Germany
4. Solling, Germany
5. Tomakomai Experimental Forest, Japan
6. Wind River Canopy Crane Research Facility, United States

Tropical Forests
7. North Queensland, Australia
8. Lambir Hills National Park Canopy Crane, Malaysia
9. Suromoni Project, Venezuela (no longer in operation)
10. Parque Natural Metropolitano, near Panama City, Panama
11. San Lorenzo Protected Area, near Colón, Panama

to Wind River. It was nonetheless situated deep within logging country, and to this day the researchers are cautious when talking to the locals about their vocation.

To make matters worse, Wind River was the habitat of the spotted owl, a bird despised by some and admired by others. The old-growth timber was disappearing to chain saws, and conservationists were using the Endangered Species Act to halt logging old growth in western Oregon and Washington.

In 2002 a fungal outbreak was detected in the forests of northern California, providing yet another threat to forest survival. Invasions by exotic pests were becoming more commonplace with the rapid transportation of people and goods between continents. Local fires too threatened some of the last giant stands. Their fate remained in jeopardy, but the Wind River canopy crane allowed a unique research opportunity in these tall canopies.

Conifers are one of the botanical wonders of the world. Consider how different a needle is from a broad leaf, and how, over evolutionary time, such variability in leaf structure occurred. Yet the end result of a needle and a leaf is the same: to take in sunlight and produce energy in the form of sugars (photosynthesis) from which all food chains originate. Conifers are skinny, elongated photosynthesis factories. They have evolved as narrow and pointy, while broad-leafed trees became wide and planar. Conifers represent some of the oldest trees on earth. The shape of conifers, as represented by the classic Christmas tree, comprises one dominant main axis with whorled branches decreasing in size toward the top.

Most conifers are evergreen, meaning they do not drop their leaves in autumn or at one specific season, but intermittently throughout the year. As with most elements of nature, exceptions to this evergreen habit are commonplace (consider the deciduous larch or the bald cypress). Conifers have enormous commercial value, and many are so fast growing that in areas such as the Pacific Northwest they represent a large part of the economy. The pollen grains of conifers are extremely long-lived in the soil, and so palynologists often use pines as indicator species to estimate the age of different ecosystems.

One conifer, the ginkgo, was alive during the Jurassic period, when dinosaurs roamed the earth. *Ginkgo biloba* (family Ginkoaceae) is often called the living fossil, one of the oldest living plants. Another group of conifers, the bristlecone pines, may boast the oldest individual plants on Earth, with specimens in California that are almost 5,000 years old. Those trees were close to 2,500 years old when the Parthenon was constructed in Greece!

The technical classification of the forest type around the Wind River crane was Douglas Fir — Western Hemlock. Tree species included western hemlock (*Tsuga heterophylla,* family Pinaceae), Douglas fir (*Pseudotsuga menziesii,* family Pinaceae), western red cedar (*Thuja plicata,* family Cupressaceae), Pacific silver fir (*Abies amabilis,* family Pinaceae), vine maple (*Acer circinatum,* family Aceraceae), Pacific dogwood (*Cornus nuttallii,* family Cornaceae), and Pacific yew (*Taxus brevifolia,* family Taxaceae).

Occasional hemlocks had severe infections of dwarf mistletoe (*Arceuthobium tsugense,* family Viscaceae), and a few firs had early signs of the silver spotted tiger moth tents that usually established in early winter. The exploits of the mistletoe were worthy of a late-night horror movie. Distributed innocently by the explosive discharge of seed from the fruit, mistletoe infected entire trees over time, exerting root-like structures into the branches of a host tree, thereby usurping its water and nutrients. Dwarf mistletoes essentially sucked all the life from a tree. But the species is now widely regarded as a natural part of Pacific Northwest forests and may enhance biodiversity.

Some mistletoes have evolved different invasive behavior: the leafy mistletoes (family Loranthaceae) in Australia mimic the foliage of the host, thereby avoiding detection until the final stages of tree death. The Wind River forest had not experienced fire for more than four hundred years, so the Douglas firs had grown to be true giants in the sky.

We drove in the dark to Cascade Locks, a tiny town of three hundred people located west of the great divide of the Cascade Mountains. This small human population contrasted strikingly with the number of needles in the local conifers, which easily exceeded 100 billion. We were in the midst of what is even today called old growth — undisturbed forest. The region clearly requires a very different fire protection policy than the controversial policies of the first Bush administration, which advocated frequent fires and logging to reduce undergrowth. The old-growth forests of the western slopes have a long history of major catastrophic fires, perhaps every several hundred years. The large Douglas firs growing in this region simply cannot burn more frequently and survive. From the perspective of a forest scientist, two hundred to three hundred stems grew per acre, with the bark of the old firs reaching as much as six inches in thickness to protect the trees from mortality by fire. (In 2002 the town paid tribute to the "pyrotechnical" hazard when it hosted a hundred-year memorial to commemorate the last huge fire that had burned over 300,000 acres.)

The town of Cascade Locks boasted a colorful cultural as well as biological history, showcased at the Forestry Service reception center. I bought a guide highlighting the Sasquatch, or Big Foot, as it was affectionately named. This beast, the American equivalent of the Loch Ness monster, was an apelike creature allegedly first sighted in 1958. The incredible dearth of data regarding Big Foot was explained in an introduction to my *Field Guide to the Sasquatch* by the offhand comment that the "absence of evidence is not necessarily evidence of any absence." The legendary beast had a suspicious relationship with an outspoken but fun-loving group of humans sometimes termed rednecks. The forestry clerk spoke with great enthusiasm about the "knuckle-draggers" who frequented the city streets after midnight on Friday nights. She also referred to them as "three-toed trouser apes," the local vernacular for troublemakers who were relatives of Big Foot. Sasquatch certainly added to the folklore of the Northwest region. Local "zoological research" had its headquarters at Big Foot Research Institute. The local tourist industry capitalized on Big Foot, advertising Big Foot Trailer Park and even the annual Big Foot Daze [*sic*], a week of celebration of this cryptic creature.

The town of Carson was the local watering hole closest to the canopy crane. Our host shared local secrets about the neighborhood as we drove through the rural landscape: in one house the owner of an equestrian center had been closed down for alleged pedophilia; a compound of four homes was empty because the owner's amphetamine production had been busted; in another compound everyone was related and had coexisted for eons. It reminded me of my childhood in upstate New York as well as my experiences living in rural Australia. Everyone who visited our rural region commented on its charm; but if you lived there, you knew its secrets.

We awoke early Monday morning, impatient to begin our mission of devising a rapid and easy method to measure the herbivory in an entire forest from a small subsample. New language ran rampant as we approached the crane site: air ball, trolley group, azimuth, go distal, hook, dendropornography, Douggies, and even pendulous erect versus lateral erect. Our team of five researchers comprised four practicing ecologists and one retired statistician. The idea for this project had begun some time back when I stood on the balcony of the Evergreen State College library with Dave Shaw (research scientist at the Wind River crane), and we both admitted that no one had ever calculated the herbivory of conifer forests with any degree of accuracy. At the time, we shrugged and laughed, wondering how anyone could be so crazy as to want to measure insect bites in tiny needles, especially when the foliage was arrayed in tight clusters that numbered in the billions, situated at enormous distances above the ground. Six years later, with GCP funding, we had accepted the challenge.

How much damage did conifer canopies suffer from insect pests? And could human eyes actually see this relatively minute damage? If we could recognize it with our eyes alone, could it be measured in some statistically reliable fashion? Could we quantify herbivory throughout a coniferous forest stand in a relatively replicable, rapid fashion? Field biology was daunting in a vast forest such as the old-growth stands of the Northwest, but fortunately the science of statistics provided a shortcut. The definition of statistics I relayed to my students was that it facilitated the quickest way to get a mathematically reliable sample with the least amount of work. That was why I have come to love statistics and the notion of subsampling. Statistics provides the system of checks and balances by which ecologists can garner accurate, relatively rapid results.

The morning was cool and the air pungent with needles. The five of us packed cameras, rulers, pens, notebooks, flagging tape, and Oreos. We donned the ten-pound harnesses and helmets that were requisite for the safety regime of the Wind River canopy crane. Dave ran through the safety protocols, which included how to exit the bucket in the event of emergency or loss of electricity (source of power for the crane motor). We were eager, almost like jockeys waiting to get out of the stalls when the race began.

The crane operator, Mark, climbed three hundred ladder steps to his operator's cab some 245 feet atop the crane arm, where he controlled our safety as well as our destiny throughout the fieldwork. The arm was well above the upper canopy, to allow the crane bucket to descend into the foliage. Mark had worked with this scientific tool since its inception, so he had a knack for driving the bucket right up to a clump of branches without touching their delicate bud tips. Silently, since the electric power had only a subtle whirring sound, he airlifted us up past the understory of vine maple and Pacific yew, past the mid-canopy with its shaded understory needles of Douglas fir and western hemlock, above the upper canopy with its artistic snags dripping in mosses and lichens, and finally to the emergent zone where the tallest tree, a Douglas fir at almost 200 feet, stood sentinel above the rest. The view from the maximum elevation of the jib was breathtaking — across 1,180 acres of the Wind River research area, then on to the 10,815-acre Gifford Pinchot National Forest. After a moment of silence to appreciate the view, we all burst into animated conversation and questions, anxious to start sampling.

I had visited this canopy crane exactly four years before, in the fall of 1998, bringing with me a group of middle-school science students as part of the Jason Expedition. Those excited students, some from underprivileged backgrounds, donned harnesses and spent a half-day in the canopy visually estimating herbivory. One youth from inner-city Washington was very uncomfortable when first confronted with the questionable privilege of holding a big, slippery banana slug; but after a day in the treetops and a climbing lesson with ropes and harnesses, he became my best biodiversity sleuth! The Jason middle-school students estimated that one needle in ten suffered approximately 10 percent defoliation. Extrapolating to the entire canopy, they calculated 1 percent defoliation. This seemed incredibly low compared to other forests around the world, and four years later, I would finally obtain a quantitative answer. How would our statistically accurate survey compare to their rapidly executed teenage approach, I wondered?

We designed our current crane study to be perfectly random, to obtain results that were unbiased and comprehensive, yet quick and easy to measure. On the computer back at the lab, we had generated random points for herbivory sampling. The points were carefully numbered with trolley (x), azimuth or radius (y), and hook or load (z). When the random point resulted in just airspace, it was termed "air ball" by the crew. Air balls constituted almost one third of our random points, so we deduced that the space above the forest floor was at least one third airspace, despite the overwhelming sense of dark canopy cover when one looked up from ground level.

When we had reached our first sample site, the gondola car stopped and we simply reached from the bucket to grab the closest foliage. If a branch was too far away to grasp, we went on to the next sample point. Our first destination was the very top of a grand fir (*Abies grandis*, family Pinaceae). This beautiful conifer with its silvery green coloration demonstrated obvious differences between the foliage in the sun (at the top) and the shade (in the understory). The sun foliage was short, yellowish, thick, and very densely arranged (ideal for water conservation). These attributes are necessary to combat the extreme winds and drought conditions existing for canopies at 150 feet in a Pacific Northwest forest.

Today, however, as the sun shone, the tree branches hung motionless. Western chickadees and red-breasted nuthatches darted about grabbing food and calling excitedly, perhaps knowing that this Indian summer day was one of their last hunting opportunities. The Indian summer conditions affected us scientists as well; we hastened to collect data "while the sun shone," a phrase attributed to the ancestral hunting instinct that remained innate despite our otherwise urbanized behaviors.

Our sampling technique was the result of almost a year of emails, reading, and discussion. Like chefs fussing to perfect a recipe, we had made minor changes and pondered ideas until satisfied with our final ingredients. We isolated replicate 10-inch cubes adjacent to the crane bucket, calculated the lengths of the branches within the cube, then measured ten areas along the branches for herbivory. We began by sampling approximately one inch of needles at each of our ten branch sections, marking each section with a tiny strand of dental floss to which we affixed a numbered piece of duct tape. (Why dental floss? In all honesty, we forgot the fishline, but Bruce had dental floss in his pocket. Here was a stellar example of improvisation in the field.)

After three trees' worth of data collection, it was lunchtime. Although we had hundreds of measurements for individual needles, we had planned to measure one hundred trees in less than a week of fieldwork, so three trees in a half-day was not even close to our estimated pace . . . Back to the drawing board. We reviewed our original ambitions, altered the "recipe," and decided to measure only five needles at each of ten branch points without leaving behind a permanent tag (which took time to affix and could cause needle mortality if the wind pushed the floss against the base of the needle).

Our original concerns about how to recognize and quantify the insect damage to conifer needles were allayed. There was almost no damage to any of the needles we surveyed. In the rare cases where damage was observed, it was either 50 percent damage where a caterpillar had voraciously nipped a clump of several needles in its travels, or 1 percent where a transient beetle appeared to have taken a tiny nibble and flown away. These levels were easy to measure accurately, and the absence of any herbivory was easiest of all to measure!

At the end of one day, we had measured 820 needles; at the end of one week, we had measured 5,640 needles with a grand mean of 0.3 percent foliage damage for the coniferous canopy (and 1.8 percent herbivory throughout the entire forest, including the broad-leafed understory trees). At this point in time, the end of the 2002 season, insect damage throughout the entire conifer forest was negligible, suggesting that the turnover of nutrients from the treetops to the forest floor occurred mainly via needle-fall but with minimal transfer through primary consumers. Notably, our Jason teenagers were incredibly close to the exact amount of 0.3 percent herbivory when they estimated 1 percent after just one day of casual observations.

The crane was the Rolls-Royce of canopy tools. Effortlessly, we would step into the bucket, with lunch and tools and all the comforts of home (or almost!) for a day's work. It was easy to descend to the ladies' room, although it was rumored that the driver kept his own aerial loo in his cabin, in the guise of a plastic bottle. The crane allowed easy access to virtually every leaf, branch, and region of a five-acre forest tract within reach of the construction crane arm. To sample fifteen hundred leaves or needles in one day distributed throughout many trees would be impossible using single-rope techniques; it would probably take closer to two weeks and require extensive physical energy. Even more exciting to the determined leaf detective, it was also possible to measure the outermost needles as well as those closer to the main trunk, including the uppermost branches of a tall tree. Such agility was not possible with the limitations of ropes.

From our comfortable gondola, we admired chickarees (Douglas squirrels, *Tamiasciurus douglasi,* family Sciuridae) whisking in and out of different canopy regions collecting their stores of Douglas fir and hemlock cones for the cold winter. We tracked vultures and ravens soaring overhead. We observed Steller's jays and various thrushes that flew in and around the dense foliage. In the distance, we noted a clump of dead trees which indicated that beavers (*Castor canadensis,* family Castoridae) had been at work in this valley. These were the true joys of field research. The view from the top was one of the special privileges of our careers.

A LOVE OF EXPLORATION

By James, aged 17

Although as a teenager I often try to deny it, it is obvious that I am related to my mother. This mysterious, evolutionary connection becomes especially clear when I find myself inexplicably embarking on my own expeditions and adventures. Now I am old enough to chart my own passage. During the summer of 2004, I traveled to rural Nicaragua with a small delegation from my church. Our mission was to assist rural farmers in shifting to sustainable shade-grown coffee operations in the highlands.

High above the cities and lowland river basins, we visited and lived with people in what some might call the real Nicaragua. These montane hillsides were no longer forested but instead were settled and farmed. Sooty and poverty stricken, the region was dotted with tin huts and dirt roads. Sometimes we traveled by donkey. The farmers were anxious to hear our opinions, hoping fervently that the American market would be happy to pay a bit more for sustainable coffee grown in the shade of regenerating forests, as compared to the cheaper coffee that is grown in cleared fields with no effort to reestablish the native vegetation. Despite limited education, the people in rural, montane Nicaragua are attempting to change their farming techniques to become environmentally friendly, and at the same time they aspire to be economically astute and create sustainable businesses. As ambassadors representing our country, we encouraged them in this endeavor and returned home eager to promote the sale of their environmentally friendly coffee.

In contrast to the steamy, humid tropics, I explored frigid Antarctica during my senior year in high school. Joining an expedition called Students on Ice, we visited icebergs, observed the antics of penguins, and witnessed first-hand the research stations where critical information on global climate change was being recorded. I earned my passage with part-time jobs as secretary, editor, or research assistant. I also sold stock in my expedition. Shareholders received a postcard from Antarctica, an educational lecture, and a slide show about the trip upon my return. Two friends, Deane and Rex Allyn, had raised millions of dollars to start the Sarasota Opera many years ago and assisted me with their fundraising prowess.

My research project in Antarctica involved studying tardigrades. These tiny, cryptic beasts live in suspended animation in extreme climates all over the world. They look like tiny water bears, but not much is known about them. According to experts, an estimated billion or more tardigrades inhabit the mosses of our local state park here in Florida. Tardigrades have been recorded in the mosses and lichens of Antarctica, but I hope to confirm this with my own collections.

My specific hypothesis was that trampled mosses, lichens, and soils hosted fewer tardigrades than untrampled areas. To verify this, I obtained collecting and importing permits and spent many hours peering down a microscope after the trip. At the time of writing, I have still not finished counting these plentiful beasts. Whether because of my mother or not, I have developed the bug for exploration (no pun intended).

On the last day of our Antarctic voyage, I wrote in my journal:

As we are completing our second crossing of the Drake Passage, the majority of us are beginning to feel less seasick and more excited about what lies ahead. I think that many felt poorly yesterday not because of the powerful swells that toy with our ship, but rather because they were upset about having to leave the majestic mystery of the Antarctic for their dreary existence back home. Today, though, many of our meetings have been about bringing what we have learned back to our homes and teaching those at home the importance of living with nature. As a result, many of us have been able to get up out of bed, as our minds and hearts are sparked by ideas of what sort of difference we can make. Tossing seas seem insignificant when revolution is in the works. Although the sky outside is gray, the atmosphere inside the ship is becoming charged with action and possibility.

12 Downsizing 101: Dynamics of the Family Ecosystem

A Nez Perce woman from Oregon once told me that there was a time when the ancient trees were living burial tombs for her people. Upon the death of a tribal elder, a great tree was scooped out enough to hold the folded body. Then the bark was laid back to grow over the small bones like a rough-hewn skin graft. "The old trees held our old people for thousands of years", she said softly. "If you cut those ancient trees, you lose all your own ancestors, everyone who came before you. Such loneliness is unbearable."

On a physical and spiritual level, we are linked to these breathing trees. And every time a great tree is cut, our kind die, too — lost and lonely and longing for what we may someday recognize as akin to ourselves.

— Brenda Peterson, *Pacific Northwest: Land of Light and Water*

Our homes constitute an ecosystem for human beings, constructed with an array of nesting materials that provide sustenance, protection, creativity, physical and emotional refuge, and space for nurturing. In my late forties, significant midlife challenges hit in close sequence: job termination, ethical issues, conservation setbacks, and the prospect of an empty nest as my sons left for college. In addition to personal unknowns, my parents faced significant changes, which inevitably affected their daughter.

Born and bred in a small town in upstate New York, they faced some complex choices in retirement, inevitably creating both financial and emotional anxiety. With the prospect of greater longevity than earlier generations, none of us is well prepared for the smorgasbord of choices for retirees. Their lifestyle complicated by threats of declining physical health, uncertain world politics, and volatile stock markets, my parents wisely sought to downsize. All of us were once children and received the wisdom of our parents; in turn, many of us eventually become advisors to our parents as they age.

An emotional moment for children and parents alike was the sale of my parents' home of fifty-three years and their subsequent move to Florida. Like a classic animal behavior scenario, their move represented the twenty-first-century senior citizen migration pattern. For me as the eldest of their three children, it seemed important to try to assist them in navigating the emotional minefield of adult changes. The sanctuary of my childhood nest was being handed over to virtual strangers. Most American families typically move several times during their lives, but my parents had never left their small town, nor moved from the hand-hewn home built at the onset of their married life. It is classic animal behavior in humans, as parents look to their children for counsel. An estimated 44 million Americans care for an elderly person, and that number is likely to increase. My peers and I find that we now spend as much time discussing the issues of our parents' welfare as we formerly devoted to discussing the pitfalls of child rearing.

October 2002. A large, mysterious box greeted me at the front doorstep. Since becoming executive director at Selby Gardens, I found that my days stretched long and hard. I often arrived home in the dark. My only consolation was that my children usually arrived even later, rowing for the regional crew team until well after dark. The exercise did them good. I can't say the same about my activities, which tended to be restricted to the padded chair; and lately my tasks were increasingly people oriented rather than science oriented.

The box on the doorstep bore the familiar handwriting of my mother in upstate New York. I talked often to my parents on the telephone, trying to offer advice as they contended with diverse "business" questions that faced senior citizens of their generation. Medical advances have added many years to our parents' expected life span, and those years create financial headaches long after professional careers are left behind. Never have the lives of human beings on the planet been as long and as healthy as those of my parents' generation. And never have so many choices existed regarding insurance, medical care, wills, property splits and sales, or even mechanisms for paying bills. Should they pay their bills over the Internet? Via automatic bank withdrawals? By check? In person? These choices seemed daunting even to my middle-aged perspective. The baby boomer generation, to which I belong, faced the first-ever mixed blessing of older parents with complex lifestyle options.

Caught in this aging process, my parents were in the midst of an enormous and painful dilemma: the possibility of downsizing and giving up the family home. It had become too large and too expensive. Our small hometown in upstate New York showed signs of turning into a ghost town. Such factors as high property taxes, an empty downtown area, the need to modernize appliances, and departure of some of their older friends gave urgency to their decision. Even worse, the near-bankruptcy of one of the major corporations, Corning Glass, economically paralyzed the region. Declines had happened in the past to other manufacturers: of typewriters, adding machines, fire extinguishers, car parts of a type that were now outmoded. Elmira had a vibrant past but a precarious future. The events of September 11, 2001, had also taken their toll on the American economy, especially in upstate New York. Few people seemed inclined to move there in the year 2002, when my parents decided to sell their house.

To retain her sanity amid the declining economy of her neighborhood, my mom wisely undertook to downsize the family's material goods. I have read about older people literally "drowning" in rooms full of collectibles — not my mother, thank goodness! She attacked her closets with zeal. The basement was devoid of anything except historical dust. I admired her. It seemed healthy to live without a warehouse of kitchen gadgets or twenty dusty photo albums of every family vacation. Mom had mailed me several boxes over the past year, exhibiting great sentiment yet zealously assaulting closets large and small throughout our home.

My dad and my grandfather had built our house in 1953, the year I was born. Each stone had a story. All the beams represented local barns. The rough brown adzed surfaces contained secrets of some past farm near Lowman, New York, our ancestral village. Educated at Princeton University, my grandfather had adapted the stone-wall construction and leaded-glass windows of his favorite Princeton architecture into all the Lowman houses. Like most retirees, my parents did not wish to remain captive to home repairs. In past generations, when families lived together, such maintenance responsibilities would appropriately be handed down to the younger generation. In our mobile American society, older citizens commonly become harnessed to property that surpasses their physical abilities. This dilemma is commonplace among the parents of my peers.

I smiled, paused, and savored the childlike pleasure of opening this new treasure box. What had Mom discovered this week? It was bittersweet to unwrap my childhood in the installments that arrived box by box. But I know that Mom was glad to provide the family memorabilia with a welcoming home. I was the family archivist, treasuring mementos such as my grandmother's recipe for hasty pudding and fabric my great-great-aunt had brought back from her legendary trip to China in 1923 (long before that was the destination of choice for any young woman).

I ripped the tape and opened the box, revealing a variety of containers within. I pulled out a plastic bag. Inside were six linen napkins embroidered with the letter M. I smiled again. My great-grandmother had had the same initial as I — what wonderful good fortune. (I suppose there may have been some careful planning on my parents' part with regard to my name. I was grateful for their choice.) Although fine linens were not essential for my field biological escapades, they were useful for the fund-raising role that I now assumed as director of the Gardens. Three heavy books came next. My theses! First a bachelor's thesis on temperate tree growth in the Williams College forest, my first piece of scientific writing. By no means a prize-winning essay, it was nonetheless a part of my long love affair with science. Second, I gently extracted my master's thesis on leaf growth and herbivores of birch trees in the highlands of Scotland. Oh, I shiver at the memories of cold camping trips to find alpine birch trees struggling to grow, their gnarled stature reflecting a constant struggle to survive the countless blizzards. My children still laugh (with slight embarrassment) at their mother's tales of eating roadkill rabbits and living on a graduate student's budget of $5 per week in rural Scotland. Last, my Ph.D. thesis on the canopy ecology of the rain forests of Australia, bound with its still-shiny gold letters, was at the bottom of the pile. I knew that Mom had tucked this weighty treatise safely away. In fact, she and Dad probably never even read it. Science was like a foreign language to my parents. They were very proud of my publications, but never quite understood the technical aspects of exploration in the jungles of the world.

The next layer in the box revealed two smaller books. I immediately recognized these rabbit-eared photo albums as my childhood herbarium. Collecting all the wildflowers within several square miles of our home, I had fastidiously pressed and glued their parts then spent many hours looking up their names and making labels. The wildflowers of upstate New York had inspired my scientific career. This collection of pressed plants was still scientifically sound in a flattened, brown-yet-recognizable state, with funny names such as live-forever, evening lychnis, lady's thumb, Indian pipe, herb Roberts, and jack-in-the-pulpit. To think that I had spent hundreds of childhood hours in the public library determining these identifications and researching the plants, when now one can go on a website and key out answers in five minutes or less.

The box seemed bottomless. Another plastic bag contained autumn foliage. My eyes welled with tears. My mother knew me like no one else. At this time of year (October) I yearned for the gorgeous fall foliage of New England. This year she had also collected some horse chestnuts — no doubt from the very tree whose fruits I had harvested when walking down Hoffman Street on my way to Miss Hill's first grade. The dogwood leaves were green intermittent with red, the birch leaves yellow, and the oaks brown and yellow. I hastily pressed them in a phone book, knowing that in a few days they would become table decorations of the most exotic nature in our subtropical Florida environs. During my childhood, I had accumulated closetfuls of roadside collectibles: dried leaves, birds' nests, stones, twigs, bark, and even dried flowers. These treasures inspired my passion for field biology, and it was a joy to receive some reminders of those early collecting days. The opportunity to observe and touch nature had served to sharpen my five senses and provided a healthy link to the natural world. Today's youth often know nature only via computer images.

A mysterious wooden box lay at the bottom of the carton. Gingerly, I lifted it over the lip of the big cardboard box. It shook like candy corn. Opening the brass clasp cautiously, I peered inside. Looking up at me were tens of tiny eyes and paws and bodies — the *sick box!* Memories came rushing back. Whenever we were sick in those ancient days before the invention of parent-approved morning television for kids, my mother would bring out our box of treasures. Inside were leaded green trees that could be set up amidst the bedcovers, creating a village. In that village wandered animals of china, lead, and wood that spanned a childhood of collectibles. For each family vacation into the small towns of upstate New York we would come home with an addition to the sick box: a Princeton tiger, a memento of attending college reunions with my father; a china cat with kittens from the Corning Museum of Glass, the institution that had been our local pride and joy; a sickly looking cloth dog that obviously had been sucked during many teething episodes; giraffe and elephant miniatures from FAO Schwarz, reminders of an outing to New York City that provided my closest encounter with African savanna ecology; a wooden pelican from Cape May, New Jersey, souvenir of my first field trip with the local Audubon Society; an ugly metal boxer dog that I always (in typical sisterly fashion) attributed to my brother's taste. Despite its threatening face, that boxer served as a loyal watchdog to protect the entrance to the blanket-villages created when I was sick in bed . . . elephant, dalmatian, owl, tiger, and leopard all came alive in imaginary villages on top of the bedcovers.

I was reminded of one of my favorite childhood books, *A Child's Garden of Verses* by Robert Louis Stevenson. Grabbing it from James's bookcase upstairs, I turned to the poem that had inspired our blanket villages:

The Land of Counterpane

When I was sick and lay a-bed,
I had two pillows at my head,
And all my toys beside me lay
To keep me happy all the day.

And sometimes for an hour or so
I watched my leaden soldiers go
With different uniforms and drills,
Among the bed-clothes, through the hills;

And sometimes sent my ships in fleets
All up and down among the sheets;
Or brought my trees and houses out,
And planted cities all about.

I was the giant great and still
That sites upon the pillow-hill,
And sees before him, dale and plain,
The pleasant land of counterpane.

Our family did not have soldiers in our "sick box" as did Stevenson; instead, we had biodiversity. Perhaps that is in part why I became a scientist and not a military hero.

I lined up my miniature bits of biodiversity across the kitchen counter, eager to share them with Eddie and James when they arrived home from crew practice. Upon coming through the door, they both offered the requisite enthusiasm, humoring me about this time capsule from my youth. After an evening of gluing the pelican's beak (the only casualty of their postal voyage), I put the sick box carefully into a cupboard, wondering if there would someday be grandchildren who might make villages on the quilts of our Florida home . . .

The box reminded me of the biological roles of children and parents in real life. For some animals, parents and offspring have relatively little interaction. For example, the Australian brush turkey de-

Meg in her childhood, sick in bed, makes "villages" with the small animals and trees of the sick box (illustration by Barbara Harrison)

serts its young, which hatch sequentially from their incubator nest of sticks and soil. The babies grow up alone, never seeing parents or siblings. Human children and parents are at the other extreme, overlapping for many years before the young leave the nest. In our generation, for the first time ever, grown children are "returning" to their parents to make hard decisions and sometimes to care physically for their adult parents. Growing old has its risks, and my parents' generation has the unenviable privilege of so many choices that the process of aging becomes almost onerous. My parents face some frightening scenarios: Will one spouse become ill? Will one partner need assisted care before the other? Will one want to travel and the other stay home? Will one want to eat home-cooked meatloaf while the other relishes tacos at a Mexican restaurant? These issues can destroy the quality of life in old age. We all want our parents to make wise choices, and execute those choices with dignity and grace. Such decision-making invariably takes a toll on the children. I was very aware of shifting my own focus from raising my children to pondering the quality of life for my parents.

Unlike many species, humans retain long-term ties between parents and offspring. I am reminded of other examples in the biological world, where communal living may serve as inspiration to humans. Ants have specific roles and interact within their complex society. Their oldest citizen, the queen, is the most revered individual in the entire community. Watching an ant colony never ceases to amaze me, in terms of how they relegate duties and create a highly efficient kingdom. Bees behave similarly in their hives, invariably impressing anyone who takes the time to observe their lifestyle.

Human beings also have complex societies, but the ancient system of extended family living together has eroded with the mobility of careers. New and relatively untested options now exist to compensate for the lack of extended family: assisted living, senior centers, home nursing care, meals on wheels, even buses that transport elders to medical appointments. What options were appropriate for my parents, I wondered, and would they receive the respect and dignity their seniority warranted?

Almost like migratory birds, many retired Americans flock to sunny climates to escape the rigors of harsh winters. This behavior mimics the behavior patterns of other animals that migrate in flocks, prides, or herds. For humans, the migration has the obvious advantages of leaving behind snow shovels, furnaces, double-glazed windows, woolen clothing, bouts of flu, icy roads, frozen pipes, road salt that rusts cars, rakes, axes, and the supreme effort required to put a garden to bed and awaken it again. Human beings, like all species, instinctively select lifestyles to ameliorate physical rigors; moving south is a biological solution.

It was difficult for our family, parents and children alike, to accept the notion of selling our family home, the nest that had nurtured all of us for over half a century. Did baby bears think the same thoughts when leaving their caves, I wondered? Did young butterfly fish lament swimming away from the coral reef of their birthplace? My address throughout childhood was the same stone house on Garden Road. Perhaps I too am an endangered species, representing the last generation of children to grow up in one abode.

Whenever I was bruised by the hardships of the world, I would seek solace in the familiar creaks of my bedroom. Each closet and loose floorboard was as familiar as my mother's recipe for apple crumble. It was always reassuring to sleep in the bed of my childhood; inexplicably, the monsters of the world never entered the room. Divorce, job searches, childhood illnesses, debts, and other crises all were lessened to some degree inside the safe walls of our family home. I was convinced that my parents experienced this security even more than we children did. After all, they had invested a lifetime in this house. But the biological clock dictated that it was time to downsize.

My parents became engaged in June 1949, when both were still in college. An engineer by trade, my grandfather immediately began to contemplate the requirements for construction of their nest: land, beams, stones. My dad remembers the day when an old family barn on the Lowman farm in Lowman, New York, was falling down, and his dad wisely requisitioned the beams before it was demolished. Father and son carted out oak timber by the truckload, exposed it to cleaning by leaving it out in the pasture for several years, prior to its new life as our living room. The beams were 12-inch-square sections of hand-hewn, hand-mortised oak, more than 125 years old. In anticipation of those oak beams, the betrothed couple spent many weekends picnicking and collecting stones. They became adept at spotting stones strewn along roadsides, construction sites, and pasturelands. It was mutualism in the biological sense, since both parties benefited.

They removed stones that were impediments to plows and traffic, and they used their collection to create walls for their nest. To this day, my father cannot resist picking up the odd stone from some deserted place. Perhaps he will continue building stone walls in his next life?

Our stone house provided a unique ecosystem for our family. It served as a hospital for one of my brothers in his many months of recovery from bronchitis and a tracheotomy; as a library for my mom, who worked late hours on her master's degree while we were asleep; and as an escape for my dad, who rode his bike home from the bank each day and rejoiced in mowing the lawn or creating a new stone wall in the garden. His stone labyrinth, if you will, became a laboratory for me as a young naturalist. I kept busy collecting old birds' nests and learning the various eggs, searching for secret locations of trillium in the swampy backyard, finding blackberry patches, pressing spring wildflowers between the pages of old telephone books, and even bandaging wounded earthworms that had passed through the lawn mower.

Arriving home in Elmira in August 2003, I slept for the last time in my childhood bed. The house had been sold. After fifty-three years, the furniture was to be transported to Florida. Estate experts would descend into the basement for the famous American tradition known as the garage sale. As the small propeller plane on which I was traveling dived into Elmira-Corning Airport, dodging the foothills of the Finger Lakes, I gazed in awe. The sultry green of late summer beckoned, despite the intermittent tired houses of a region that had seen a great economic downturn. Early tinges of red and yellow foliage frosted the hillsides like ornaments on a Christmas tree.

My brother Ed returned too for this poignant weekend. We photographed everything we saw, told tales of our favorite stones, and recaptured moments in the history of this house that had nurtured, coddled, comforted, warmed, and buffered us from the outside world. We paid homage to every room and held own quiet rites of passage, touching the stones and timbers of our childhood. Emotional moments abounded. My dad misplaced the fifteen-year-old sneakers that he wanted to take to Florida. Ed almost undercut the notion of a garage sale, in that he tried to take home every sentimental artifact he could lay his hands on: some green glass of no known function, a rake with only six tines, a bent snow shovel, Dad's ancient lawn mower, and Mom's rusted metal garden heron. A large trunk of items was shipped to our brother in Germany. Everyone remained surprisingly buoyant and chipper as the paperwork of moving to a new address consumed Dad, and the organizational elements of the garage sale required Mom's complete attention. Ed and I smiled. In my generation, a few milestones stand out over the rest: the birth of a child, college graduation, marriage, and most recently, moving parents into their retirement nest.

I am very proud of my parents. They executed their move with grace and sensibility. It is my hope that they can live out their last chapter with sunshine, with exercise, with fewer daily chores, in simpler surroundings, and in closer proximity to family. No scientific study has yet determined the long-term impact of downsizing on our beloved senior citizens, but I look forward to becoming a guinea pig in that research in my own later years.

Postscript, 2004

James and I had just completed a tour of college campuses, a special mother-son journey. We spent hours in our rental car discussing the pros and cons of engineering versus physics, of big versus small student bodies, of rural versus urban university settings. Three generations of my family met in Stowe, Vermont, for several days of fresh air and reunion. On the last day, I joined my father for the morning calisthenics he faithfully completed each and every day of the year. Gasping for breath after twenty pushups, forty leg lifts, and sixteen other bodily stretches and contortions, I was full of respect for my 79-year-old patriarch. With my mother, we hiked along a trail that led us up several 1:4 inclines, through a maze of gooey cow pies, and over and under several barbed wire fences that would dismay a West Point freshman. My parents were hardly breathless. I have renewed respect for the aging process as my parents — in their late seventies — navigate life's pitfalls (both physical and cerebral) with dignity and agility.

ODE TO SPECIAL PLACES

By James, aged 17

For the past six summers, I have been fortunate to return to Coopers Cove, West Virginia, one of my favorite places in the world. A wildlife camp was established in 1965, so long ago that my mom was a camper there and then a staff member. Now I too have experienced the cove as both camper and staff during summers. The director, Vini Schoene, wrote: "We cannot describe the special quality of our favorite spots at the cove any more than we can explain art. But they tug at you and you have to go back." She says it so well. I feel this way about many places at the cove: Fern Valley, the pond, the top of Ben's Knob, and one of the newest special places, which is a canopy walkway. From its upper platform I can see the entire valley just as our resident red-tailed hawk must view it. My brother loves lying in a hammock that is suspended over a gurgling stream, where he feels surrounded by air, foliage, and water.

Perhaps even more poignant to me is not just the notion of a physical place as special, but a special moment that embodies the mood and atmosphere of the entire summer. I will always cherish a moment in time when, after a night of raucous singing down at the Big Barn, the campers were all hiking back to the dormitories. Those teenagers fell under the spell of an undiminished night sky and a whip-poor-will's call echoing over the valley.

What makes the cove so amazing, though, is that moments like that one are extraordinarily common. You have to grasp them when they occur and treasure them like jewels. When not in the heat of activity, I frequently find myself taking a quiet moment to reflect on the natural beauty of this place.

MOM-IDIOSYNCRASIES

By Eddie, aged 19

When James and I reflect on the years spent with our mother, we tend to remember mostly fun and happy adventures, with little contention between us. When we are hard pressed, however, that is not a complete portrayal of our family life. It neglects the occasional moments of embarrassment and frustration my brother and I shared on our journey to independence. I somehow believe that my mother's shy and eccentric childhood as a lonely naturalist left her clueless about some of the finer points of teenage socialization. For instance, when I had a female guest for dinner one time, my mom did not quite comprehend the inappropriateness of making bifurcated snake penises the topic of discussion. (Or was she testing my date in some macho-scientific fashion?)

Our mom's career path has honed her five senses to a greater degree than in other mothers. She woke up when a snake was slithering across her bedroom carpet (and that is not very much noise); and a bird watching through the window as she slept jolted her awake. These uncanny powers of observation certainly did put a damper on any nocturnal pursuits my brother and I sought, especially when we had friends over.

Perhaps the most consistent source of embarrassment is our mother's obsession with the consumption of insects. Don't get me wrong, I think eating bugs is cool too. But her ability to bring up this topic at the most inopportune times was astounding. Once while my brother was visiting some college students he greatly admired, the topic of senior theses came up in discussion. Without missing a beat, my mother blurted, "James, you could write about eating bugs — for life!!!" The look of horror on my brother's face at the mention of this absurd proposal will forever be imprinted in my memory. Often when new friends arrived at our house, it was not uncommon for our mom to offer them cookies or candy — in which crickets were one of the main ingredients. My brother and I considered it a miracle if that friend ever returned to our house after such a traumatic experience.

As I look back, these events often seem trivial. But in the limited world of our teenage minds, these embarrassing moments seemed bigger than life. Certainly every family has its disputes; ours simply revolved around the unlikely subjects of snake anatomy and insect nutrition.

13 Coming Full Circle: Linking the Green and Brown Food Webs

It probably doesn't matter if, while trying to be modest and eager watchers of life's many spectacles, we sometimes look clumsy or get dirty or ask stupid questions or reveal our ignorance or say the wrong thing or light up with wonder like the children we all are. It probably doesn't matter if a passerby sees us dipping a finger into the moist pouches of dozens of lady's slippers to find out what bugs tend to fall into them, and thinks us a bit eccentric. Or a neighbor, fetching her mail, sees us standing in the cold with our own letters in one hand and a seismically red autumn leaf in the other, its color hitting our senses like a blow from a stun gun, as we stand with a huge grin, too paralyzed by the intricately veined gaudiness of the leaf to move.

— Diane Ackerman, *A Natural History of the Senses*

I do not know what makes me agree to crazy adventures, but in January 2004 for the third time in my life I found myself packing an odd assortment of luggage on behalf of science education for young people. My list included penetrometers, Off! repellent, climbing harnesses, turkey basters, plastic measuring cups, bandanas, hats, more Off!, Wellington boots, sneakers, The Flora of Barro Colorado Island *by Tom Croat, film, cameras, binoculars, Swiss army knife, pens and markers, field notebooks, ropes, carabineers and descending devices of all kinds, binoculars, graph paper, plastic poop-catching trays, string to suspend plastic poop-catching trays, hypsometer, thermometer, pH meter, flagging tape, measuring tape, tree-diameter tape, first aid kit, extra stocks of Benadryl and Cipro, Itch Off, butterfly net, beating tray, aspirators, helmet, toiletries,* Birds of Panama *by Robert Ridgely and John Gwynne, and of course my laptop computer so I could continue to keep my diary.*

I was off to Barro Colorado Island in Panama, for three weeks on a "movie set" for science television. My luggage was like a portable field laboratory, from which I hoped I could create an hour of action-packed science education programs for kids who might someday become scientists themselves, if motivated by the role models and sense of exploration that they experienced during the Jason broadcasts. It took many days to prepare the household for my departure: I had to pay all bills both current and in advance, make arrangements for lawn work and repairs, find rides for James, reset the phone and computer messages, anticipate birthdays, anniversaries, as well as requests from Eddie at college for money or forgotten clothes, bake extra cookies for James after school, leave a macaroni and cheese casserole in the refrigerator so that my bachelors would have a nutritional start to their month, and attend to any other details that required attention. I do not mean to imply that the men in my house were not totally competent, but somehow I remained the family logistics coordinator.

My destination was the Jason XV Expedition in the tropical rain forests of Panama, similar in scope to Jason V in Belize in 1994 and Jason X in Peru in 1999. The Jason distance-learning expeditions were an excellent platform for me to wear a public scientist hat and advocate for ecology and conservation. Jason XV, aired in 2004, aimed to give several million students and teachers a better understanding of the links between the tropical tree canopy and the forest floor. This theme was also the topic of a National Science Foundation research project that several colleagues and I had just completed in forests of Puerto Rico.

Barro Colorado Island (BCI) in Panama was blessed with its comfortable living, its laboratory facilities, and a wealth of tropical ecology. The advantages of living and working in a place with strong logistic support, easy access from airports, and a wealth of well-funded projects by Smithsonian scientists have made it a mecca for field biologists since 1923. Is it possible to call a tropical rain forest research station luxurious? To tumble out of bed in an air-conditioned room, grab hot breakfast on a tray, leave equipment in a laboratory overnight, and walk to work only five minutes away *is* luxury for a rainforest biologist. My colleagues and I are impressed by hot running water and overwhelmed by washing machines. We are dumbstruck at the thought of a computer in a rain forest.

BCI offers such conditions and more. Perhaps most important is a biological field station that encourages the camaraderie and exchange of information that make research more productive. Nonetheless, BCI was recently isolated by the construction of the Panama Canal. Scientists cannot help pondering how the island's artificial formation may affect long-term populations of animals and their interactions. The impact of isolation by a water barrier could potentially skew some of the natural dynamics observed by scientists.

Some three million years ago the Isthmus of Panama rose to form a barrier between the Pacific and Atlantic oceans, and a land bridge between North and South America. This unique land formation, called Panama, became home to more than 10,000 species of plants, 900 species of birds, 225 species of mammals, and 360 species of reptiles and amphibians. Of those, approximately 1,368 plants, 366 birds,

93 mammals, and 90 reptiles inhabited the island of Barro Colorado. This small sanctuary was isolated by water that, with the completion of the Panama Canal in 1914, formed Lake Gatun. Suddenly the large expanse of rain forest through the center of Panama became a divided cluster of islands, and the exchange of species between North and South America was barricaded forever.

One of the few other drawbacks to BCI was its healthy population of ticks and chiggers. I cannot help speculating that the population of chiggers may have become unbalanced owing to some consequences of island biogeography. Was it an island phenomenon? Had the chigger predators been barricaded from the island by the formation of the canal? Or would this seasonally dry tropical rain forest have been an epicenter for tick populations even without isolation by the Panama Canal? I did not wish to devote more flesh and blood to a long-term study of the distribution of chiggers throughout Panama, but they certainly were a test of strength during the broadcasts. To scratch or not to scratch on live TV — that was my dilemma.

Students listening to this fifteenth Jason expedition via satellite probably imagined they were participating in research in Panama's tropical rain forests. Our specific focus was the connection between the green and brown food webs. The student/teacher teams were led by "Dr. Dirt" of the University of Oklahoma (Mike Kaspari) and "Lady Liana" from New College of Florida (me). Although I had never used the term "green food web" before, it was an apt description for middle schoolers, especially when compared to the brown food web that included dirt, decaying leaf litter, and other ground elements on the forest floor. Other scientists tackled anthropology, the engineering of the Panama Canal, satellite imagery to measure deforestation, ethnobotany, and the brown food web.

Jason in the rain forest was known affectionately as "the big sweat."

To film fifty-five live broadcasts, complete with sound, props, and un-rehearsed actors — and to retain high standards for the level of sci-ence — challenged both the actors and the crew. The weeks on BCI were some of the hottest live broadcasts I experienced in my three years of Jason. We exhausted the stock of bottled water and Gatorade throughout Panama. Despite the heat, Jason expeditions gave stu-dents a firsthand sense of scientific research and exposure to the rig-ors of designing experiments to answer questions. During our on-air investigations we discovered that *Clusia* sp. (family Clusiaceae) was the toughest leaf in the neotropical rain forest. We recorded monkeys breaking branches and tearing leaves from trees (not actual herbivory, but definitely a reduction in leaf area), discovered new insect herbi-vores feeding on specific canopy plants, and monitored leaf-cutter ants both above and below ground.

Even our lunch breaks were lessons of learning about the interac-tions within the rain forest. One notable memory derived from spi-der monkeys who came for lunch at our broadcast site. It all started when one of our scientists was whacked on the head with a *Dipteryx panamensis* (family Leguminosae) seed. The woody *Dipteryx* seeds were shaped like large almonds and fell in masses during the dry sea-son (January–April) that ensured them a next generation in the rain-forest canopy. Monkeys obviously assisted in the distribution, in this case by throwing seeds at scientists on the forest floor. Only one shot successfully intercepted a human being, but the clever monkeys made many attempts.

One sultry day, a large troop appeared just as the smells of our lunches escaped from their plastic bags. The noisy monkeys got closer and closer, until one brazen fellow hung on a vine just over our tarp, ready to swipe a sandwich. Cowering in anticipation of receiving a scat bath, we were impressed by the diligent vocal efforts of these monkeys to show us who was boss. The furry, adept climbers had the audacity to clip branches — sometimes as long as 5 feet — and fling them at us. I bemoaned the fact that the primates had defoliated well over three hundred leaves from our *Anacardium excelsum* (family Anacardiaceae) tree. One leaf usually represented several days of feasting for an insect.

The Jason XV Expedition was a never-ending series of questions. The press asked questions of everyone, students posed questions to scientists, scientists asked questions of students, scientists questioned one another, teachers and students posed questions to the researchers, and back in the classroom teachers posed questions to their students. Here was the essence of science: inquiry and hypothesis. It was exciting to engage in this exchange, especially with a program that could well inspire a new generation of students to consider science as a career. The broadcasts themselves ran on questions. Scientists posed questions to our students in the field, and subsequently the students in the distance-learning audience posed questions to us (asking live from their satellite network links).

In a typical day of five hour-long broadcasts, the material covered was staggering. Here are a few examples:

What tools do you use to study the green food web?
As a canopy biologist, I rely on tools to study the treetops. Devices such as construction cranes, hot-air balloons and inflatable rafts, bridges and platforms, and the adaptation of mountaineering hardware with ropes all represent new tools essential for study of the treetops. Equipment such as graph paper, leaf-area meters, penetrometers, and notebooks constitute my tool kit for measuring herbivory of foliage. More recently, the advent of satellite imagery has provided new ways to view the forest canopy and increased our ability to assess defoliation.

How are the green and brown food webs connected?

Several types of material fall from the canopy to the forest floor, including green leaves, insect bodies, throughfall (rainwater augmented by nutrients from washing over the surfaces of leaves and stems), and insect frass. Frass is the technical term for insect poop; I used to think it was the literal term "from your xxx (rear end)," until I learned that it is a German word related to digestion by animals. The disappearance of forest canopy due to fires or clearing not only means loss of the green food web, but also means loss of the brown food web and its inhabitants on the forest floor. Soil decomposers are often overlooked in assessing the challenges of regenerating a forest, but they are essential to the health of the trees. Scientists tend to specialize in either the canopy or the forest floor, but over the past four years I have received a grant from the National Science Foundation to study the links between these two important regions of the forest. Logically, we need to look at both together, not just one at a time.

What is the rate of rain-forest deforestation?

Rain forests are disappearing faster than we can study them. The estimated losses, calculated from satellite surveys of tropical forests, are approximately 1 percent annually. That figure may not sound large, but deforestation has been occurring for fifty years, or even more, in some countries. For several reasons, it is difficult to measure deforestation accurately. Satellite imagery is only beginning to have a level of precision that allows us to determine whether green vegetation represents primary forests or grass, agricultural crops or secondary forest. Certain data are not reported accurately because selective cutting or partial logging is not defined by some foresters as deforestation. Sometimes forests are cut illegally and are not recorded. In short, there are many reasons why we are likely to have underestimated the rate of rain-forest clearing.

What is your favorite insect?

My personal favorite is the giant stinging tree beetle, which lives exclusively in the foliage of the giant stinging tree in Australia. Despite the physical and chemical defenses in the leaves of the giant stinging tree, this shiny beetle is adapted to digest these leaves and eat them voraciously, consuming up to 40 percent leaf-area loss per year. Its gorgeous metallic green carapace is camouflaged perfectly by the giant stinging tree leaf color. Such host-specific relationships, where one insect eats only one species of tree, are less common than I thought when I first started canopy research twenty-five years ago.

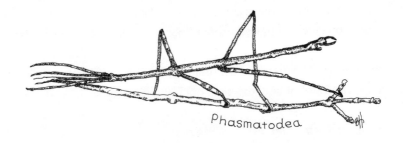

Phasmatodea

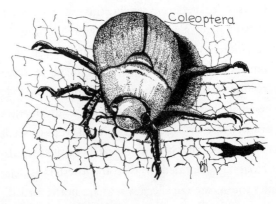

Coleoptera

Meg's favorite insects: the walking stick above, and the giant stinging tree beetle, below (illustrations by Barbara Harrison)

The more common insects are what I call guild feeders: groups of insects that feed on similar-but-different vegetation. An example of a guild feeder, and my second-favorite insect, is the walking stick or stick insect. It looks just like a tiny branch of a tree, and it can easily hide from predators. In Australia, walking sticks ate the foliage of a range of tree species, but usually ate leaves of the same age, at a similar height in the forest, and of the same toughness (to chew).

How long do leaves live in the canopy?

From long-term canopy studies completed in Australia, I found leaves that lived as little as three months (giant stinging tree or *Dendrocnide excelsa,* family Urticaceae) and others that lived as long as nineteen years (sassafras or *Doryphora sassafras,* family Monimiaceae). To calculate their lives, I marked many leaves with waterproof marking pens and returned monthly to survey them. I never expected to continue these observations for nineteen years. Like many biologists who come from the temperate zones, I had imagined that leaves probably lived at most two or three years. Was I ever wrong!

How many plants live on Barro Colorado Island?

Over one thousand plants inhabit BCI. The most recent survey estimated 1,368 species, of which over half are trees. This is astounding compared to the mere seven hundred species of plants throughout all of North America, a land area many times larger than BCI, which covers only 1,564 hectares (or 3,865 acres). Up to ten thousand species of plants are recorded for all of Panama, a very small country compared with North America.

Are there questions in your research that no one has answered?

Many questions concerning tropical rain-forest canopies have not been answered. A friend of mine has devoted his entire life to answering the question, "What is the most common tree in the tropical rain forest?" No one knows the answer to even that basic question. A recent challenge in my work has been to measure the insect poop falling from the canopy to the forest floor. It is an important element of nutrient cycling, but to date no scientist has successfully collected and extracted the relatively tiny pieces of insect waste material that look almost identical to the many other particles falling to the forest floor. I mentioned this dilemma to Jason students, who proceeded to experiment with different tools to measure insect frass. They laid plastic on the forest floor, but managed to collect only large amounts of branch and leaf material that displaced the tiny pieces of frass. Next they placed small plastic trays under *new* leaves in the forest of BCI, hoping to catch the frass of any voracious insect that came along to munch on the new leaves (which are usually preferred because they are softer). After one week, the results were disappointing: the frass and other litter were lost in the soup of rainfall. We have gone back to the drawing board on this unsolved challenge of designing a tool to measure frass.

What is your favorite tree?

My favorite is the fig tree. I have always thought that the fig tree will someday become the dominant species in the rain forest. In *Life in the Treetops* I paid tribute to the fig: "Figs [are] perhaps my favorite trees in the rain forest because of their unique lifestyle. They grow down from the top, thereby guaranteeing a high rate of success in obtaining a canopy position; and they surround and suffocate the host tree, further ensuring a permanent position in the forest canopy. They are important food sources for many birds, insects, and animals. Because of their incredible success, I secretly believe that figs may someday dominate the rain forest." And perhaps best of all, figs are lots of fun to climb!

How do you go to the bathroom in the canopy?

Almost every classroom and every student who writes to me asks this question! Like the sloth, I have to return to the forest floor to go to the bathroom. Other scientists and friends have tried to invent portable potties for the canopy, but I have not yet seen a reasonable design. Although sloths also come down to the forest floor to go to the bathroom, they have a more efficient system than mine; they only descend from the canopy approximately once a week. I usually have to come down to the forest floor at least once a day.

How much herbivory occurs in a forest?

Biologists used to think that 5–7 percent of the foliage was eaten annually by herbivores. This figure was calculated by picking up leaves either from the forest floor or from the lower branches of a tree, so obviously it was not really representative of the whole forest. When I first began climbing to the top and then measuring leaves over their whole life span, I was able to calculate that leaves were 95 percent or even 100 percent consumed. I found that earlier studies had greatly underestimated this forest process. Herbivory throughout the canopy ranged from as low as 1 percent for fir trees in the Pacific Northwest, to 20 percent in the tropical rain forests of Panama and Belize, to as high as 300 percent per year in the eucalyptus forests of Australia. How can a tree be 300 percent eaten? In this case, Christmas beetles and other herbivores sometimes ate foliage not once but three sequential times throughout a single year. Each time, the tree grew new foliage and the beetles consumed the second and third flushes. This is *extreme* herbivory!

Have you ever fallen from a tree?

Once I had a close call. I fell about 15 feet from a eucalypt tree because I was hurrying to finish my research before a thunderstorm. I was not careful and failed to check the carabiner that attached my harness to the rope. Down I came, with a few bruises but otherwise safe. It was a humbling lesson for me, a reminder that tree climbing requires attention to safety rules and a buddy present! A few research colleagues have had similar falls, but climbing gear is extremely safe. When the equipment is used properly, climbing is probably safer than crossing a city street.

How can students in middle school help conserve the rain forest?
You students are already helping by participating in the Jason Expedition. You are learning the facts about tropical rain forests so that you can make wise decisions in the future. Education is a valuable tool for conservation, and I hope that students will share their knowledge with friends and family. Another way that students can contribute to rain-forest conservation is by advocating for careful shopping. Encourage your parents to buy shade-grown coffee; its beans are grown in the understory of native forest rather than in open areas where the forest has been cleared. Shade-grown coffee costs a bit more, but it provides habitat for songbirds, prevents soil erosion, and protects the biodiversity of the tropics. Families should also recycle, carpool, and seek other ways to consume less fossil fuel, and buy products such as certified timber that support rain-forest conservation. If you are planning a family vacation, go to a national park or visit a forest instead of giving your money to an amusement park. Your economic support of natural ecosystems instead of artificial entertainment will help reinforce the importance of conservation. Last but not least, read, read, read! Educate yourself about the latest findings in science and the newest discoveries that will help you to become wise stewards of the planet's natural resources. And someday, a few Jason students may choose a career in science and become my newest canopy colleagues.

SKATEBOARDING AS AN EXPLORATION OF EARTH'S SURFACE

By James, aged 16

As the skateboard begins to wobble beneath my feet, I immediate realize that I am going to fall — and at this speed, the fall will likely leave a mark. I sense time slowing down. I am experiencing vastly heightened sensitivity in all five senses. I see every jagged chunk of shell mixed into the asphalt to help car tires grip the street. I feel each small wobble and shift of balance in my precarious position atop the board. Then, as my head moves toward the ground at close to 15 miles per hour, time stretches to its fullest to encompass an instant of unconsciousness that feels like an eternity. I float in this timeless, ageless realm and finally jerk back into consciousness with all the abruptness of a rubber band snapping back into position after being held stretched. I am awake, unable to believe that I fell, unable to believe that the blood covering my face is mine, and with my mind full of the horror that my brain or other important parts of me may be damaged. I am still.

Similar thoughts must go through the minds of explorers who stumble while climbing Everest or canopy biologists who fall from trees. With my mom I have met such heroes: Don Perry, who fell from a tall tropical tree in Costa Rica; Hal Heatwole, who endured the bite of a sea snake out on the Great Barrier Reef; Mark Moffett, who witnessed a colleague fatally wounded by a juvenile viper in Myanmar. This field biology stuff that my mom pursues is dangerous business, but as a kid it has been a great and adventurous way to grow up. After climbing tall trees in a jungle or stalking a tarantula, skateboarding seems kind of tame.

14 Global Citizens: An Environmental Ethic for Families

Consider two aspects of globalization: first, planes exploding as they slam into the World Trade Center, and second, the emission of carbon dioxide from the exhausts of gas-guzzling sport utility vehicles. One brought instant death and left unforgettable images that were watched on television screens all over the world; the other makes a contribution to climate change that can be detected only by scientific instruments. Yet both are indications of the way in which we are now one world, and the more subtle changes to which sport utility vehicle owners unintentionally contribute will almost certainly kill far more people than the highly visible one. When people in rich nations switch to vehicles that use more fuel than the cars they used to drive, they contribute to changes in the climate of Mozambique or Bangladesh — changes that may cause crops to fail, sea levels to rise, and tropical diseases to spread.

— Peter Singer, *One World: The Ethics of Globalization*

It is Mother's Day 2004. As I write this, eighteen such celebrations have come and gone in my short life as a parent. I wonder anxiously about the American moms who are in Iraq struggling to do battle on soils that are not home; their children must miss them. And what about the Iraqi moms who live in fear each and every day, wondering if their children will ever be safe? Considering the fate of these mothers, I recognize that my life has been spent in a very different battle — not one with imminent bloodshed, but one with slow, yet irreversible environmental degradation that will lead to great loss of life. The ecological battle is a subtle and insidious war, in which science education is one of the most powerful weapons. Yet most global citizens have not been educated about the workings of their environment or how to keep it healthy. Like the engine of an automobile, our global machinery — manifested in nutrient cycling, water flow, flowering, decay, bird migration, and other incredibly complex cycles — requires maintenance to keep it in working condition. Unlike auto maintenance, though, our ecosystems will operate well only if we leave a portion of them alone.

As a parent, I feel a strong biological instinct to keep these cycles intact and assure a safe and healthy home for my children and their children. As a scientist, I consider it a professional priority to detect problems and achieve solutions as an ecological steward of this planet. My children have developed their own ethics about caring for the world around them. One has integrated religion and science into a strong love of nature and will no doubt use that sensitivity to be a true steward of the natural world. The other wishes to go a step beyond his mother's detective work and engineer sound technology to solve the environmental threats to our quality of life. Suddenly my sons are at an age where I learn more from them than they learn from me.

My children are nearing the end of their teen years. At this writing, my elder son is as old as my longest-lived leaf, found in the Australian rain-forest understory. And who knows, perhaps some of its cohorts in different parts of that tree lived even longer. I wonder if a sassafras tree is cognizant of birthing and rearing a nineteen-year-old leaf. Actually, I do hope that trees experience some sense of maternal pride or appreciation of their progeny in their sylvan efforts.

Trees and mothers have a great deal in common. Trees are the heart of productivity of many ecosystems, just as mothers function as the biological center of birth and life. Like motherhood, trees provide energy and nutrients for their entire community. They provide sustenance. They provide shelter and stable homes for those around them. Most important, they quietly drive important functions that make all life possible in the surrounding ecosystem. Consider the amazing functions that trees perform: production of sugars from sunlight, transport of water over long distances, cycling of energy from the tree-tops down to the forest floor, prevention of soil erosion, filtration, provision of a home to biodiversity, cleansing of pollution from the air, and moderation of the harmful solar rays that would otherwise desiccate the forest floor. In the midst of this busy schedule of vital activities, trees produce their next generation without a fuss. I laugh when I contemplate the relatively trivial nature of human daily functions. We fret over the grocery list, dentist appointments, paying the mortgage, buying school supplies, or removing spam from our email accounts. In contrast, without fanfare, trees produce energy as the basis of all food chains on planet Earth.

On Mother's Day, I cannot help pondering my maternal contributions to my children's quality of life and comparing myself to the successful tree. If only I could have achieved as much as the tree! If I could have reduced pollution, saved biodiversity, found cures for diseases, reversed global warming, or conserved soils. But I have not. I have whittled away at relatively small goals in comparison to the grander accomplishments of a tree. Still, I hope that my personal achievements will strengthen conservation for the next generation. In my scientific role, I have managed to discover a few new species; pioneered some innovative approaches to forest ecology through canopy access; left a legacy of treetop walks encircling the globe to encourage eco-tourism instead of chain saws; and talked to several million young people—perhaps inspired a few—through distance learning. In my parental role, I have sought to connect my children to nature and to remind them that their health links directly to the environment, not the state of their computers or cell phones. Children and their parents need to understand that we are *part* of our ecosystem, not outside it.

Like most working parents, I wear two hats. In my case, I am a parent and a scientist. My goal for scientists is to work together to invoke effective stewardship of our planet. Looking back at the many scientific conferences, speeches, and publications in which I have participated during my lifetime, I am puzzled why scientists have not made more positive changes in the state of our global environment as a result of our collective efforts. We ecologists feel disheartened that thousands of research projects in tropical rain forests have not reversed the decline of this precious habitat. We voice frustration that our multimillion-dollar pharmaceutical industry has not yet analyzed even 2 percent of the botanical species in tropical forests as potential medicines. We share disappointment that we do not even know the most common tree in South America, nor do we have any idea how many creatures live in our own backyards. Yet we know the chemicals that compose Mars, the structure of an electron, and the genetic makeup of a mosquito. Science has advanced in many arenas, but the ability to understand the machinery of our "home" is still lacking.

Perhaps my most valuable legacy will be a simple but effective suggestion, intended to impart a change in perspective to those who are parents or scientists (or both). Contemplate the current scenario: Scientists are busily cataloguing and observing the species in tropical rain forests, yet the habitat around them continues to shrink; parents are busy buying groceries for their children, but they have forgotten how to grow vegetables. Perhaps we need a different approach. Once again, I suggest borrowing the church's concept of tithing. What if all scientists gave 10 percent of their research time directly to conservation and science education, in addition to their pure research? And what if parents pledged to spend 10 percent of their family time rediscovering nature?

In my corner of the scientific world, I interact with tropical biologists, ecologists, botanists, and canopy scientists. We are just beginning to use our collective voices to advocate for global change. If every research grant included a component of conservation, or education outreach to youth, and if tenure and promotion included a requirement for public science, then we might indeed achieve the underlying goal that inspired us to become scientists in the first place: a healthy planet. Both scientists and parents must take the initiative. As parents, we need to allow our children to get muddy, at least once in a while. The natural world exists everywhere: in sidewalk cracks, mold in refrigerators, ants at a picnic, spittlebugs on a goldenrod stalk, and in the pages of *National Geographic* read aloud. "Conservation over conversation" is perhaps the most meaningful take-home lesson for all of us.

SCIENCE AND SPIRIT

By Eddie, aged 17
(Adapted from Eddie's application to the Youth Theological Initiative at Emory University, which he attended during the summer of 2002)

Most of my classmates know me as a crazy-haired Australian chemistry whiz with a fondness for hacky-sack. Beside the long hours of crew practice and sporadic forays into the jungle, these classmates know nothing of my intense spiritual life. They do not know my long history of attending church, playing in the handbell choir, and contemplating my own faith through self-reflection, prayer, and fellowship. Most of all, they do not understand how my faith has grown from my love for nature.

In years past, my faith grew most readily as I traveled with my mother to distant rain-forest ecosystems. The Peruvian Amazon in particular helped me to appreciate the true wonder of God's creation. Toucans, monkeys, butterflies, and vines filled the vast jungle cathedral towering overhead — individual parts of this masterful machine working in unison. What a treasure we have in this Earth, not only practically, scientifically, and aesthetically, but spiritually as well!

Upon returning from my journeys to Peru, I started thinking more about how my faith has been enriched by these intimate experiences with biodiversity. I came to realize also that science, rather than being an enemy to spirituality, can be a tool to interpret and glorify God's creation. My participation in the natural world has only served to strengthen my beliefs as a Christian. Furthermore, through my own thoughts I have helped others, including my mother, to integrate the concepts of science and religion without betraying either — something often rendered impossible by technical training in either discipline.

One of my strongest convictions regarding religion is the importance of knowledge. Knowledge can empower belief by providing a basis and a goal for further spiritual exploration. Thus, the more we understand through science about how our world functions, the better we can appreciate both science and spirit. In addition, it is our duty to spread our knowledge by teaching others to recognize the miracles of biodiversity on our planet.

After visiting the Peruvian Amazon, I feel an urge to teach others to respect and care for our natural world. Though humanity has faltered in its stewardship of the creation that sustains us, I think we can remedy this neglect through education and sharing of knowledge about the environment's beauty, economic and spiritual importance, and biological function. Our lives depend on it.

CICADAS: SEVENTEEN YEARS UNDERGROUND

By James and Eddie, aged 16 and 17

Recently, the seventeen-year cicadas hatched. This special type of insect burrows underground, where it remains until its biological clock tells it that seventeen years have passed. Thousands of these cicadas then emerge in a chaotic three-week stint of mating, buzzing, and crashing into windshields. Needless to say, this unique behavior draws a lot of attention from the public. Cicadas are hard to miss, with their constant drone in the background and their squished guts on sidewalks and windshields.

We have noticed two basic reactions to the cicada phenomenon. The first is revulsion. Most people we know are repulsed by the multitude of these creatures. The other sentiment toward the cicadas is one of excitement. This latter feeling is shared primarily by the other half of our acquaintances, who are eccentric scientists. They would rather collect these critters than exterminate them. They delight in the evolutionary genius of the cicadas, whereby they avoid predators through their seventeen-year cycle. We think the two perspectives on cicadas provide a lesson for any of life's problems: Attitude is everything. Even the smallest matters in life, such as tiny insects, will elicit a response that is either critical or enthusiastic. And as our mom once said, it is better to exclaim than to complain.

Appendix

Useful Equipment Handy for a Field Biologist in the Rain Forest

Comfortable shoes

Long pants and long-sleeved shirt (in Australia, I sewed my canvas boots to my pants, to minimize leech invasions)

Rain coat

Rain hat (a visor is useful for those who wear glasses)

Handkerchiefs (to wipe off perspiration)

Sunglasses

Water bottle

Small fold-up umbrella to hold over data sheets during rain

Hand lens

Swiss army knife

Daypack for supplies

Camera and film

Compass

Tape measure

Flashlight (for late returns)

Binoculars

Notebooks and pencils

Field notes and field guides for species identification

Waterproof magic markers to label plants

Vials to hold insects or other unidentified objects

Permits (if collecting or working in a restricted area)

Maps and checklists for site

First aid kit

Insect repellent

Toilet paper

Plastic bags

Tarp (to sit on during lunch and to minimize the dirt, ticks, and leeches that tend to lodge in one's private parts)

Energizers (Oreo cookies are still my favorite)

Glossary

agouti a large rabbit-like rodent of Central and South America

ant plants tropical plants that house ants in pockets or swollen nodes and in turn are protected by the ants, resulting in a mutualistic relationship whereby both parties benefit

arachnologist a scientist who studies spiders and their biology

arthropods invertebrates such as spiders, insects, and crustaceans of the phylum Arthropoda that feature a segmented body, jointed legs, and a hard exoskeleton

biomass the weight of living matter in a habitat, usually expressed as dry weight of plant material, dry weight of insects, and the like

biome a biotic community with its own characteristic species and climate

bromeliad an epiphyte or air plant that lives in the canopies of trees (but is not parasitic), commonly structured as a rosette of stiff leaves surrounding a central water tank; occasionally exists as a ground-dwelling plant

brown food web the interconnected chain of organisms responsible for decay on the forest floor, a region that tends to be predominantly brown in color

buttress the woody growth at the base of some tropical trees that flares out from the main trunk and appears to offer structural support or to channel rainfall down to the roots

canopy the green leafy portion of a plant or tree, often supported by woody structures, that contains chlorophyll for photosynthesis

carabiner an oval metal device used to fasten ropes or secure attachments points in mountaineering, caving, or tree climbing

cauliflory the characteristic of some tropical trees whereby the flowers are borne on the trunk (rather than on the branch tips), presumably to facilitate pollination by understory creatures such as bats

conifers evergreen trees with needles (not leaves) that typically produce naked seeds in cones

cotyledons two leaves produced by a seed upon germination

decomposition the process whereby dead material breaks down and recycles back into the soil as nutrients

drip tip a feature of leaves of tropical trees whereby the point is elongated to a sharp point, presumably to channel water off the leaf during rain showers

ecosystem a biotic community characterized by a group of organisms and their interactions with one another and with the regional climate

emergent a tropical tree that grows above the height of the forest canopy

entomologist a scientist who studies insects and their kin

epiphylly the covering on leaf surfaces, especially in moist tropical forests, composed of a diversity of organic matter including mosses, lichen, fungi, and the microorganisms inhabiting them

epiphyte a plant that lives in the canopies of trees, procuring its nutrients and water from the air and using its host tree only for physical support

ethnobotanist a scientist who studies the economic uses of plants (such as medicines, foods, and materials)

flush the event of leafing out synchronously

frass the German-derived term for insect defecation (poop)

goanna a large monitor lizard native to Australia

green food web the chain of organisms involved in photosynthesis and interactions within the forest canopy *hacky-sack* a small, woven bag that is tossed between players (or sometimes by just one player) with the foot

hammock an ecosystem in which forests exist on slightly elevated patches of land, usually surrounded by wetter ecosystems such as marshes; occurs in Florida

herbarium a standardized collection of dried plants, labeled for use in scientific study

herbivore an animal (such as the sloth or beetle) that consumes green leafy tissue

herbivory the process by which animals consume green foliage

host specific descriptive of an organism that is specific to one food plant and will die without it

island biogeography the biological concept that explains why smaller isolated spaces have fewer species than larger tracts

Jason Expedition (formerly Jason Project) the distance-learning program founded by Robert Ballard, whereby students explore remote regions of the world to study science via satellite telecommunication from classrooms or museums

jumar a toothed metal device utilized in mountaineering, caving, or tree climbing to ascend a rope

kava a South Pacific ceremonial drink, made from the roots of a native shrub

lava lava an item of Samoan clothing worn wrapped around the waist like a skirt

liana woody vines of the tropical rain forest

life-list a comprehensive list of the species of birds seen throughout one's lifetime

mutualism a relationship between two organisms in which both benefit

mycorrhizae fungi that live in association with the roots of a plant and may confer an advantage to that individual by enhancing nutrient and water uptake

nutrient cycling the movement of organic compounds from living organisms to dead and decaying material, usually through a circular pattern: production in green plants, growth, death on the forest floor, decomposition in the soil, and uptake back into green plants

orependula a tropical bird that builds a pendulous nest in a communal setting (ten or more birds per tree crown) and has a unique melodious call

palynologist a scientist who studies the history of plants by analyzing pollen grains from deposits such as sediments in lakes or cores in soil

penetrometer a standardized device to estimate the physical pressure required to bite through a leaf; used to gauge the toughness of a leaf that a herbivore tries to eat

photosynthesis the process whereby the cells in the green tissue of plants utilize the energy of sunlight to manufacture the organic compounds that form the basis of all food chains

pioneer species a colonizing or early-settler species on a disturbed or open tract of land, usually succeeded by late-successional species

pollinator organism that aids in plant reproduction by transferring pollen

predator an organism that survives by feeding or in some way preying on other organisms

pteridophytes the scientific term for ferns

rain forest the kind of forest typified by complex structure and physiognomy, and more than 65 inches of rainfall annually

replication the part of a scientific experiment that involves repeated units or treatments

Rivereños people who live along the Amazon River

shade leaf a leaf grown in the shaded region of a plant, with physiological characteristics such as large, thin, and soft that are functional in conditions of low light

shaman the term for a village leader who knows the medicinal attributes of plants and applies them when people are ill

species reservoir potential availability of species to a region, as a factor of rates of immigration and extinction and, on an island, as influenced by its size and relative distance from the mainland

subtropical rain forest the forest type that boasts tropical features (such as high diversity of plant forms and species, with buttresses, drop tips, and other traits) but is situated in a subtropical latitude

succession the gradual changes in ecosystem composition that occur over time

sun leaf a leaf grown in the sunny region of a plant, with physiological characteristics such as small, thick, and tough that are functional in conditions of strong light

tardigrades microscopic invertebrates that inhabit every continent of the world and have the unique ability to exist in suspended animation when conditions are unfavorable

taxonomist a scientist who classifies organisms

terra firma forest a forest located above the water table that therefore does not flood

throughfall rain that hits the canopy and then trickles through the leaves and branches to the understory below, sometimes bringing additional nutrients absorbed as particles on the plant surfaces

transect in ecology, a line (usually marked with a tape measure) upon which species are counted or specific variables are surveyed

tropical rain forest the most complex forest type, characterized by high rainfall, homogeneous climate throughout the year, warm and humid conditions, a large variety of plant forms, high diversity, and plant species that have tropical origins

Selected Bibliography

Introduction

Leopold, A. *A Sand County Almanac.* New York: Oxford University Press, 1949.

Seuss, Dr. *The Lorax.* New York: Random House, 1971.

Chapter 1. Why Canopies Are Exciting

Doris, E. *Life at the Top.* Austin, Tex.: Steck-Vaughn, Smithsonian Institution, 2001.

Lasky, K. *The Most Beautiful Roof in the World.* Orlando, Fla.: Gulliver Green, Harcourt Brace, 1997.

Linsenmair, K. E., A. J. Davis, B. Fiala, and M. R. Speight, eds. *Tropical Forest Canopies.* Norwell, Mass.: Kluwer Academic Publishers, 2001.

Lowman, M. D. *Life in the Treetops.* New Haven: Yale University Press, 1999.

Lowman, M. D., and H. B. Rinker, eds. *Forest Canopies.* San Diego: Elsevier, 2004. See especially pp. 453–465.

Mitchell, A. W. *The Enchanted Canopy.* Glasgow: William Collins, 1986.

Mitchell, A. W. *The Global Canopy Handbook.* Oxford: Halifax House, Oxford University, 2002.

Moffett, M. W. *The High Frontier.* Cambridge, Mass.: Harvard University Press, 1993.

Perry, D. *Life Above the Jungle Floor.* New York: Simon and Schuster, 1986.

Wilson, E. O. *The Diversity of Life.* Cambridge, Mass.: Belknap Press of Harvard University Press, 1992.

Wilson, E. O. *The Future of Life.* New York: Alfred A. Knopf, 2003.

Chapter 2. Canopies for Conservation

Akerele, O., V. Heywood, and H. Synge. *Conservation of Medicinal Plants.* Cambridge: Cambridge University Press, 1991.

Cox, P. A., and S. A. Banack, eds. *Islands, Plants and Polynesians.* Portland, Ore: Dioscorides Press, 1991.

Elmquist, T., P. Cox, W. Rainey, and E. Pierson. *An Introduction to the Rain Forest Preserves on Savai'i, Western Samoa.* Savai'i: Fa'asao Savai'i Society, 1993.

Erbacher, J., and S. Erbacher, *Survival in the Rainforest.* Cambridge: Cambridge University Press, 1991.

Gutmanis, J. *Kahuna La'au Lapa'au.* Aiea, Hawaii: Island Heritage Publishing, 1995.

Lowman, M. D., and H. B. Rinker, eds. *Forest Canopies.* San Diego: Elsevier, 2004.

Martin, G. J. *Ethnobotany.* London: Chapman and Hall, 1995.

Plotkin, M. J. *Tales of a Shaman's Apprentice.* New York: Viking Penguin, 1993.

Plotkin, M. J. *Medicine Quest.* New York: Viking Penguin, 2000.

Powledge, F. *Pharmacy in the Forest.* New York: Atheneum Books, Simon and Schuster, 1998.

Reader's Digest. *Magic and Medicine of Plants.* Pleasantville, N.Y.: Reader's Digest Association, 1986.

Schultes, R. E., and R. F. Raffauf. *The Healing Forest.* Hong Kong: Dioscorides Press, 1990.

Vaughan, J. G., and C. A. Geissler. *The New Oxford Book of Food Plants*. Oxford: Oxford University Press, 1997.

Whistler, W. A. *Polynesian Herbal Medicine*. Hong Kong: Everest Printing, 1992.

Chapter 3. Indoor Canopies

Beattie, A., and P. R. Ehrlich. *Wild Solutions*. New Haven: Yale University Press, 2001.

Hawken, P., A. Lovins, and L. H. Lovins. *Natural Capitalism*. Boston: Little, Brown, 1999.

Lowman, M. D., and H. B. Rinker, eds. *Forest Canopies*. San Diego: Elsevier, 2004.

Marino, B. D. V., and H. T. Odum. *Biosphere 2*. San Diego: Elsevier, 1999.

Meadows, D. H. *The Global Citizen*. Washington, D.C.: Island Press, 1991.

Primack, R. B. *Essentials of Conservation Biology*. Sunderland, Mass: Sinauer Associates, 1993.

Wilson, E. O. *The Future of Life*. New York: Alfred A. Knopf, 2003.

Chapter 4. Orchid Farming in Africa

Kingdom, J. *Island Africa*. Princeton: Princeton University Press, 1989.

Lowman, M. D. *Life in the Treetops*. New Haven: Yale University Press, 1999. See especially chapter 7.

Martin, C. *The Rainforests of West Africa*. Basel, Switzerland: Birkhauser, 1991.

Weber, W., L. J. T. White, A. Vedder, and L. Haughton-Treves. *African Rain Forest Ecology and Conservation*. New Haven: Yale University Press, 2001.

Chapter 5. An Emmy Award for the Treetops

Hallé, F. *In Praise of Plants*. Portland, Ore.: Timber Press, 1999.

Hallé, F., and O. Pascal. *Biologie d'une canopée de forêt équatoriale. II. Opération, canopée,* Lyon, France: Opération Canopée, 1992.

Lowman, M. D. *Life in the Treetops.* New Haven: Yale University Press, 1999.

Lowman, M. D., and H. B. Rinker, eds. *Forest Canopies.* San Diego: Elsevier, 2004.

Tripp, J. L. *La Croisière verte.* Grenoble, France: Glénat Publishers, 1992.

Chapter 6. Canopy Walkways

Benschoff, P. *Myakka.* Sarasota, Fla.: Pineapple Press, 2003.

Carr, A. *A Naturalist in Florida.* Gainesville: University of Florida Press, 1961.

Lowman, M. D. *Life in the Treetops.* New Haven: Yale University Press, 1999.

Lowman, M. D., and H. B. Rinker, eds. *Forest Canopies.* San Diego: Elsevier, 2004.

McDade, L. A., K. S. Bawa, H. A. Hespenheide, and G. S. Hartshorn. *La Selva.* Chicago: University of Chicago Press, 1994.

Mitchell, A. W. *The Global Canopy Handbook.* Oxford: Halifax House, Oxford University, 2002.

Moffett, M. *The High Frontier.* Cambridge, Mass.: Harvard University Press, 1993.

Chapter 7. Of Tarantulas, Teenagers, and Turkey Basters

Ackerman, D. *A Natural History of the Senses.* New York: Random House, 1990.

Ackerman, D. 1995. *The Rarest of the Rare.* New York: Random House, 1995.

Berenbaum, M. R. *Buzzwords.* Washington, D.C.: John Henry Press, 2000.

Carson, R. *The Sense of Wonder.* New York: HarperCollins, 1956.

Castner, J. L. *Explorama's Amazon*. Gainesville, Fla.: Feline Press, 2000.

Forsyth, A., and K. Miyata. *Tropical Nature*. New York: Macmillan, 1984.

Gentry, A. H. *A Field Guide to the Families and Genera of Woody Plants of Northwest South America*. Chicago: University of Chicago Press, 1993.

Jason Project Curriculum. Waltham, Mass.: Jason Foundation, 1999 (*www.jason.org*).

Lowman, M. D. *Life in the Treetops*. New Haven: Yale University Press, 1999, ch. 9.

Chapter 8. International Powwows

Forster, E. M. *A Passage to India*. Orlando, Fla.: Harcourt, 1924.

Ganeshaiah, K. N., R. U. Shaanker, and K. S. Bawa. "Tropical Ecosystems: Structure, Diversity, and Human Welfare." International Conference on Tropical Ecosystems July 15–18, 2001, Bangalore, India.

Mehta, G. *Raj*. New York: Fawcett Columbine, 1989.

Chapter 9. Colorful Bodies

Bierregaard, R. O., C. Gascon, T. E. Lovejoy, and R. Mesquita. *Lessons from Amazonia*. New Haven: Yale University Press, 2001.

Brummitt, R. K. *Vascular Plant Families and Genera*. Kew, England: Royal Botanic Gardens, 1992.

Clements, J. F., and N. Shany. *Birds of Peru*. Temecula, Calif.: Ibis Publishing Company, 2001.

Jacobs, M. *The Tropical Rain Forest: A First Encounter*. Berlin: Springer-Verlag, 1981.

Kricher, J. C. *A Neotropical Companion*. Princeton: Princeton University Press, 1989.

Richards, P. W. *The Tropical Rain Forest*. Cambridge: Cambridge University Press, 1952.

Stap, D. *A Parrot Without a Name*. New York: Alfred A. Knopf, 1990.

Chapter 10. Down from the Treetops

Abrahams, J. *The Mission Statement Book*. Berkeley, Calif.: Ten Speed Press, 1999.

Bernardt, P. *Wily Violets and Underground Orchids*. New York: William Morrow, 1989.

Bernardt, P. *Natural Affairs*. New York: Villard Books, 1993.

Drucker, P. *The Effective Executive*. New York: HarperCollins, 1966.

Drucker, P. *Managing the Non-Profit Organization*. New York: Harper-Collins, 1992.

National Center for Nonprofit Boards. Governance Series (10 volumes covering a range of topics) and Committee Series (8 volumes including Audit, Development, etc.), and Strategic Issues Series (4 volumes). Washington, D.C.: National Center, 1995.

National Center for Nonprofit Boards. *Board Passages*. Washington, D.C.: National Center, 1995.

National Center for Nonprofit Boards. *The Troublesome Board Member*. Washington, D.C.: National Center, 1995.

National Center for Nonprofit Boards. *The Legal Obligations of Nonprofit Boards*. Washington, D.C.: National Center, 1995.

Orlean, S. *The Orchid Thief*. New York: Random House, 1998.

Veverka, J. A. *Interpretive Master Planning*. Tustin, Calif.: Acorn Naturalists, 1994.

Chapter 11. Billions of Needles

Basset, Y., V. Horlyck, and S. J. Wright. *Studying Forest Canopies from Above*. Panama: Smithsonian Tropical Research Institute and United Nations Environmental Programs, 2003.

Doris, E. *Life at the Top*. Austin, Tex.: Steck-Vaughn, Smithsonian Institution, 2001.

Gordon, D. G. *Field Guide to the Sasquatch*. Seattle: Sasquatch Books, 1992.

Lowman, M. D., and H. B. Rinker, eds. 2004. *Forest Canopies.* San Diego, Calif: Elsevier, 1992.

Mitchell, A. W., K. Secoy, and T. Jackson, eds. *The Global Canopy Handbook.* Oxford: Global Canopy Programme, 2002.

Pojar, J., and A. MacKinnon. *Plants of the Pacific Northwest Coast.* Redmond, Wash.: Lone Pine Publishing, 1994.

Smithson, M. *Olympic.* Helena, Mont.: American and World Geographic Publishing, 1993.

Chapter 12. Downsizing 101

Lindbergh, A. M. *Gift from the Sea.* New York: Pantheon Books, 1955.

Lowman, S. 1938. *The Lowmans in Chemung County.* Elmira, N.Y.: Commercial Press, 1938.

McCarthy, J. F., and L. B. McCarthy. *The Finger Lakes.* Toronto: Oxford University Press, 1984.

Pilcher, R. *Winter Solstice.* New York: St. Martin's Press, 2000.

Stevenson, R. L. *A Child's Garden of Verses.* Heritage Press, 1944.

Viorst, J. *Necessary Losses.* New York: Simon and Schuster, 1986.

Weiner, J. *Time, Love, Memory.* New York: Random House, 1999.

White, E. B. *Essays of E. B. White.* New York: Harper Colophon Books, 1977.

Chapter 13. Coming Full Circle

Gentry, A. H., ed. *Four Neotropical Rainforests.* New Haven: Yale University Press, 1990.

Leigh, E. G., Jr. *Tropical Forest Ecology.* New York: Oxford University Press, 1999.

Leigh, E. G., Jr. *A Magic Web.* New York: Oxford University Press, 2004.

Leigh, E. G., Jr., A. S. Rand, and D. M. Windsor, eds. *The Ecology of a Tropical Forest.* Washington, D.C.: Smithsonian Institution Press, 1982.

Mulkey, S. S., R. L. Chazdon, and A. P. Smith. *Tropical Forest Plant Eco-physiology.* New York: Chapman and Hall, 1996.

Royte, E. *The Tapir's Morning Bath.* New York: Houghton Mifflin, 2001.

Wong, M., and J. V. Ventocilla, with O. Acevedo. *A Day on Barro Colorado Island.* Smithsonian Tropical Research Institute, Panama City: Polygraphica, 1995.

Chapter 14. Global Citizens

Beattie, A., and P. R. Ehrlich. *Wild Solutions.* New Haven: Yale University Press, 2001.

Daily, G. C., and K. Ellison. *The New Economy of Nature.* Washington, D.C.: Island Press, 2002.

Hawken, P., A. Lovins, and L. H. Lovins. *Natural Capitalism.* Boston: Little, Brown, 1999.

Lowman, M. D., and H. B. Rinker, eds. *Forest Canopies.* San Diego, Calif.: Elsevier, 2004.

Meadows, D. H. *The Global Citizen.* Washington, D.C.: Island Press, 1991.

Primack, R. B. *Essentials of Conservation Biology.* Sunderland, Mass.: Sinauer Associates, 1993.

Singer, P. *One World: The Ethics of Globalization.* Yale University Press, 2003.

Vermeij, G. J. *Nature.* Princeton: Princeton University Press, 2004.

Wilson, E. O. *The Diversity of Life.* Cambridge, Mass.: Belknap Press of Harvard University Press, 1992.

Wilson, E. O. *The Future of Life.* New York: Alfred A. Knopf, 2003.

Index